JOURNAL FOR THE STUDY OF THE OLD TESTAMENT
SUPPLEMENT SERIES
193

Editors
David J.A. Clines
Philip R. Davies

Executive Editor
John Jarick

Editorial Board
Richard J. Coggins, Alan Cooper, Tamara C. Eskenazi,
J. Cheryl Exum, John Goldingay, Robert P. Gordon,
Norman K. Gottwald, Andrew D.H. Mayes,
Carol Meyers, Patrick D. Miller

Journal for the Study of the Old Testament
Supplement Series 193

The Opponents of Third Isaiah

Reconstructing the Cultic History
of the Restoration

Brooks Schramm

Journal for the Study of the Old Testament
Supplement Series 193

For Gammy

ἀρκούμενοι τοῖς παροῦσιν!

BS
1520.5
.S370
1995

Copyright © 1995 Sheffield Academic Press

Published by Sheffield Academic Press Ltd
Mansion House
19 Kingfield Road
Sheffield, S11 9AS
England

Typeset by Sheffield Academic Press
and
Printed on acid-free paper in Great Britain
by Bookcraft
Midsomer Norton, Somerset

British Library Cataloguing in Publication Data

A catalogue record for this book is available
from the British Library

ISBN 1-85075-538-8

CONTENTS

ACKNOWLEDGMENTS

The present work is a revision of my doctoral dissertation submitted to the University of Chicago in 1993 and entitled, 'The Opponents of Third Isaiah: A Contribution to the Social History of the Restoration'. My doctoral advisor was Jon D. Levenson. His teaching and guidance I regard as priceless. Arthur J. Droge of the University of Chicago and Wolfgang Roth of Garrett-Evangelical Theological Seminary served as readers. They provided me with sound advice and encouragement to persevere. I would also like to mention my other teachers at Chicago: Gösta W. Ahlström, Hans Dieter Betz, W. Randall Garr and Norman Golb.

The editors of Sheffield Academic Press, and especially the desk editor of this monograph, Steve Barganski, have been a pleasure to work with. In addition, the Press's anonymous reader provided me with several valuable insights and criticisms. One of these was the suggested change in subtitle from '*Social* History' to '*Cultic* History'. I was never comfortable with the original subtitle, because I was not convinced that I was really doing 'social history'. This slight change, I think, accurately reflects what this work is about. I would also like to thank Paul Spalding of Illinois College and my colleague here at Lutheran Theological Seminary, Eric Crump, for advice on rendering into English certain knotty German phrases.

My parents, Bennie and Lynn Schramm, my parents-by-marriage, Gene and Mary Tully, and my wife, Mary Beth, have supported me continuously from the first day of graduate school until today. I owe each of you a debt that cannot be repaid.

This book is dedicated to my grandmother, Mrs Delta Anthis, in honor of her ninetieth birthday, September 4, 1994.

Gettysburg
November 10, 1994

ABBREVIATIONS

AB	Anchor Bible
AnBib	Analecta biblica
ARM	Archives royales de Mari
ARW	*Archiv für Religionswissenschaft*
BA	*Biblical Archaeologist*
BARev	*Biblical Archaeology Review*
BASOR	*Bulletin of the American Schools of Oriental Research*
BETL	Bibliotheca ephemeridum theologicarum lovaniensium
BHK	R. Kittel, *Biblia hebraica*
BHS	*Biblia hebraica stuttgartensia*
BHT	Beiträge zur historischen Theologie
Bib	*Biblica*
BWANT	Beiträge zur Wissenschaft vom Alten und Neuen Testament
BZ	*Biblische Zeitschrift*
BZAW	Beihefte zur *ZAW*
CAP	A. Cowley (ed.), *Aramaic Papyri of the Fifth Century BC*
CBQ	*Catholic Biblical Quarterly*
CRINT	Compendia rerum iudaicarum ad Novum Testamentum
ExpTim	*Expository Times*
GKC	*Gesenius' Hebrew Grammar*, ed. E. Kautzsch, trans. A.E. Cowley
HAR	*Hebrew Annual Review*
HSM	Harvard Semitic Monographs
HTR	*Harvard Theological Review*
HUCA	*Hebrew Union College Annual*
IDB	G.A. Buttrick (ed.), *Interpreter's Dictionary of the Bible*
Int	*Interpretation*
JAOS	*Journal of the American Oriental Society*
JBL	*Journal of Biblical Literature*
JNES	*Journal of Near Eastern Studies*
JPSV	*Jewish Publication Society Version*
JQR	*Jewish Quarterly Review*
JR	*Journal of Religion*
JSOT	*Journal for the Study of the Old Testament*
JSOTSup	*Journal for the Study of the Old Testament*, Supplement Series
JSS	*Journal of Semitic Studies*
JTS	*Journal of Theological Studies*
KAT	Kommentar zum Alten Testament
LCL	Loeb Classical Library

NCB	New Century Bible
OBO	Orbis biblicus et orientalis
OTL	Old Testament Library
RB	*Revue biblique*
SBLMS	SBL Monograph Series
SBS	Stuttgarter Bibelstudien
SJT	*Scottish Journal of Theology*
StudOr	*Studia Orientalia*
TLZ	*Theologische Literaturzeitung*
TQ	*Theologische Quartalschrift*
TSK	*Theologische Studien und Kritiken*
TZ	*Theologische Zeitschrift*
UF	*Ugarit-Forschungen*
VT	*Vetus Testamentun*
VTSup	*Vetus Testamentum*, Supplements
ZAW	*Zeitschrift für die alttestamentliche Wissenschaft*
ZTK	*Zeitschrift für Theologie und Kirche*

Chapter 1

INTRODUCTION: THIRD ISAIAH?

Problems of Literary Criticism, Dating and Authorship

It is customary in biblical studies to refer to the last eleven chapters of the book of Isaiah as 'Third' Isaiah. This designation goes back to Bernhard Duhm's famous commentary on Isaiah.[1] In spite of various modifications in Duhm's argument, the vast majority of scholars accept the proposition that from the point of view of literary criticism, Isaiah 56–66 is to be separated from Isaiah 40–55. The purpose of this chapter will be to survey and highlight the course of the scholarly discussion on Third Isaiah since Duhm, with particular emphasis on the questions of the unity, authorship and date of the material.[2]

---

1. B. Duhm, *Das Buch Jesaia* (Göttingen: Vandenhoeck & Ruprecht, 5th edn, 1968). Although Duhm actually spoke of 'Trito' Isaiah, it has been customary in the English speaking world to use 'Third'. The commentary was first published in 1892. Duhm was not the first, though, to claim that Isaiah 40–66 could not all be attributed to Second Isaiah. This honor must go to the Dutch scholar, Abraham Kuenen. See the discussion by A. Rofé, 'How is the Word Fulfilled? Isaiah 55.6-11 within the Theological Debate of its Time', in *Canon, Theology, and Old Testament Interpretation: Essays in Honor of Brevard S. Childs* (ed. G.M. Tucker, D.L. Petersen and R.R. Wilson; Philadelphia: Fortress Press, 1988), pp. 246-61, esp. pp. 255-56, 260.

2. By far the best survey of scholarship on Third Isaiah is that contained in K. Pauritsch, *Die neue Gemeinde: Gott sammelt Ausgestossene und Arme (Jesaia 56–66)* (AnBib, 47; Rome: Biblical Institute Press, 1971), pp. 1-30. Pauritsch deals with virtually all the problems involved in the study of Third Isaiah, whereas I will focus on a more limited set of questions that are directly related to the thesis of this paper. In addition, several books and articles relating to Third Isaiah have been published since 1971. Another good survey of the literature may be found in P.D. Hanson, *The Dawn of Apocalyptic* (Philadelphia: Fortress Press, rev. edn, 1979), pp. 32-46. Hanson's summary is not so detailed as that of Pauritsch, but he covers all of the major issues and presents the various alternatives possible in the current study of

The existence of a Third Isaiah is obviously dependent on there being a Second Isaiah. One of the major results of the early historical-critical investigation of the Hebrew Bible was the conclusion that chs. 40–66 of Isaiah should not be assigned to the eighth-century prophet, Isaiah of Jerusalem, but rather to an anonymous, sixth-century prophet. The theory was developed by Döderlein and Eichhorn at the end of the eighteenth century.[1] By the time of Duhm's commentary, the division of Isaiah into two parts had achieved virtual consensus status among scholars.[2] But Duhm challenged the consensus by arguing that three different authors are represented in Isaiah 40–66:

> The oldest of these is the so-called Second Isaiah, the author of chapters 40–55, excluding the later insertions. He is writing around the year 540 BC, probably in a place located in Lebanon, or perhaps in Phoenicia. Later, and in any case post-exilic, are the Servant Songs: 42.1-4; 49.1-6; 50.4-9; 52.13–53.12. All of these undoubtedly come from one poet and probably constitute only a portion of his poems; those that were not included may have been lost early on, or, due to their too personal tone, may not have been suitable for inclusion in the prophetic writing. These Songs are probably older than the third writing, chapters 56–66, which according to form and content shows itself to be the product of a single author, whom, for the sake of brevity, we call Third Isaiah. The two halves of this writing, chapters 56–60 and chapters 61–66, have perhaps been transposed by the redactor. It was written just before the activity of Nehemiah, in Jerusalem.[3]

Duhm's hypothesis of a Third Isaiah had three major implications. First, chs. 56–66 were not written by Second Isaiah. Secondly, they were not written in exile, but rather in Jerusalem itself. Thirdly, the texts reflect the problems and concerns of the restoration community, separated by almost a hundred years from the writings of Second Isaiah.

In order to emphasize the differences between Second and Third Isaiah, Duhm wrote,

> As a writer, Third Isaiah differs from Second Isaiah as strongly as possible... In contrast to Second Isaiah, Third Isaiah speaks more often of himself. He designates as his task: informing the people of their sins,

Third Isaiah. The newest survey can now be found in S. Sekine, *Die Tritojesajanische Sammlung (Jes 56–66) redaktionsgeschichtlich untersucht* (BZAW, 175; Berlin: de Gruyter, 1989).

1.   B.S. Childs, *Introduction to the Old Testament as Scripture* (Philadelphia: Fortress Press, 1979), p. 316.

2.   Childs, *Introduction to the Old Testament as Scripture*, p. 317.

3.   Duhm, *Das Buch Jesaia*, pp. 14-15 (translation mine).

bringing the gospel to the poor, announcing the year of salvation and the day of vengeance. All of these tasks are foreign to Second Isaiah.[1]

Although there has been a small but persistent group of scholars that has questioned the existence of a Third Isaiah,[2] Duhm's basic argument has stood the test of time. The initial course of the debate after Duhm wrote was confined to the question of the literary unity of Isaiah 56–66 and also to the related question of when to date the oracles. Duhm argued for the unity of the material and a mid-fifth century dating, claiming that the chapters reflect a long-established community, rebuilt temple and city, and a community beset by many internal problems, especially with regard to the 'Schismatiker' (schismatics).[3] Decisive for Duhm is the reference in 66.1 to a conflict over temple building, which he believed referred to the Samaritans, and the phrase in 66.21 which reads: וגם מהם אקח לכהנים ללוים אמר יהוה ('and I will also take some of them to be levitical priests, says YHWH'). According to Duhm, because the Masoretic Text lacks a ו before לוים, the Pentateuchal distinction between Priests and Levites was not yet known, and is evidence, therefore, that the passage predates the work of Ezra.[4]

It was soon noticed, however, that the material in Isaiah 56–66 was of a much more varied nature than that in 40–55. Budde and Volz claimed that this divergence is best explained by viewing 56–66 as the work of several prophets who spoke and wrote over a period of several centuries.[5] Volz isolated thirteen oracles, the earliest being 56.9–57.5, 57.6-13 (seventh century) and the latest 66.3-4, 17, 5-6, 66.7-24 (third

---

1. Duhm, *Das Buch Jesaia*, p. 419 (translation mine).

2. For instance, it was claimed that the divergence in subject matter between Isa. 40–55 and 56–66 was best explained by positing a change in the geographical location of Second Isaiah, i.e., that Second Isaiah had returned home from exile and was now prophesying in a new, post-exilic situation. See Pauritsch, *Die neue Gemeinde*, pp. 20-21. Among the works that directly challenge the hypothesis of a Third Isaiah are: C.C. Torrey, *The Second Isaiah* (New York: Charles Scribner's Sons, 1928); J.D. Smart, *History and Theology in Second Isaiah* (Philadelphia: Westminster Press, 1965); F. Maass, 'Tritojesaja?', in F. Maass (ed.), *Das ferne und nahe Wort: Festschrift für L. Rost* (BZAW, 105; Berlin: de Gruyter, 1967), pp. 153-63; A. Murtonen, 'Third Isaiah—Yes or No?', *Abr-Nahrain* 19 (1980–81), pp. 20-42.

3. Duhm, *Das Buch Jesaia*, p. 418.

4. Duhm, *Das Buch Jesaia*, p. 418. The reading of LXX, ἱερεῖς καὶ Λευίτας is usually viewed as reflective of the time of the translation.

5. Pauritsch, *Die neue Gemeinde*, p. 24.

century).[1] In support of Duhm and in direct opposition to Budde and Volz was Elliger. He viewed Third Isaiah as a disciple of Second Isaiah, who edited the work of his master and whose own words are found in Isaiah 56–66. His work remains the most ardent defense of the literary unity of Third Isaiah.[2]

This debate over 'Einheit' led to a virtual stalemate in the study of Third Isaiah. Volz and Elliger were arguing mutually exclusive positions, with each having much to commend itself. Elliger wrote,

> The 13 passages from chapters 56–66 all come from the productive period of one man; the terminus a quo is the year 538, and the terminus ad quem is roughly 500; consequently, Third Isaiah was active +/– 520.[3]

In response to Elliger, Volz wrote,

> When one can assert that '63.1-6 and 63.7-64.11 exhibit the most and the strongest agreements', this proves to me how completely the spiritual differences between the individual sections are misunderstood... In reality, the differences within the sections with respect to contemporary history, style, mentality, and religion are so great that, in my view, a unity of personage as well as of time-period is out of the question.[4]

In the same way that Duhm had argued that the divergence in subject matter between Isaiah 40–55 and 56–66 demanded assigning the latter to a different author, so Volz argued that the divergence in subject matter within 56–66 demanded assigning several authors and dates to 56–66. Volz's logic is clear:

> The poet, who portrays YHWH as a blood dripping wine-press treader, and the psalmist, according to whose word the Holy One on high dwells with the shattered and the humble, cannot be the same; the singer, who views foreigners merely as subservient instruments of Jerusalem's glory, would

1. D.P. Volz, *Jesaja II* (KAT, 9; Leipzig: A. Deichertsche Verlagsbuchhandlung D. Werner Scholl, 1932), p. 200.
2. K. Elliger, *Die Einheit des Tritojesaja (Jes 56–66)* (BWANT, 45; Stuttgart: Kohlhammer, 1928); *idem*, 'Der Prophet Tritojesaja', *ZAW* 49 (1931), pp. 112-40; *idem, Deuterojesaja in seinem Verhältnis zu Tritojesaja* (Stuttgart: Kohlhammer, 1933). For a new, critical look at the arguments of Elliger, see Sekine, *Die Tritojesajanische Sammlung*, pp. 239-84.
3. Elliger, *Die Einheit des Tritojesaja*, p. 76 (translation mine).
4. Volz, *Jesaja II*, p. 199 (translation mine).

not have written at the same time in favor of the admission of proselytes; whoever rejects temple-building as such, cannot at the same time desire all kinds of precious objects for the Jerusalem sanctuary, etc.[1]

At this point in the history of the discussion of Third Isaiah there were three major alternatives. Duhm saw Isaiah 56–66 as a literary unity dating to the mid-fifth century; with Duhm, Elliger also viewed the chapters as a unity, but assigned them to the early restoration period, c. 520 BCE; Volz rejected the unity of the chapters and spread the oracles over a period of some five centuries. The only other alternative was to deny the basic thesis of Duhm and argue that there is no Third Isaiah. Obviously, if one accepts either Duhm or Volz, then Second Isaiah could not have composed chs. 56–66. On the other hand, Elliger's claim that the chapters date to the early restoration period makes possible the argument that Second Isaiah could have written them.

In spite of all the controversy over 'Einheit', the most difficult problem in the study of Third Isaiah is that of when to date the various oracles. The material is notorious for its lack of any sort of concrete historical reference. Neither foreign nor native Judean rulers are mentioned. Coupled with our general lack of knowledge of the historical events that took place in the late sixth and early fifth centuries in Judah, the problem is compounded.[2] As a result, interpreters are forced into subtle arguments in order to arrive at approximate dates. Do the chapters know of the rebuilding of the temple?[3] Have the walls of Jerusalem been rebuilt?[4] Does the material know of the P-document's

1. Volz, *Jesaja II*, pp. 199-200 (translation mine).
2. See Chapter 2.
3. Williamson has recently drawn attention to the slippery nature of this question by showing that Isa. 60.13 has been used to 'prove' both that the temple was standing and that it was yet to be rebuilt. H.G.M. Williamson, 'The Concept of Israel in Transition', in R.E. Clements (ed.), *The World of Ancient Israel* (Cambridge: Cambridge University Press, 1989), pp. 141-61.
4. This question is especially problematic. The Bible knows only of the rebuilding under Nehemiah, but it is highly unlikely that the walls would have remained in ruins after the re-establishment of the community and the building of the temple under Darius I. It is possible that the walls were built and rebuilt several times during the restoration period, being necessitated by numerous Arab/Idumaean raids. See M. Smith, *Palestinian Parties and Politics that Shaped the Old Testament* (London: SCM Press, 2nd edn, 1987), p. 97. Support for Smith's position can be found in Josephus, *Ant.* 11.159-63. Another possibility is that the walls which Nehemiah found in ruins had been destroyed during the revolt of satrap Megabyzus

distinction between Priests and Levites?[1] Do the chapters reflect an exilic or a Palestinian provenance? Has there been a return of the גולה ('exiles')? Is Isa. 65.17 and its reference to שמים חדשים וארץ חדשה ('new heavens and a new earth') to be interpreted in apocalyptic terms, and if so, does that imply a Hellenistic date for the passage? Does Isa. 66.1 refer to the rebuilding of the second temple in Jerusalem, or does it refer to some other temple, or is it purely theoretical and, hence, refers to no temple in particular? All of these questions have been raised time after time, but few if any can be regarded as having been definitively answered. It is evident that an impasse has been reached, and the result is a daunting array of interpretations of Third Isaiah, all fundamentally shaped by the question of dating, and all dependent on either Duhm, Elliger or Volz. It is undoubtedly correct to say that these three scholars were all partially correct, and this accounts for the fact that variations on their respective theses still continue to appear in the literature.[2]

At this point a sampling is offered of scholars who have written on Third Isaiah and the dates they have proposed for the various oracles. The purpose is to show that, in spite of significant disagreements, the discussion has moved in a common direction.

Elliger[3]

Between 538 and 519 BCE:	63.7–64.11
	63.1-6
Around 515:	60–62
	57.14-19
Not long after 515:	56.1-2
	58
	59.1-20

in 448 BCE. See E. Stern, 'The Persian Empire and the Political and Social History of Palestine in the Persian Period', in W.D. Davies and L. Finkelstein (eds.), *The Cambridge History of Judaism*. I. *Introduction; The Persian Period* (Cambridge: Cambridge University Press, 1984), pp. 70-87.

1.   Another problematic question. Even if it can be answered, what to do with this information is dependent on when to date P, and even that depends on a historical reconstruction of the priesthood in Israel.

2.   See Hanson, *Dawn*, p. 40.

3.   Elliger, *Die Einheit des Tritojesaja*, pp. 116-17.

Later, but before 500:	56.9–57.13
	65.1-7
	65.8-12
	66.1-4
	65.13-25
	66.5-17

Redactional, between 520 and Ezra:	56.3-8
	66.18-22
	57.13c
	57.20-21
	58.13-14
	59.21

Volz[1]

Pre-exilic:	56.9–57.5
	57.6-13
Around 585, beginning of exile:	63.7–64.11
Early post-exilic:	60
	62
	59.1-3
Around 520:	66.1-2
Between 500 and 450:	63.1-6
5th century?:	56.1-8
	57.14-21
	58.1-12
	58.13-14
	59.9-20
	61
	65
Hellenistic:	66.3-4
	66.17
	66.5-6
	66.17-24

Fohrer[2]

| Mid-6th century: | 63.7–64.11 |
| 520: | 66.1-4 |

1. Volz, *Jesaja II*, p. 200.
2. G. Fohrer, *Introduction to the Old Testament* (trans. D.E. Green; Nashville: Abingdon Press, 1968), p. 388.

Early post-exilic:	60–62
Beginning of 6th century:	56.1-8
	56.9–57.13
	59
Post-exilic:	57.14-21
	58.1-12
	58.13-14
	63.1-6
4th century:	65
3rd century:	66.5-24

Soggin[1]

Possibly late pre-exilic:	63.7–64.11
Before 520:	66.1-2a
Contemporary with Haggai and Zechariah:	56.1-8
	57.14-19
	60–62
	66.3-17
	58
	59.1-15a
Before Ezra–Nehemiah:	56.9–57.13
	65
Cannot be dated:	63.1-6
	59.15b-20
Redactional:	66.18-24

Westermann[2]

Around 530:	60.1-11, 13-18, 21–62.12
	59.1, 9-20
	63.7–64.11
	57.14-20
	65.16b, 18-24
	66.7-14
	58.1-12

1.   J.A. Soggin, *Introduction to the Old Testament* (trans. J. Bowden; Philadelphia: OTL; Westminster Press, 1976), pp. 336-37.

2.   C. Westermann, *Isaiah 40–66* (trans. D.M.G. Stalker; OTL; Philadelphia: Westminster Press, 1969), pp. 296-308.

Later:	56.9–57.13
	57.21
	59.2-8
	65.1-16a
	66.3-4
	66.5, 17

Later:	60.12
	63.1-6
	66.6, 15-16, 20, 22-24
	60.19-20
	65.17, 25

Framework:	56.1-2, 3-8
	58.13-14
	66.18-19, 21
	66.1-2

Pauritsch[1]

587:	63.7–64.11
520:	56.9-12
	57.1-13
	60–62
	65
	66.1-4
515:	56.1-8
	57.14-19
	66.6-16
Early post-exilic:	58
No date:	59
Later hand:	57.20-21
Apocalyptic:	63.1-6

Hanson[2]

Early post-exilic:	60–62
	57.14-21
	63.7–64.11
	58.1-12

1. Pauritsch, *Die neue Gemeinde*, pp. 219-26.
2. Hanson, *Dawn*, pp. 32-208. The only absolute date Hanson offers is that for 66.1-16, 520 BCE. All other oracles are dated forward or backward from this date. The parameters are from approximately 530 to approximately 500.

	59.1-20
	65.1-25
520:	66.1-16
	56.9–57.13
Contemporary with 60–62:	63.1-6
Redactional framework, possibly 475–425:	56.1-8
	58.13-14
	66.18-24

The seven scholars surveyed here cover the whole period of research on Third Isaiah. One could double or even treble the size of the list, but the results would be essentially the same. The survey reveals certain commonalities. There is general agreement about the extent of the various units, with the exception of chs. 59, 65 and 66. The following units can be regarded as fairly well established: 56.1-8; 56.9–57.13; 57.14-19; 58.1-12, (13-14); 60–62; 63.1-6; 63.7–64.11. Elliger is the only one in the group listed above who argues for unified authorship; the others posit several authors. In summarizing the present state of the debate, Pauritsch has written, 'As the more recent Old Testament introductions confirm, today the majority of exegetes tends toward the view that the book of Third Isaiah goes back to several chiefly post-exilic authors'.[1] This summary statement could be pushed even further by arguing that most exegetes date most of the oracles of Third Isaiah to the *early* post-exilic period.[2]

Although a small minority persists in seeking to establish authorial unity,[3] Volz's hypothesis of multiple authorship appears to have won the day, but with one major modification. Scholars are reluctant to date the oracles over a period of several centuries, as Volz did, but instead come to the conclusion that the subject matter of the bulk of the oracles fits nicely into the early restoration period. Isa. 63.7–64.11 and sections of ch. 66, particularly 66.18-24, tend to be the exceptions. The former is

---

1. Pauritsch, *Die neue Gemeinde*, p. 4 (translation mine).

2. The two major exegetical works on Third Isaiah from recent times, Pauritsch's *Die neue Gemeinde* and Hanson's *The Dawn of Apocalyptic*, both support this dating. This is also true of Sekine's redaction-critical study, *Die Tritojesajanische Sammlung*.

3. See W. Kessler, *Gott geht es um das Ganze* (Die Botschaft des Alten Testaments, 19; Stuttgart: Calwer Verlag, 1960); H.-J. Kraus, 'Die ausgebliebene Endtheophanie: Eine Studie zu Jesaja 56–66', *ZAW* 78 (1966), pp. 317-32.

usually dated earlier because of its similarities to the book of Lamentations, and the latter later because of its similarities to the first chapter of Isaiah.

The resulting view is a synthesis of the insights of Duhm, Elliger and Volz. With Duhm, the partitioning off of Isaiah 56–66 from 40–55 is accepted. With Elliger an early post-exilic dating is accepted. And with Volz multiple authorship is accepted. As is the case with the designation 'First' or 'Proto' Isaiah, 'Third' Isaiah has come mainly to designate a corpus of writings, as opposed to a particular personage. A common view is that of Westermann who identifies 60–62, 59.1, 9-20, 63.7–64.11, 57.14-20, 65.16b, 18-24, 66.7-14 and 58.1-12 with an actual person, Third Isaiah, but assigns the remaining oracles to later authors. The impasse described above is overcome by means of compromise.

A Challenge to the Consensus

As has already been stated, there have been a few scholars who continue to challenge the Third Isaiah hypothesis. The possibility that Second Isaiah could have written Isaiah 56–66 should not be readily dismissed, especially now, given the fact that the majority view dates Isaiah 56–66 to the early restoration period. Chapters 40–55 and 56–66 are now generally dated close enough together chronologically that one person could conceivably have been responsible for them. This chronological factor should play a major role in the literary critical debate, since arguments based on compatibility of subject matter, or lack thereof, are notoriously subjective. It is simply wrong for a modern interpreter to assume that an ancient Hebrew prophet could not have changed his style or even his message over the course of a career. Even what a modern person would view as blatant contradiction should not be regarded as automatic grounds for positing multiple authorship.[1]

Any standard introduction to the Old Testament reports that Second Isaiah lived and prophesied in Babylon, but because chs. 56–66 of Isaiah

---

1. The arguments put forward during the debate over Third Isaiah are amazingly similar to those put forward in the debate over the Pastoral Epistles in the New Testament. Arguments that confine themselves to questions such as 'Is it "Pauline" or not?' are circular and prove nothing. It is not the subject matter as such of the Pastorals which identifies them as non-Pauline, but rather the types of church structures that they presuppose, structures that could only have developed over a rather extended period of time. Unlike the Pastorals, however, there are no two passages in Isa. 40–66 that reflect a community situation so disparate that the career of a single prophet could not have encompassed them.

clearly do not reflect a Babylonian background, the Third Isaiah hypothesis offers itself as a way to account for this divergence. What is often overlooked, however, is that the initiator of the Third Isaiah hypothesis, Duhm, did not locate Second Isaiah in Babylon, but rather in Phoenicia.[1] Duhm had seen something which those who would later challenge his hypothesis also saw: there is no compelling reason that Isaiah 40–55 need have been spoken in Babylon. Although the change from Babylon to Jerusalem has come to be the most common reason for separating Isaiah 56–66 from 40–55, this was not Duhm's argument at all. Duhm argued mainly on the basis of change in style and subject matter. In addition, the presence of prose or prose-like material in 56–66 played a major role in his argument:

> As a writer, Third Isaiah differs from Second Isaiah as strongly as possible. To be sure, he frequently takes loftier flight at the beginning of a poem, and at those times he is somewhat reminiscent of his predecessor, but usually he sinks down into versified prose.[2]

He also saw in Third Isaiah a 'spiritualizing' of the message of Second Isaiah: 'The tendency is for citations from Second Isaiah to be spiritualized (cf. 57.14; 58.8; 62.10-11)'.[3]

The discussion subsequent to Duhm makes use of his arguments but tends to place the major emphasis on a change from Babylon to Jerusalem. There are indeed references in Second Isaiah to Babylon, to the כשדים ('Chaldeans') and to the Babylonian gods בל ('Bel') and נבו ('Nebo'), but the common recipients of the prophet's message throughout Isaiah 40–55 are identified as: Zion, Jerusalem, Judah, Jacob, Israel, my servant and the איים ('islands'). This lack of internal evidence demonstrating Babylonian provenance leads Torrey to claim, 'There is not a word in II Isaiah which could be said to point plainly to Babylonia as the place of its composition'.[4] Torrey's goal is twofold. He wants to show that Second Isaiah was neither spoken in Babylon nor was it concerned with the return of the Babylonian גולה. He even goes so far as to say that a massive return of Babylonian exiles was a literary fiction created by

---

1. Duhm, *Das Buch Jesaia*, pp. 14-15.
2. Duhm, *Das Buch Jesaia*, p. 419 (translation mine).
3. Duhm, *Das Buch Jesaia*, p. 419 (translation mine). This idea has been expanded by W. Zimmerli, 'Zur Sprache Tritojesajas', in *Gottes Offenbarung: Gesammelte Aufsätze zum Alten Testament* (Munich: Chr. Kaiser Verlag, 1963), pp. 217-33.
4. Torrey, *The Second Isaiah*, p. 20.

the Chronicler. In writing against the consensus position that Second Isaiah was a prophet to the Babylonian exiles, Torrey states his thesis as follows:

> As for the sixth century BC, and a return of the Babylonian Golah, the entire unequivocal evidence consists of the mention of Cyrus twice by name, and the presence of the names 'Babylon' and 'Chaldaea' in three other passages which speak of a 'flight' from a land of bondage. These proper names are all palpable interpolations, as will be demonstrated in the following chapter. Drop them from the text in the five passages mentioned, and there is not a word or phrase anywhere, as I shall show, to indicate that the prophet had ever heard of Jewish exiles in Babylonia. This is a striking fact, to say the least, when one remembers what the mission of the Second Isaiah is supposed to be![1]

Torrey's position is known, but it is usually dismissed as too extreme. For instance, Hanson evaluates Torrey negatively on the grounds that Torrey's interpolation theory requires 'massive surgery on the text'.[2] In actuality, Torrey's 'surgery' is quite delicate. The argument that his interpolation theory is not supported by any of the versions is not conclusive either; surely interpolations occurred in the Hebrew text prior to the rise of the versions. Another common attack on Torrey is that he has forced the text to fit his hypothesis. But Torrey claims that it was the other way around; it was the Babylonian hypothesis of the majority that was forcing the text into a particular mold. Evidence for this is the tendency of scholars gradually to reduce the amount of material in Isaiah 40–66 that is to be assigned to the prophet Second Isaiah. Initially, Second Isaiah was identified with the whole of chs. 40–66. Then Stade reduced it to chs. 40–62.[3] Then followed Duhm who reduced Second Isaiah still further to chs. 40–55, excluding the four 'Ebed-Jahwe-Lieder' (servant songs).[4] At that point everyone agreed with Duhm that chs. 56–66 were not Babylonian, but rather Palestinian. General agreement in subject matter between 40–55 and 56–66 was accounted for by the claim that the latter were written in imitation of the former. Finally, Cheyne limited Second Isaiah to chs. 40–48.[5] In every case this shrinkage was necessitated by the Babylonian hypothesis. If one started with the

1. Torrey, *The Second Isaiah*, pp. 20-21.
2. Hanson, *Dawn*, p. 36.
3. Torrey, *The Second Isaiah*, p. 6.
4. Duhm, *Das Buch Jesaia*, p. 19.
5. Torrey, *The Second Isaiah*, p. 12.

assumption that Second Isaiah lived and prophesied in Babylon, then those passages that clearly do not reflect a Babylonian background had to be assigned to a later author(s) or imitator(s).

The Babylonian hypothesis did not develop out of thin air. It was the twin references to Cyrus in 44.28 and 45.1 that gave rise to it. But after viewing the steady shrinkage of oracles assigned to Second Isaiah, Torrey decided to challenge the hypothesis itself. He wryly observed that if the reductionistic tendency continued

> it seems possible to foresee the day when the genuine writings of the 'Great Unknown of the Exile' will be reduced by this same utterly logical process of criticism to the two verses 44.28 and 45.1 (the two which contain the name of Cyrus), with or without their immediate context.[1]

It was out of this situation that he developed his interpolation hypothesis, the express intent of which was precisely to allow the text to speak instead of forcing it to fit a scholarly construct. True, the result of his procedure was the excision of a few words of text, but in Torrey's view he was performing minor corrective surgery as opposed to amputation. It is worth looking again at his proposed interpolations.

Torrey isolates five texts as interpolations: 44.28; 45.1; 43.14; 48.14; 48.20. The first two passages contain the name כורש ('Cyrus') and the final three contain the names בבל ('Babylon') and כשדים ('Chaldeans'). In analyzing these texts, Torrey relies to a large extent on a rather rigid metrical theory, the same theory that is so in evidence in the third edition of Kittel's *Biblia Hebraica*. With the publication of the *Biblia Hebraica Stuttgartensia*, that theory has come to be viewed as far too extreme.[2] It was not the meter of the passages in question, however, which originally suggested to Torrey that they contained interpolations, but rather that the references to Cyrus and to Babylon/ Chaldea come as a surprise to the careful reader; he speaks of these passages as being 'a slap in the face rather than a light to the eyes'.[3] In his opinion the references to Cyrus and to Babylon/Chaldea render the message of Second Isaiah inexplicable.[4]

In Isaiah 40–43 it is always Jacob/Israel who is the object of God's concern and the instrument through which God will act. But suddenly,

---

1. Torrey, *The Second Isaiah*, p. 13 (parentheses mine.)
2. For a current discussion of this issue, see J.L. Kugel, *The Idea of Biblical Poetry: Parallelism and its History* (New Haven: Yale University Press, 1981).
3. Torrey, *The Second Isaiah*, p. 35.
4. Torrey also viewed Isa. 34–35 as the work of Second Isaiah.

in 45.1, the Persian king, Cyrus, takes the place of Jacob/Israel. Torrey sees this as making the message of the prophet strikingly inconsistent, and he inquires whether the phrase in 45.1, לכורש ('to Cyrus'), might not be an interpolation. Basing his argument upon the inner logic of the text and upon metrical analysis, he concludes that it is. The rationale for making such an interpolation would have been an attempt to interpret the cryptic and provocative למשׁיחו ('to his messiah'). He then proposes that the correct reading of the verse is: כה אמר יהוה למשׁיחו אשׁר החזקתי בימינו ('Thus saith Yahwe, to his Anointed, to him whose right hand I hold').[1] The interpolation is to be seen as the work of a person who was influenced by the Chronicler's pattern of destruction, exile, return and restoration under the Edict of Cyrus, and who was attempting to make Second Isaiah's prophecy more concrete.

Torrey supports his position by claiming that the idea of 'return' that occurs in Second Isaiah is something quite different from the Chronicler's schematized return from Babylon. He claims that, apart from the five passages that refer to Cyrus and Babylon/Chaldea, Second Isaiah consistently refers to a 'return' from the four corners of the earth.[2] According to Torrey, the 'return' of which Second Isaiah speaks is his solution to the problem of the threatened dissolution of the people of Israel, brought about by the continued deportations and migrations of the people to other nations, a phenomenon that had been going on steadily since 722 BCE.[3] Thus, Torrey refers to Second Isaiah as 'the Prophet of the Dispersion'.[4] It is this attempt to bring the prophecies of Second Isaiah into harmony with the Chronicler's scheme that explains why the interpolation in 45.1 was made, but the result of the interpolation is logical inconsistency in the prophet's message.[5]

1. Torrey, *The Second Isaiah*, pp. 40, 238.
2. Cf. Isa. 43.6; 49.12. The same idea is expressed in Ezek. 11.17; 37.21.
3. For Torrey, the actual restoration itself was more generalized than that which is presented by the Chronicler, and had little to do with Babylon. He states his position as follows: 'Jews who had taken temporary refuge in Ammon, Moab, Edom, and other neighboring regions (cf. Jer. 40.11-12), as well as the large body that fled to Egypt (with the expressed intention of returning, Jer. 44.14), must have constituted the majority, in and near Jerusalem. This was the actual "restoration". Foreigners also poured in, as was inevitable.' Torrey, *The Second Isaiah*, p. 29; see also pp. 59-67.
4. Torrey, *The Second Isaiah*, p. 64. He chooses this designation as opposed to the traditional 'prophet of the exile'.
5. Attempts to make prophecies more concrete by means of scribal interpolations are recognized in other parts of the Hebrew Bible, but in each case the inner logic of

It has long been observed that the second half of 44.28 repeats what had just been stated in 44.26. Torrey sees the first half of the verse as just as repetitious, but with כורש taking the place of עבדו. The solution is that the whole of 44.28 was inserted to prepare the way for 45.1. For Torrey, this is evidence that more is going on than simply the accidental incorporation of a marginal gloss. All of 44.28 and the phrase לכורש in 45.1 were inserted 'in the interest of a theory'.[1] The result is that the reader is forced to conclude that the prophet successfully predicted in advance the overthrow of Babylon by Cyrus and his subsequent policy of allowing release to the exiles and the rebuilding of their city and temple, exactly as it is described by the Chronicler. In Torrey's view, a large leap of faith is required in order to accept such a proposition.

The results achieved in his exegesis of 45.1 lead Torrrey to look for other passages where the same theory appears to be in evidence. He finds three: 43.14; 48.14; 48.20. In each of these the words בבל and כשדים occur.[2] The effect of these words is again to concretize the prophecy by allusion to the 'land of exile'.[3] Torrey does use metrical analysis in his argument, but only as a supplement to the internal evidence of the passages themselves.[4]

The context surrounding Isa. 43.14 speaks of a great and joyous homecoming, and 43.14 itself speaks of this as taking place באניות ('in ships'). What could possibly be meant by a homecoming from Babylon that was supposed to take place in ships? For Torrey, the present text of

---

the passage is confused. Torrey lists several examples of this phenomenon. Isa. 7.17: את מלך אשור ;Isa. 7.20: במלך אשור ;Isa. 8.7: את מלך אשור ואת כל כבודו ;Isa. 8.6: את מלך אשור ;Isa. 7.20: את מלך אשור ;Isa. 8.7 נבוכדראצר מלך בבל ;Ezek. 26.7: החזים and את הנביאים ;Isa. 29.10: את רצין ובן רמליהו Nah. 3.18: מלך אשור ;Hos. 13.7: אשור ;Neh. 8.9: התרשתא הוא נחמיה ;Neh. 10.2: נחמיה התרשתה ;Isa. 45.13 (LXX): βασιλέα. Torrey, *The Second Isaiah*, pp. 42-43.

1. Torrey, *The Second Isaiah*, p. 44. The theory in question is that of the interpolator, namely, that the prophecies of Second Isaiah refer to the return of the Babylonian גולה as described in the work of the Chronicler.

2. That the words בבל and כשדים were of particular interest to ancient scribes is evident from Jer. 25.26 and Jer. 51.1, which appear to be instances of the phenomenon known as 'athbash'. In the former ששך is the equivalent of בבל, and in the latter לב קמי is the equivalent of כשדים.

3. Torrey, *The Second Isaiah*, p. 44.

4. 'There are few, if any, examples of interpolation in the Hebrew Old Testament more interesting and instructive than these; nor, it may safely be asserted, are there any which from internal indications alone, unaided by the testimony of parallel passages or versions, can be more certainly demonstrated'. Torrey, *The Second Isaiah*, pp. 44-45.

Isa. 43.14 is not only illogical, but as it stands it is also impossible to translate. Delete the two words בבלה and כשׂדים, however, and the verse makes perfect sense and fits logically into its surrounding context: למענכם שלחתי והורדתי בריחים כלם באניות רנתם ('For your sake I will send, and cause all the fugitives to embark, with shouts of rejoicing, in their ships').[1]

The second occurrence of the word-pair Babylon/Chaldea is in 48.14. The context is similar to that of ch. 41, with the prophet describing the history of God's dealings with his chosen people Israel, beginning with the call of Abraham and the promises made to him and to his offspring. As the text now reads, it refers to God's coming vengeance on Babylon and implies that this vengeance would demonstrate his right to be Israel's God. Torrey is unable to accept such an idea, claiming that 'a promise of vengeance on Babylonia would be too pitiful an anticlimax to be credible'.[2] To his mind, a triumph of Jews over Babylonians would prove nothing. Remove the word-pair Babylon/Chaldea, however, and the resulting text is consistent with parallel passages: הקבצו כלכם ושמעו מי בהם הגיד זאת האל יהוה אהבו יעשׂה חפצו וזרעו ('Assemble, all ye, and hear! What one among them foretold this? The One God, Yahwe, loves him, he will execute his pleasure and his might').[3]

The final place in which Torrey sees an interpolation is at 48.20. The text as it now stands lends credence to the prevailing theory that the mission of Second Isaiah was directed toward the Babylonian exiles. The commands צאו מבבל ('go out from Babylon') and ברחו מכשׂדים ('flee from the Chaldeans') appear to be incontrovertible evidence in support of the theory. But it is at least curious that the removal of the word-pair Babylon/Chaldea, as in the previous two examples, produces a strikingly rhythmic and sensible verse: צאו ברחו בקול רנה הגידו השמעו זאת הוציאוה עד קצה הארץ אמרו גאל יהוה עבדו יעקב ('Go forth, flee, with a shout of joy; proclaim this, make it known; Bring it forth to the end of the earth: Yahwe redeems his servant Jacob!').[4] Torrey's argument is the same as before:

---

1. The reference would then be a reference to a joyous return from the four corners of the earth. Torrey, *The Second Isaiah*, p. 234.

2. Torrey, *The Second Isaiah*, p. 48.

3. Torrey, *The Second Isaiah*, p. 48. In addition to the proposed interpolation Torrey also emends את אלה to זאת האל, based upon Isa. 43.9 which contains the phrase: מי בהם יגיד זאת. The text is now consistent with Isa. 41.8-10; 43.1-13; 44.1-8.

4. Torrey, *The Second Isaiah*, p. 245.

The incident of a portion of the Jewish colonists in Babylonia migrating to join their fellow countrymen in Judea would not impress 'the ends of the earth' in the least. As has already been shown, the argument, truly valid, which the prophet repeatedly presents, is based on something more substantial: the call of Abraham from a distant land, and the promises made to him; the escape from Egypt and the journey to the Promised Land; the mission of the Servant, now plainly appearing; the certain accomplishment, in the future, of the One God's eternal plan. The parallel between vv. 14-15 and vv. 20-21 is obvious, and hence the interpolator treated the two neighboring passages alike.[1]

In addition to the five passages singled out as interpolations, Torrey's thesis also receives support from the taunt against Babylon in Isaiah 47. There Babylon is clearly the subject. Interestingly, however, no mention is made of Cyrus, nor of any Babylonian captivity,[2] nor of a return from Babylon. The implication of the chapter is that 'the doom of Babylon is contemporary with the restoration of Israel—whatever that may mean'.[3]

Torrey posits a single individual living in a time later than Second Isaiah who, in reflecting upon the prophecies of Second Isaiah, and being under the influence of the Chronicler's scheme of the return of the גולה from Babylon, made a few small insertions in those prophecies in order to bring them into harmony with the systematic scheme of the Chronicler with which he was familiar. The interpolator undoubtedly believed that he was performing an act of clarification as opposed to one of deception; his procedure served only to concretize the prophecies and to bring out their true meaning. Whether he actually inserted the interpolations into the text, or simply wrote them in the margins, is a moot question. But, according to Torrey, the result of this procedure was actually to obscure the prophet's message by making it appear that the context is the Babylonian exile. Scholars who do not recognize the interpolations are then forced to reduce the number of oracles in Isaiah 40–66 assigned to Second Isaiah, and to posit another prophet (or prophets) who imitated the work of his (their) master.

Torrey emphasizes again and again that all theories of a Third Isaiah turn on the proposed change of background from Babylon to Jerusalem. In attempting to show that the only concrete evidence for a Babylonian background of any of the oracles is dependent upon five passages that

---

1.   Torrey, *The Second Isaiah*, p. 49.
2.   Isa. 47.6 refers only to the destruction of Jerusalem by the Babylonians and not to the exile.
3.   Torrey, *The Second Isaiah*, pp. 41-42.

are arguably interpolations, he hopes to defeat once and for all all theories of a Third Isaiah.[1] Isaiah 40–66 (and 34–35) is to be read as the unified work of a single author, Second Isaiah. Duhm had argued that Isaiah 56–66 presupposes a well-established community in Palestine and a rebuilt temple. With the excision of the five interpolations, chs. 40–55 would also fit into this same context. Therefore, Torrey proposes that Isaiah 34–35 and 40–66 were written by the same author, in Jerusalem, in approximately 400 BCE.[2]

By deleting the two references to Cyrus, Torrey proposes a complete revision in the common reading of Second Isaiah. The prophet was not to be viewed as merely proclaiming a military victory over Babylon under the leadership of a foreign king. Rather, he was proclaiming something much more radical, namely, the speedy advent of the Kingdom of God which was to be ushered in by God's מׁשיח ('messiah'):

> Second Isaiah is indeed a prophecy of release from bondage and a triumphant return of 'exiles' to Jerusalem by sea and land; but the prophet is looking to the ends of the earth, not to Babylonia. There is indeed prediction, definite and many times repeated, of the speedy advent of a great conqueror and deliverer, the restorer of Israel and benefactor of the world; but the prophet is speaking of the Anointed Servant of the Lord, the Son of David, not the son of Cambyses.[3]

Not only is Second Isaiah the prophet of the dispersion, he is also the one who gave the term מׁשיח ('messiah') the meaning of the coming ideal ruler who shall preside in the messianic age.[4] But in Torrey's view, if the messiah is Cyrus, then the interpreter is forced to conclude that Second Isaiah was at worst deluded, and at best disappointed.

The only scholar who has picked up on Torrey's thesis in a systematic way is Smart.[5] Like Torrey he emphasizes the lack of evidence in support of a Babylonian background for Isaiah 40–55 and accepts

---

1. Torrey's thesis has recently received indirect support from H.M. Barstad, 'Lebte Deuterojesaja in Judäa?' *Norsk Teologisk Tidsskrift* 83 (1982), pp. 77-86; *idem*, 'On the So-called Babylonian Literary Influence in Second Isaiah', *SJT* 2 (1987), pp. 90-110.

2. Torrey, *The Second Isaiah*, p. 53.

3. Torrey, *The Second Isaiah*, p. 37. Torrey also points to the curious tendency of scholars to leave Isa. 61.1ff. out of discussions on the so-called Servant Songs.

4. Torrey, *The Second Isaiah*, pp. 149-50.

5. Smart, *History and Theology in Second Isaiah*. Although Torrey had assigned Isa. 34-35 to Second Isaiah, Smart does so only with ch. 35.

Torrey's proposed interpolations.[1] He also concurs that the restoration
that is described in Isaiah 40–66 lies in the future and is yet to be
accomplished.[2] He points to passages such as 56.8, 60.3-22, 61.5-6, 62.4-
5, 10-12 and 66.23 which indicate that the prophet was still looking
forward to the ingathering of both Jew and Gentile.[3] Smart, however, is
not so constrained as Torrey was to demonstrate the total coherence of
the proclamation of Isaiah 40–66. For him, the hypothesis of a Third
Isaiah was not completely ill-conceived, because there are differences
between Isaiah 40–55 and 56–66, the most significant being that Isaiah
56–66 does appear to be addressed to a concrete community living in
Jerusalem, whereas Isaiah 40–55 is more generalized. But he does not
account for this difference in the usual way by positing a Third Isaiah.
Instead, he argues that this can be accounted for by taking seriously the
differences between oral and written speech. He points out that the text
of Isaiah 40–55 is in a much better state of preservation than that of
Isaiah 56–66. The text of Isaiah 56–66 is poorly preserved because the
oracles were originally spoken by the prophet directly to his contem-
poraries living in Jerusalem, and his words were then written down at a
later date. In contrast, the text of Isaiah 40–55 is well-preserved because
the prophet himself wrote down these words in order that they be circulated among his compatriots who were scattered throughout the
surrounding nations.[4]

The only point on which Smart differs from Torrey in a significant
way is in regard to the dating of Second Isaiah. He locates Second Isaiah
at a point no later than 538 BCE, and argues that the material does not
reflect a well-established community and rebuilt temple. The historical
background for all of the oracles is 'the direct continuation of the

---

1.   Refusal to accept the Cyrus passages as interpolations results, according to
Smart, in an absurdity, namely, that the prophet 'expected a Persian conqueror to
inaugurate a new era in which all nations would find their salvation in the acknowledgment of the sole sovereignty of Israel's God'. Smart, *History and Theology in
Second Isaiah*, p. 19.

2.   This is in contrast to Duhm who claimed that the major difference between
Isa. 40–55 and 56–66 was that the latter presupposes an already re-established
community, while the former only looks forward to this.

3.   The prophet may well have reckoned with a return of Babylonian exiles, but
they are not the object of his proclamation. With Torrey he argues that the prophet
had something much greater in mind than merely a return of exiles from Babylon.
Smart, *History and Theology in Second Isaiah*, pp. 234-35.

4.   Smart, *History and Theology in Second Isaiah*, pp. 35-36.

Jerusalem community as we see it at the beginning of the sixth century in the books of Jeremiah and Ezekiel'.[1] Smart supports this view by referring to Isa. 56.9–57.13, a passage that is often assigned a pre-exilic date.[2] The passage does have much in common with pre-exilic prophecy, but Smart warns that we should be careful to distinguish between epochal boundaries drawn by historians (e.g., pre-exilic, post-exilic) and actual life as it is experienced by individuals and communities.[3] What Isa. 56.9–57.13 demonstrates is this:

> The impression of a 'preexilic' community is actually evidence that the community addressed by the prophet was the sixth-century continuation of the shattered Jerusalem and Judah that Jeremiah had known. For those who remained in Palestine it was still 'preexilic' times.[4]

In summarizing the positions of Torrey and Smart, one must question their animosity toward the figure of Cyrus. It is certainly true that the references to Cyrus make it more difficult to understand the message of Second Isaiah because they force the interpreter to hold side by side the figures of כורש משיחי ('Cyrus, my Messiah') and ישראל עבדי ('Israel, my servant'). But it is also surely true that no single theory can resolve the problems involved with the עבד יהוה ('servant of YHWH') in Second Isaiah. Torrey and Smart would also have us believe it completely implausible for the prophet to have spoken of Cyrus as he does in 44.28–45.1. But Second Isaiah's 'Cyrus-theology' is in harmony with First Isaiah, Jeremiah and Ezekiel. Just as God in the past used a foreign ruler as the instrument of his wrath, so he is now using a foreign ruler as the instrument of his mercy.[5] In addition to this theological prejudice of the two scholars, their interpolation hypothesis borders upon circular argumentation. The only way that they are able to claim that there is no evidence of a Babylonian provenance for the oracles of Isaiah 40–55 is by removing the meager evidence that does exist.

That the theories of Torrey and Smart have received so little attention

---

1. Smart, *History and Theology in Second Isaiah*, p. 232.
2. For example, see Volz, *Jesaja II*.
3. The same thing could be said about our habit of saying that life in the eighteenth century was like this, whereas life in the nineteenth century was like that. It may be a helpful way of learning history, but it is not an accurate way of assessing life as it was actually experienced by real people who lived during these two centuries.
4. Smart, *History and Theology in Second Isaiah*, p. 238.
5. It must be acknowledged, however, that none of these other prophets refers to the foreign ruler as משיח

in the literature is unfortunate but understandable, considering the way both men appear to hold in contempt all other scholars who have written on Isaiah 40–66. It is interesting, though, how the knotty problem of dating the oracles in chs. 56–66 again comes to the forefront, even in two people who obviously share such basic presuppositions.[1]

The most recent attempt to win Isaiah 56–66 for Second Isaiah is the study by Murtonen.[2] He has rightly seen that an early post-exilic dating of chs. 56–66 raises the possibility that these passages could have been written by Second Isaiah.[3] The value of Murtonen's work is that unlike Torrey and Smart his argument is not dependent on undermining the traditional picture of Babylonian exile followed by return and restoration. Nor is he at pains, as was Torrey, to deny the possibility that some of the prophecies of Second Isaiah (specifically those contained in chs. 40–55) proved to be failures.[4] Starting with the datum that Isaiah 40–55 and 56–66 are now commonly located close together chronologically, he raises the question whether one can make the case for unified authorship based upon the vocabulary and semantics of the two sections.[5] Murtonen provides an exhaustive list of the vocabulary of Isaiah 56–66, together with the frequency of occurrence of each word; he also tabulates the number of times that each of these words occurs in chs. 40–55.[6] After

---

1.   Both scholars hold to unified authorship for Isa. 40–66 and deny a Babylonian provenance for Isa. 40–55. But even with these two major agreements their dates for Isa. 40–66 diverge by about a century and a half: 538 BCE for Smart and 400 BCE for Torrey. This, of course, has obvious implications for the kind of historical and social background an interpreter can posit for Isa. 40–66.

2.   Murtonen, 'Third Isaiah—Yes or No?'

3.   Murtonen, 'Third Isaiah—Yes or No?', p. 22.

4.   When reading Torrey, one senses a need on his part to exalt Second Isaiah to an almost divine status. At the time of his writing he claimed that Second Isaiah had come to be viewed as a 'spineless and morally deficient sky-gazer'. In attempting to reclaim the whole of Isa. 40–66 for Second Isaiah, Torrey hoped to restore Second Isaiah to his 'rightful' position of being the greatest of the Hebrew prophets. But in order to do this, he felt constrained to explain away any possibility that the prophet may have been misguided, deluded or just plain wrong. Torrey, *The Second Isaiah*, pp. 13-19.

5.   Murtonen thinks the use of the term 'author' is inappropriate in this context because of 'the relatively modest extent of the corpus'. Murtonen, 'Third Isaiah—Yes or No?', p. 28. I fail to see the problem.

6.   This same information is now available in an even more exhaustive form, and in a much more readable format, in J. Bastiaens, W. Beuken and F. Postma, *Trito-Isaiah: An Exhaustive Concordance of Isa. 56–66, Especially with Reference to*

applying a rather complex system of statistical analysis to his data, he concludes that 'the result is fully compatible with the assumption of one single author for all the chapters involved, i.e., of the identity of the "Third" with the "Second" Isaiah'.[1] Words that occur only in Isaiah 40–55 and not in 56–66 and vice versa, and words that occur in both sections but with different meanings, should not lead to the assumption of multiple authorship. The vast majority of these are readily explained by the traditional view of the change of provenance from Babylon to Palestine. For example, 'the relatively less frequent appearance of the names, Jerusalem and Zion, before ch. 60, would seem to be due to the absence from the relevant locality'.[2] That certain words take on different meanings in Isaiah 56–66 from those they had in 40–55 has long been an argument in favor of multiple authorship.[3] Murtonen, however, offers some interesting and persuasive arguments to the contrary. He shows how words often take on different meanings *within* each of the respective sections. In 56–66 for example, the word אב has the following meanings: 'God', 'ancestor', 'patriarch'. In short, it is too simplistic to focus only on change in nuance for words common to Isaiah 40–55 and 56–66 once it is recognized that changes of this sort already occur within each section. Just as the use of אב with three different meanings in 56–66 does not require the critic to posit three different authors to account for this variation, in the same way the use in 56–66 of אב to refer to God, while 40–55 never does so, cannot be taken as evidence of separate authorship for the two sections.[4]

Murtonen proposes seeing Isaiah 56–66 as the continuation of the prophecy of Second Isaiah and that the 'oracles were spoken partly in Babylonia on the eve of the departure, partly on the way to Palestine and/or through it, and partly in or near Jerusalem, between 538 and 518 BC'.[5] The oracles and their locale divide up as follows:

Deutero-Isaiah: An Example of Computer Assisted Research (Amsterdam: VU Uitgeverij, Free University Press, 1984).

1. Murtonen, 'Third Isaiah—Yes or No?' pp. 34-45.
2. Murtonen, 'Third Isaiah—Yes or No?' p. 36.
3. See Elliger, *Deuterojesaja*; Zimmerli, 'Zur Sprache Tritojesajas', pp. 217-33.
4. Murtonen, 'Third Isaiah—Yes or No?', p. 37.
5. Murtonen, 'Third Isaiah—Yes or No?', p. 38. He also claims that the oracles were written down by someone in the prophet's audience and that we now have these oracles in the chronological order in which they were spoken.

Babylon:	56.1-8; 56.9–57.13; 57.14-21
On the way to Palestine:	58.1-12; 58.13-14; 59.1-14
Palestine:	59.15-20; 59.21
Jerusalem:	60.1-22; 61.1-11; 62.1-9; 62.10-11; 63.1-6; 63.7-14;
	63.15-19; 64.1-11; 65.1-7; 65.8-25; 66.1-4; 66.5-24[1]

A New Direction

If one accepts the dominant view today that most of Isaiah 56–66 dates to the latter part of the sixth century BCE, then one is forced to admit that, purely on chronological grounds, unified authorship for Isaiah 40–66 is at least a possibility. Everyone will grant this. But why, then, do those who actually argue for unified authorship comprise such a small minority in the scholarly community? One answer may be that once a scholarly hypothesis achieves virtual consensus status, as Duhm's Third Isaiah hypothesis very quickly did, the hypothesis becomes a presupposition, as opposed to something that must always be hammered out anew. If the Third Isaiah hypothesis is to be maintained today, it must be supported by evidence that can answer the challenges of people like Torrey, Smart and Murtonen.

In my view, such evidence has been provided by Hanson in *The Dawn of Apocalyptic*. Hanson has argued that the various interpretations of Isaiah 56–66 have been marred by an almost total concentration on the question of authorship. He is in agreement with Duhm and Elliger that the material does reflect a distinctive unity, but the unity is of a kind that cannot be adequately explained by recourse to debates over authorship. The express goal of Hanson's work is, therefore, to move the study of Third Isaiah in a new direction.

Those who see Isaiah 40–66 as a unified work, those who see Isaiah 56–66 as the work of a Third Isaiah, and those who see Isaiah 56–66 as a composite work subsequently added on to the oracles of Second Isaiah, are all partially correct in Hanson's view. But what has not been adequately dealt with is the fact that Isaiah 40–66 is an anonymous collection of oracles. Failure to appreciate this fact has served as a major hindrance in the interpretation of the material. The anonymous nature of the collection points to a time when the production of prophetic literature was becoming a collective or community phenomenon.[2] Hanson's

---

1.   Murtonen, 'Third Isaiah—Yes or No?', pp. 39-41.
2.   Hanson, *Dawn*, p. 41.

proposal is that Isaiah 56–66 represents the growth of 'a common
tradition' arising out of 'a common community situation'.[1] His explication of the nature of this community situation and a critique of that
explication will be the subject matter of Chapters 3, 4 and 5. For the
present, I will focus only on Hanson's criteria for separating Isaiah 56–
66 from 40–55.

Hanson's methodology for dealing with this strictly literary-critical
question involves a combination of prosodic analysis and a typology of
prophetic genres. In applying these methods to Isaiah 56–66, he dis-
covers two parallel phenomena: (1) a breakdown of the classical poetic
canons and the rise of more prosaic forms, and (2) the evolution of
classical prophetic eschatology into apocalyptic eschatology.[2] These
parallel phenomena, in evidence in Isaiah 56–66, serve to separate this
material from chs. 40–55.[3]

Hanson has stated that in the sixth and fifth centuries BCE, Hebrew
poetry was undergoing significant structural changes. Classical Hebrew
poetry was characterized by 'the dominance of the parallel bi- and
tricolon',[4] and this same style dominates Isaiah 40–55. After Second
Isaiah 'the development is in the direction away from the dominance of
the simple bi- and tricolon toward longer, more baroque prosodic
units',[5] and this is precisely what is found in Isaiah 56–66. It is on the
basis of this development that Hanson proposes to date the oracles of

1.   Hanson, *Dawn*, p. 41. The common tradition is the tradition of Second Isaiah,
and the common community situation is the struggle for control of the temple in
Jerusalem in the early restoration period.

2.   The distinction between these two forms of eschatology consists in the fact
that in the former the divine vision/word is translated 'into the terms of plain history,
real politics, and human instrumentality', whereas in the latter the vision/word is not
translated 'into the terms of plain history, real politics, and human instrumentality'.
Hanson, *Dawn*, p. 11. Hanson designates the eschatology of Second Isaiah as 'proto-
apocalyptic' and that of Isa. 65–66 as 'early apocalyptic'. A prophet like Isaiah of
Jerusalem would represent classical prophetic eschatology, where the cosmic is fully
translated into the realm of everyday life and politics. Conversely, an example of 'full
blown' apocalyptic eschatology is represented by Zech. 14, where no attempt at all is
made to relate the cosmic to the mundane.

3.   Hanson uses the term 'Third Isaiah' to refer to Isa. 56–66, but he does not
use it to imply anything about authorship. For him, 'Third Isaiah' implies 'a unity of
tradition'. Hanson, *Dawn*, p. 60.

4.   Hanson, *Dawn*, p. 47.

5.   Hanson, *Dawn*, p. 47.

Isaiah 56–66. Stated in a simple way, breakdown of meter and internal structure implies a later date.[1]

The best place to see Hanson's methodology at work is to look at his treatment of chs. 60–62. Of all the oracles in Isaiah 56–66, these three chapters contain material that most closely parallels the style and thought of Isaiah 40–55. As a result they have often been assigned to Second Isaiah. But Hanson sees in these chapters the beginning of a process that will eventually result in the early apocalyptic eschatology of Isaiah 65–66. Analysis of the internal structure of chs. 60–62 reveals multiple affinities with chs. 40–55. The bicolon predominates throughout, as does a regular meter.[2] But there are 'features which foreshadow the development seen in later parts of Third Isaiah toward a more irregular, baroque style'.[3] Examples of this are the prose-like list in 60.17 and what he calls 'the grotesque mixing of metric patterns found in the last half of the fifth strophe of chapter 60 and in the first half of the second strophe of chapter 61'.[4] Thus, on the basis of metrical and structural analysis alone, Isaiah 60–62 occupies a transitional position between Isaiah 40–55 and the later oracles of Third Isaiah. When Isaiah 60–62 is examined with regard to its *content*, the very same pattern emerges. As in Second Isaiah, salvation is proclaimed to the entire nation and multiple parallels with chs. 40–55 can be adduced:

60.10b, 15	=	40.1-2; 44.22; 54.7-8
60.4, 9	=	43.5-7; 49.12, 18, 22
60.5-7, 16	=	45.14
61.10-11	=	49.7b, 23
60.13, 17	=	54.11-12
60.12, 14; 62.8	=	41.11-13; 51.21-23; 54.1b-3
61.8	=	54.10; 55.3
60.3	=	49.6
62.4-5	=	45.17; 54.4-8
60.16, 21	=	48.11; 49.26b[5]

1.   Hanson admits that this method can only yield a relative chronology rather than an absolute chronology.

2.   Hanson's metrical analysis is based on syllable count.

3.   Hanson, *Dawn*, p. 59.

4.   Hanson, *Dawn*, pp. 59-60. He also points out that metrical and structural change away from the style of Second Isaiah also brings with it the development of new themes characteristic of the Third Isaiah material.

5.   Hanson, *Dawn*, pp. 60-61.

In addition, three major themes of the remainder of Third Isaiah do not occur in chs. 60–62: (1) the delay of salvation/restoration,[1] (2) the positing of a new, 'future judgment which must precede the restoration', and (3) restriction of the announcement of salvation to a particular group within the people of Israel.[2] These parallels serve to link Isaiah 60–62 closely with Second Isaiah. But there are subtle differences. The prophetic task of relating the cosmic to the mundane is beginning to be severed. This can be seen in ch. 60, where the restoration described is not tied to any historical personages or events, as was the case in Second Isaiah where everything was linked to the advent of Cyrus and the fall of Babylon. Another subtle difference can be seen in Isa. 60.21 and 61.7 with the introduction of the new theme of possession of the land. Lastly, chs. 60–62 lack any polemic against foreign gods.[3] Hanson summarizes the thematic similarities and differences between Second Isaiah and Isaiah 60–62 as follows:

> Indeed, one can perhaps best describe the difference between Second Isaiah and Isaiah 60–62 by characterizing the former as the prophet's announcement of the imminent second exodus-conquest whereby Yahweh would lead the exiles back to Zion in a manner reminiscent of the first exodus, and by characterizing the latter as a program of restoration written by a group which has returned to Zion, a program based to be sure on the earlier message of Second Isaiah.[4]

His subsequent treatment of the remaining passages in Third Isaiah shows how the subtle changes that are evident in chs. 60–62, changes in meter and internal poetic structure, and changes in the overall theme of the prophecy, come to be more and more overt.

On the basis of these parallel changes Hanson proposes a theory for establishing a relative chronology for the oracles in Third Isaiah. Isaiah 60–62, which represents the beginning of the transition, reflects the earliest stage, whereas 56.9–57.13, in which the transition is far advanced, reflects the latest.[5] The only oracle for which Hanson proposes an

---

1. For an exposition of Third Isaiah based upon this particular theme, see Kraus, 'Die ausgebliebene Endtheophanie'.

2. Hanson, *Dawn*, p. 61.

3. Hanson, *Dawn*, pp. 62-63.

4. Hanson, *Dawn*, p. 64. The group that is responsible for the production of Isa. 56–66 is identified by Hanson as 'the Visionary Disciples of Second Isaiah'.

5. Isa. 56.1-8 and 66.18-24 are regarded as a 'redactional framework' and are not considered part of the same process. Hanson, *Dawn*, pp. 162, 388-89.

absolute date is 66.1-16. He argues that the בַּיִת ('house') which occurs in
66.1 is best understood as referring to the new, Persian period temple,
the construction of which was encouraged by Haggai.[1] Hanson is, therefore, able to state that 66.1-16 'can be dated with confidence circa 520
BC, that is, in the period of the rebuilding of the temple'.[2] By establishing this one absolute date, he is then able to set parameters for the
relative chronology that his method had previously yielded. Those
oracles that are less developed with regard to internal structure and
prophetic genre are to be dated earlier than 520, and those that are
more developed are to be dated later. The result is that the oracles of
Third Isaiah, excluding 56.1-8 and 66.18-24, span the period of time
from roughly 538 to 500 BCE.

As previously stated, Hanson traces a parallel development in Isaiah
56–66: (1) a breakdown of the classical poetic canons and the rise of
more prosaic forms, and (2) the evolution of classical prophetic eschatology into apocalyptic eschatology. His analysis of the first of these
developments has not escaped criticism.[3] But in spite of the immense
amount of labor that was required for this part of his book, the most
persuasive arguments for reading Isaiah 56–66 as a unit, separate and
distinct from 40–55, come from his exposition of the transition in
prophetic genres that can be observed in chs. 56–66. Although not
evident in 60–62, the most dominant characteristic of the Third Isaiah
material is its polemical nature. Unlike Second Isaiah, however, which is
also highly polemical, the polemic is not directed outwardly, that is,
toward foreign nations, but rather toward groups within the restoration
community. In his exegesis of 56.9–57.13, 58.1-12, 59.1-20, 65.1-25 and
66.1-16, Hanson shows how words of salvation and judgment are no
longer delivered along national lines (e.g., salvation for Israel and judgment for the nations, or vice versa), 'rather the line cuts through one
nation, and thus in an oracle delivered to that nation, salvation and

---

1.   For other interpretations of בַּיִת in Isa. 66.1, see Hanson, *Dawn*, pp. 168-70;
Pauritsch, *Die neue Gemeinde*, p. 198.

2.   Hanson, *Dawn*, pp. 172-73.

3.   Hanson admitted that his using an analysis of the 'development of the canons
of poetic composition' as a tool for dating biblical poetry could only be regarded as a
tentative attempt. But he does operate out of the conviction that prose or prose-like
material is, relatively speaking, evidence of lateness. This distinction between Hebrew
poetry and Hebrew prose, however, rests upon various metrical theories that have been
severely challenged by Kugel, *The Idea of Biblical Poetry*.

judgment words' occur side by side.[1] He refers to the juxtaposition of
salvation and judgment words within a single oracle as a 'salvation-
judgment oracle'.[2] This juxtaposition does not occur uniformly throughout Third Isaiah, but rather is a developing process. For example, it is
nowhere to be found in Isaiah 60–62 or 57.14-21. The beginnings of a
rift within the community, however, can be seen in 63.7–64.11 and in
chs. 58–59. And in 65.1-25, 66.1-16 and 56.9–57.13 the fusion of salvation and judgment words is complete. This can be clearly observed in
65.13-14 with its rapid oscillation between salvation for 'my servants'
(עבדי) and judgment for 'you' (אתם).

Hanson's work in illustrating the emergence of the salvation-judgment
oracle in chs. 56–66 provides the surest evidence for rejecting the thesis
that Isaiah 40–66 is to be treated as a single unit written by a single
individual, Second Isaiah. Whether one accepts his analysis of the internal structure of the poetry or not, the existence of this new kind of
oracle in chs. 56–66 requires a much more dynamic explanation to
account for it than the theory of unified authorship for Isaiah 40–66 is
able to provide. The genius of Hanson's approach is that it shows how
the critical insights in the history of scholarship on Third Isaiah that have
traditionally been regarded as mutually exclusive, at least with regard to
the literary-critical question, can be synthesized in such a way that the
insights are taken seriously, and that the discussion can then be moved
in a new and fruitful direction. The traditional Second Isaiah-Babylonian-

---

1.   Hanson, *Dawn*, p. 150. That the nation as a whole is no longer considered to
be the recipient of the proclamation of salvation can be seen in Isa. 65.10. In this
verse, the common national designation, עמי ('my people'), has to be qualified by the
additional phrase, אשר דרשוני ('who seek me'). In full-blown apocalyptic eschatology
the traditional distinction between Israel and the nations gives way completely to the
new distinction between the צדיקים ('righteous') and the רשעים ('wicked').

2.   The traditional method for dividing the oracles of Third Isaiah was based on
the distinction between salvation and judgment, that is, oracles were understood to be
either salvation oracles or judgment oracles, and no mixing of the two was allowed. A
classic example of this procedure is found in Westermann's treatment of Isa. 66.18-
24. He claims that this passage is made up of two distinct oracles, 66.18-19, 21 and
66.20, 22-24, which have been secondarily fused. Because the former breathes a spirit
of universalism and the latter a spirit of particularism and judgment, they must have
been originally separate. See Westermann, *Isaiah 40–66*, pp. 423-29. But Hanson
has demonstrated that the themes of salvation and judgment are so intimately intertwined in many of the oracles of Third Isaiah that division of the oracles based purely
upon this distinction not only is illegitimate but also completely misses the sense of
the oracles.

Third Isaiah-Palestinian dichotomy is upheld. As regards the unity of Third Isaiah, he shows how Elliger and Volz could have arrived at such (seemingly) contradictory conclusions. Elliger is correct in pointing out the manifold similarities among the oracles in Isaiah 56–66, but in Hanson's view these similarities are better explained by seeing a common tradition at work rather than a single author. On the other hand, it is Volz who shows that in spite of certain similarities, internal differences on the level of style and theological outlook make it highly questionable whether these can be accounted for by the thesis of unified authorship. The weakness in Volz's position is that he ends up denying even the most basic insights of Elliger by treating the oracles of Third Isaiah as if each one were completely isolated from the rest. He is led to this extreme position by his attempt to link some questionable historical references in Third Isaiah to known historical people, places and events. But because our historical knowledge of the post-exilic period is so sparse, he is forced to arrive at widely divergent dates for each of the oracles. Hanson's approach incorporates the basic insights of Volz with regard to dissimilarity among the oracles, but he is able to show that recourse to widely divergent dates is unnecessary. Such differences can be accounted for when the material is viewed as the production of a distinct group within the post-exilic community whose message is developing dynamically in response to a variety of sociological and theological factors.

Isaiah 56–66 and the Scroll of Isaiah

A great number of works dealing with Third Isaiah that have been written since Hanson have begun to talk about Third Isaiah within the context of the Isaiah scroll as a whole. The impetus for this shift in focus has no doubt arisen from the renewed interest in reading biblical texts in their literary context. Studies such as Hanson's and Westermann's are attempts to recover the original sequence in which the oracles of Third Isaiah were delivered, but they offer little help for understanding the oracles in the context in which they now stand.[1] Childs, drawing upon the anonymous nature of Isaiah 40–66, calls attention to the almost total lack of historical references within the second major division of Isaiah. He argues that the scroll as a whole has been structured along the lines

---

1.   A good example is the fact that Hanson does not even exegete Isa. 56.1-8 and 66.17-24, identifying them (negatively) as a redactional framework.

of prophecy and fulfillment, and in that sense, it has a self-consciously theological structure. To be sure, no one would deny that theological reflection has often interfered with the actual history of biblical texts and that it is important not to confuse the two, but Childs argues that it is also a mistake to regard the present structure of the Isaiah scroll as merely a 'historical fiction'.[1] Chapters 40–66 have an explicitly theological function within the Isaiah scroll, and this theological function requires that the original historical background of the material be subordinated. Childs's thesis is that the overarching theological structure of the scroll (judgment and salvation, prophecy and fulfillment, exile and return, destruction and restoration) serves to bind it together as the unified חזון ישעיהו ('vision of Isaiah').[2]

These insights lead Childs to ask the following question:

> In the light of the present shape of the book of Isaiah the question must be seriously raised if the material of Second Isaiah (i.e., chapters 40–66) in fact ever circulated in Israel apart from its being connected to an earlier form of First Isaiah.[3]

In other words, it is conceivable that the material in Isaiah 40–66 was, from the beginning, composed in conscious dialogue with First Isaiah. In support of this position, Childs argues that

> the force of much of the imagery of both Second and Third Isaiah is missed unless the connection with First Isaiah is recognized. The schema of before and after, of prophecy and fulfilment, provides a major bracket which unites the witnesses.[4]

All of this produces the question as to whether it is appropriate, even on historical grounds, to speak of the 'book' of Second or Third Isaiah.[5]

---

1. Childs, *Introduction to the Old Testament as Scripture*, p. 325.
2. On this phrase as the possible original title of the work, see 2 Chron. 32.32; Sir. 48.22.
3. Childs, *Introduction to the Old Testament as Scripture*, p. 329 (parentheses mine).
4. Childs, *Introduction to the Old Testament as Scripture*, pp. 329-30.
5. There is no concrete evidence that a book of Second or Third Isaiah ever circulated independently. However, the text of 1QIsa has a break of three lines at the end of ch. 33. This may imply a tradition of dividing Isaiah into two parts or halves. See W.H. Brownlee, *The Meaning of the Qumran Scrolls for the Bible: With Special Attention to the Book of Isaiah* (New York: Oxford University Press, 1964), pp. 247-59. But this says nothing about the independent circulation of the two parts; even if a definite division was intended, it remains a manifestly internal one. The same could be

That such a question can be seriously considered is an illustration of how
far the study of the Hebrew Bible in general, and of Isaiah in particular,
has come. No longer is the present form of Isaiah viewed as having
resulted 'from an accidental linkage of two separate manuscripts (Isa.
1–39; 40–66)'.[1] On the contrary, Isaiah is seen as a document that intri-
cately interweaves historically disparate traditions. Not only does it
appear that the second major division (40–66) was composed in dialogue
with the first, but also that the first division was fundamentally shaped
by the concerns of the second.[2] That the latter is the case is clear from
the fact that Isaiah 1–39 contains a wealth of material that is not of pre-
exilic origin but rather speaks the idiom of Second or Third Isaiah.[3] The
intimate interconnectedness of the whole of Isaiah is asserted by Childs
when he claims that 'Second Isaiah begins in ch. 1', the chapter that
provides 'a theological summary of the message of the entire Isaianic

---

said of Josephus's remark about Ezekiel that he 'left behind him in writing two
books', *Ant.* 10.79-80. On the other hand, a passage like Isa. 8.16, צור תעודה חתום
תורה בלמדי ('Bind up the testimony, seal the teaching among my disciples'), implies a
collection of sayings of Isaiah of Jerusalem. See also Isa. 30.8, עתה בוא כתבה על לוח
אתם ועל ספר חקה ותהי ליום אחרון לעד עד עולם ('Go now, write it upon a tablet before
them, and inscribe it on a scroll, so that it will be an eternal witness for a later time').
It should be noted that Brownlee did attempt to provide evidence for an independent
book, Second Isaiah. In 'The Manuscripts of Isaiah from which DSIa was Copied',
BASOR 127 (1952), pp. 16-21, he argues that chs. 1–33 and 34–66 of 1QIsa reflect
different textual traditions, and this would seem to imply that the scribe who copied
the Great Isaiah Scroll had before him two separate 'books' of Isaiah.
    1.   Childs, *Introduction to the Old Testament as Scripture*, p. 330 (parentheses
mine).
    2.   Childs, *Introduction to the Old Testament as Scripture*, p. 333. Childs affirms
that the material commonly referred to as Third Isaiah may have originally been
dependent upon Second Isaiah, but in their present context both Second and Third
Isaiah have the same function within the book as a whole. Thus, he often uses the
designation 'Second' Isaiah, to refer to Isa. 40–66, but when he speaks specifically of
chs. 56–66 he uses 'Third' Isaiah. The common function that Isa. 40–55 and 56–66
serve in their present context goes a long way toward explaining why scholars
continue to emerge who argue against separating Isa. 56–66 from 40–55.
    3.   The best examples are Isa. 1, 34–35 and to a lesser extent Isa. 13–14, 24–27.
On the post-exilic dating of Isa. 13–14, see now B. Gosse, *Isaïe 13, 1-14, 23 dans la
tradition littéraire du livre d'Isaïe et dans la tradition des oracles contre les nations*
(OBO, 78; Freiburg: Universitätsverlag; Göttingen: Vandenhoeck & Ruprecht, 1988).
Gosse links Isa. 13–14 to the same post-exilic concerns which shape Isa. 24–27; 34–
35, 60–62.

corpus by using material from several periods of Isaiah's ministry'.[1]

Childs's work on Isaiah emphasizes the thoroughgoing theological concerns that gave final shape to the book. These concerns were such that virtually all historical particularity in chs. 40–66 has been suppressed in an attempt to link the entire book together as a coherent whole. He also argues that the various semantic, stylistic and theological nuances are so intertwined in the book that none of the individual sections (1–12, 13–39, 40–55, 56–66 or any variation thereof) can, as it were, stand on its own.

As regards Third Isaiah, it is clear that it contains the majority of the latest material in Isaiah. But how far removed, chronologically speaking, is Third Isaiah from the final editing of the Isaiah scroll? That the distance is not far at all can be inferred from the fact that many of the concerns that surface in Third Isaiah are the very same concerns that shape the whole of Isaiah. This, in turn, implies that what is going on in Third Isaiah is an integral part of a process that eventually led to the creation of the entire book of Isaiah.[2] Any interpretation of Third Isaiah that does not take this into account does not do justice to the material.

The views of Childs have received direct support from other scholars who have begun to focus on the book as a whole. Ackroyd, Rendtorff and Clements have all sought to show how chs. 1–39 have been shaped by the exilic and post-exilic theological concerns of the second part of the book. Ackroyd argues that the present structure of Isaiah 1–39 has reinterpreted the negative prophecies of Isaiah in such a way that they are (ultimately) to be understood as prophecies of salvation.[3]

Clements has devoted much effort to the question of the unity of Isaiah, and in this regard he is a pioneer in the new approach to Isaiah.[4] He does not deny validity to previous (predominantly literary) research on Isaiah, but he insists that it has neglected all of the things that bind

1. Childs, *Introduction to the Old Testament as Scripture*, p. 331.
2. See M.A. Sweeney, *Isaiah 1–4 and the Post-Exilic Understanding of the Isaianic Tradition* (BZAW, 171; Berlin: de Gruyter, 1988).
3. P.R. Ackroyd, 'Isaiah I–XII: Presentation of a Prophet', in J.A. Emerton *et al.* (eds.), *Congress Volume, Göttingen 1977* (VTSup, 29; Leiden: Brill, 1978), pp. 16-48.
4. R.E. Clements, 'Beyond Tradition History: Deutero-Isaianic Development of First Isaiah's Themes', *JSOT* 31 (1985), pp. 95-113; *idem, Isaiah and the Deliverance of Jerusalem* (JSOTSup, 13; Sheffield: JSOT Press, 1980); *idem, Isaiah 1–39* (NCB; repr.; London: Marshall, Morgan & Scott; Grand Rapids: Eerdmans, 1987); *idem,* 'The Prophecies of Isaiah and the Fall of Jerusalem in 587 BC', *VT* 30 (1980), pp. 421-36; *idem,* 'The Unity of the Book of Isaiah', *Int* 36 (1982), pp. 117-29.

the book together. In addition, Clements argues against trying to establish
the unity of the book as a unity based on authorship.[1] The problem with
this approach is that it does not require 'any truly intrinsic connection of
content between various blocks of material'.[2] For Clements, the unity of
Isaiah is to be conceived as a redactional unity, and he has attempted to
describe the redactional process through which the book received its
final form.[3] The major impulse leading to the present structure of the
book was when scribes came to understand certain prophecies of Isaiah
of Jerusalem as having been fulfilled in the events of 587 BCE.[4]
Evidence that this interpretive step was actually taken can be seen in a
group of systematic additions to the words of Isaiah, all of which have
the express purpose of reinterpreting words originally spoken about the
Assyrians as words that now reflect the Babylonian destruction.[5] The
effect of this interpretive step was to link Assyrian Isaiah with the
Babylonian period.[6]

It has long been recognized that the overall structure of the book of
Isaiah reflects an Assyrian–Babylonian dichotomy, but the problem has
been the question of how to account for this structural phenomenon.
Clements has forcefully argued that the key to understanding how such
chronologically disparate periods came to be united under the heading of
a single prophetic figure lies in the scribal reinterpretation of the words

1.   In this he is not referring to an anti-critical position that would seek to establish a single author for chs. 1–66, but rather to the common 'discipleship' or 'school'
hypothesis originally championed by Mowinckel.

2.   Clements, 'Beyond Tradition-History', p. 97.

3.   In a significant departure from Childs, Clements wants to keep separate the
redactional activity that shaped Isaiah and the issue of canonization. That this is a
necessary distinction is clear from the fact that 'the book of Isaiah had acquired its
present shape by the time the limits of the canon were determined'. Clements,
'Beyond Tradition History', p. 112.

4.   Clements 'The Prophecies of Isaiah'.

5.   Isa. 1.9; 2.18-19; 2.20-21; 6.12-13; 8.19-20; 8.21-22; 17.7-8; 17.9; 22.5-8a;
22.8b-11; 22.24-25; 23.13. It was also at this time, according to Clements, shortly
after 587 BCE, that Isa. 2.6–4.1 was placed in its present position. This section, containing the harshest words that Isaiah uttered against Judah and Jerusalem, took on
the role of a preface to Isa. 5.1–14.27 and served to make clear that Isaiah had
predicted the destruction of Jerusalem at the hands of the Babylonians.

6.   This linkage is even more explicit in 2 Kgs 20.12-19 = Isa. 39, the story of
the visit of the emissaries from Merodach-baladan. A parallel process can be observed
in Jer. 26 where the eighth-century words of Micah (Mic. 3.12) are understood to
receive their fulfillment in the Babylonian period.

of Isaiah of Jerusalem in the light of the destruction of the city and the
temple in 587 BCE. In his words, 'Isaiah's prophecies were felt to have
an important bearing upon the fate of Jerusalem and the Davidic
dynasty'.[1]

But how is the predominantly positive nature of the prophecies in
chs. 40–66 to be explained? This can only be answered from an analysis
of the material traditionally known as Second Isaiah. Clements sees three
possibilities for explaining the relationship of chs. 40–55 to 1–39. The
first is that Isaiah 40–55 was originally a completely independent
collection. The second is that the juxtaposition of chs. 1–39 and 40–55
was the work of a scribe who viewed chs. 40–55 as a suitable sequel to
the prophecies of Isaiah. The third 'is that, from the outset, the material
in chs. 40–55 was intended to develop and enlarge upon prophetic
sayings from Isaiah of Jerusalem'.[2] It is Clements's contention that the
third option is the most probable. His position is based upon an examination of two major themes in chs. 40–55 that appear to be developments
or elaborations of elements in chs. 1–39. The first is the theme of the
blindness and deafness of the people that occurs in Isa. 42.16, 42.18-19,
43.8 and 44.18. Unless one is familiar with the call narrative in Isaiah 6,
such a theme seems to be totally unexpected within the context of
chs. 40–55. The second is the theme of the divine election of Israel that
Second Isaiah stresses in a variety of phrases, for example: 40.1; 41.8-9;
42.1-4; 43.6-7; 43.20-21; 44.1-2; 44.5, 21-22; 45.4, 9-10; 51.4, 16; 52.5.
Clements demonstrates that Second Isaiah's election language was
designed to counter the specific claim of Isaiah that God had in fact
rejected Israel.[3] He summarizes his position by stating that Second Isaiah
did not have 'an entirely independent and self-contained message of his
own to declare'.[4] On the contrary, the largely promissory material in
Second Isaiah was never intended to be understood apart from its

1. Clements, 'The Prophecies of Isaiah', pp. 434-35.
2. Clements, 'Beyond Tradition History', p. 100-101.
3. See Isa. 2.6, כי נטשתה עמך בית יעקב ('For you have rejected your people, the
house of Jacob'). Additional evidence of thematic development is also noted. Isa.
43.10, 12, 44.8, 55.4 are dependent on the reference to עדים ('witnesses') in Isa. 8.2.
Isa. 42.4, 21 pick up on the reference to תורה ('teaching') in Isa. 8.16. Isa. 44.26 is a
reversal of Isa. 6.11. Isa. 49.22-23 refers to YHWH's נס ('standard') which he will
use to summon the nations; such a usage seems to be dependent on the Isaianic
saying in Isa. 5.26. One could also add to this list Isa. 62.10. Clements, 'Beyond
Tradition History', pp. 106-109.
4. Clements, 'The Unity of the Book of Isaiah', p. 128.

relationship to the more primary units in chs. 1–39.[1]

Although Clements has concentrated mainly on the relationship between Isaiah 1–39 and 40–55, his work has obvious implications for the question of Third Isaiah. If Clements is correct that Isaiah 40–55 cannot stand alone, then, קל וחמר, neither can Isaiah 56–66.[2]

A somewhat different approach to Isaiah is represented by Rendtorff.[3] Whereas Childs, Ackroyd and Clements reflect variations on the traditional view that some collection of the words of Isaiah of Jerusalem represents the core of the book and that it was this core that generated subsequent reinterpretation, Rendtorff sees Isaiah 40–55 as the actual core of the book. His position is based upon an examination of key words and ideas from Second Isaiah that occur in the other major sections of the book.[4] He summarizes the results of his study as follows:

> First of all, it has been shown, in my view, that the second part of the book, chs. 40–55, occupies a dominant position in the book as a whole. Both in the first and in the third part it is clearly evident that the compositional work takes its bearings from the second part, either drawing on it directly or orientating its own utterances toward it. This is confirmed by the insight (acquired independently of this postulate) that chs. 40–55 present a unified

1. This is essentially the position of Childs as well, who argued that Second Isaiah's references to the ראשנות ('former things') can only be understood as referring 'to the prophecies of First Isaiah'. Childs, *Introduction to the Old Testament as Scripture*, p. 329. The difference is that for Clements this unity of message is not confined to a 'canonical' reading, but is already apparent in the redactional growth of the book.

2. This is true whether or not one accepts Zimmerli's view that Third Isaiah represents a 'spiritualization' of the language of Second Isaiah. Whatever one thinks of Zimmerli's thesis, it is clear that he has demonstrated an intrinsic relationship between the language of Second and Third Isaiah. Clements has drawn attention to a particular passage in Third Isaiah that demands to be understood in the context of the book as a whole, Isa. 62.6-12. With its picture of a gloriously restored Jerusalem it serves as an effective redress to the dire oracles uttered against the city in Isa. 1–32. Clements, 'The Unity of the Book of Isaiah', pp. 128-29.

3. R. Rendtorff, 'The Composition of the Book of Isaiah', in *Canon and Theology: Overtures to an Old Testament Theology, Overtures to Biblical Theology* (trans. M. Kohl; Minneapolis: Fortress Press, 1993), pp. 146-69.

4. Focusing mainly on Isa. 40, he analyzes נחם ('comfort'), Zion/Jerusalem, the coming of the Lord's כבוד ('glory'), and עון ('transgression'), all of which play significant roles elsewhere in the book.

and self-contained unit. Consequently it would seem reasonable to assume
that chs. 40–55 form the heart of the present composition and that the two
other parts have been shaped and edited in its light, and point toward it.[1]

Although Rendtorff's position represents a significant departure from
the traditional view of the growth of the book, his work confirms
Childs's argument that Isaiah 1–39 was fundamentally shaped by the
concerns of the second half of the book. Where he differs from Childs is
in his claim that Isaiah 40–55 could theoretically have had an independent
existence.

Rendtorff's work also has implications for the study of Third Isaiah.
Based upon the manifold relationships between Third Isaiah and the rest
of the book, he argues that an independent existence of the former is
'hardly conceivable'.[2] In addition, and perhaps more importantly, he
claims it to be very likely that those responsible for the final form of
Isaiah 56–66 also played a major role in the final redaction of the book
as a whole.[3] This implies that the concerns reflected in Third Isaiah are
not far removed from the concerns of the final form of the book.

The cumulative insights of Childs, Ackroyd, Clements and Rendtorff
have been taken up by Sweeney in a detailed study designed to demonstrate the redactional unity of Isaiah.[4] Sweeney has called attention to
five major lines of evidence that serve to unify the book. First, the anti-
Babylonian oracle in Isaiah 13–14, coming as it does in the section of the
book that deals exclusively with Assyria, serves to link chs. 1–39 with
40–66. Secondly, Isaiah 36–39 forms a transition between 1–35 and 40–
66 by providing a context for the latter. Isaiah's prophecy of the coming
exile of the house of Hezekiah is to be understood as specifically referring
to the Davidic dynasty, and in Sweeney's words, this 'paves the way for
the "democratized" Davidic covenant in Second Isaiah'.[5] Thirdly, Isaiah
35 serves as a transitional chapter in that it anticipates major themes in
the second part of the book, for example, the transformation of the

1.   Rendtorff, 'The Composition of the Book of Isaiah', p. 167.
2.   Rendtorff, 'The Composition of the Book of Isaiah', p. 169.
3.   This is also the position of Roth who places the composition of the entire
book around 520 BCE. See W. Roth, *Isaiah* (ed. J.H. Hayes; Knox Preaching
Guides; Atlanta: John Knox Press, 1988).
4.   Sweeney, *Isaiah 1–4*.
5.   Sweeney, *Isaiah 1–4*, p. 17. For the particular notion of a democratized
Davidic covenant, see O. Eissfeldt, 'The Promises of Grace to David in Isaiah 55.1-
5', in B.W. Anderson and W. Harrelson (eds.), *Israel's Prophetic Heritage: Essays
in Honor of James Muilenberg* (New York: Harper & Row, 1962).

wilderness and the creation of a highway (מסלול), and it also summarizes themes from the first part of the book, for example, the blindness/ deafness of the people and the Exodus motif. Fourthly, 'Isa. 1 and 65–66 form an inclusion which is intended to unite the entire book of Isaiah'.[1] Fifthly, the material in chs. 1–39 'has been presented in such a way as to anticipate the concerns of the second part of the book'.[2] Sweeney's major thesis is that the book as a whole reflects the concerns of the late exilic and post-exilic periods, and that 'in essence, the concerns of the latter part of the book dictated the final redaction of the first part'.[3]

With regard to Isaiah 56–66 Sweeney shows how these chapters present a coherent message, but nevertheless a message that demands to be understood as a part of the overall message of the book. This overall message Sweeney entitles 'Exhortation to the People of Jerusalem/Judah to Return to YHWH as their God'. In order to show how chs. 56–66 function within the context of the overall message of the book, I will give Sweeney's structural analysis in full.[4]

Exhortation to the People of Jerusalem/Judah
to Return to YHWH as their God (1–66)

I. Prologue: Exhortation: YHWH's Offer of
    Redemption to the People (1)

II. Elaboration: Exhortation to People to
    Participate in YHWH's Plan for New World
    Order (2–66)

    A. Announcement of YHWH's plan for New
       World Order centered in Zion (2–35)

       1. Announcement concerning the cleansing
        of Zion for its role (2–4)

       2. Elaboration on implementation of plan to achieve
        new world order under YHWH (5–35)

          a. chastisement of Israel/Judah and
            the nations (5–27)
          b. announcement of YHWH's assumption of
            kingship in Zion (28–35)

1. Sweeney, *Isaiah 1–4*, p. 24.
2. Sweeney, *Isaiah 1–4*, p. 24.
3. Sweeney, *Isaiah 1–4*, p. 185.
4. Sweeney, *Isaiah 1–4*, p. 98.

B. Transition: Narrative Explanation for Delay
   in implementation of Plan (36–39)

C. Exhortation to Participate in YHWH's
   Renewed Covenant (40–66)

   1. Announcement that YHWH is reestablishing
   His covenant with Zion (40–54)

     a. announcement proper: prophet's commission
   to announce YHWH's return to
   Zion (40.1-11)

     b. substantiation: YHWH is renewing His
   covenant with Zion (40.12–54.17)

   2. Exhortation proper to join covenant (55–66)

For Sweeney, chs. 56–66 represent the goal toward which the book as a whole is striving, namely, the attempt to persuade the people to join YHWH's renewed covenant. The chapters are unified by their concentration upon the requirements for membership in this new covenant community.[1]

For our purposes it is highly significant that Sweeney places the final redaction of the book of Isaiah in the late fifth century, around the time of Ezra and Nehemiah.[2] If one accepts the most common dating of the material in chs. 56–66, this means that the final redaction of the book was not far removed chronologically from much of the material in Isaiah 56–66, and it should therefore come as no surprise that the dominant concerns of chs. 56–66—elucidating the criteria for determining who will be a part of the new covenant community and who will not—also come to expression elsewhere in the book.[3]

---

1.   Sweeney, *Isaiah 1–4*, p. 88. He acknowledges the traditional view that ch. 55 originally served as the epilogue of Isa. 40–55, but in its present position, having much in common with what follows, it forms a 'bridge' between chs. 40–54 and 56–66. Sweeney's discussion of the issue helps explain why a small but significant group of scholars has continually resisted the practice of separating Isa. 56–66 from 40–55.

2.   Sweeney, *Isaiah 1-4*, p. 99.

3.   Sweeney argues that the final form of the book presupposes Persian rule. This is supported by the consistently positive references to the Medes (Isa. 13.17; 21.2) and to Cyrus (Isa. 44.28; 45.1) as the instruments through which Babylon would be overthrown, by the fact that Persia/Media is not condemned in Isa. 13–23, and by the fact that the book does not know Greece as a major world power. In addition, the word תורה ('Torah') in Isaiah is always used in a general way and never takes on the

Summary

Is it legitimate to continue to speak of a Third Isaiah? The answer can only be yes and no. Duhm was correct to see a different historical background behind Isaiah 56–66 from that of chs. 40–55. But his contention that a single prophetic figure, Third Isaiah, was responsible for chs. 56–66 is to be rejected. In this regard, the designation 'Third Isaiah' remains a helpful one if it is understood to refer to a section of the book of Isaiah and not to a particular historical personage. In addition, Third Isaiah is not to be viewed as an independent collection. Those scholars who have continually opposed the attempt to separate Isaiah 56–66 from 40–55 are correct, but for reasons different from those they proposed. The relationship of these two sections cannot be decided by resorting to arguments about authorship. Apart from the question of authorship, the issue is whether or not Isaiah 56–66 came into existence independently of chs. 40–55. The answer is probably no. The issues and themes of Isaiah 56–66 demand to be read against the background of chs. 40–55 and can be understood as continuations, extensions and reinterpretations thereof. Isaiah 56–66 is, therefore, dependent upon 40–55.

But what of the relationship between Isaiah 40–66 and 1–39? This is the question that much work on Isaiah is presently attempting to solve. Childs's question as to whether chs. 40–66 ever circulated independently of an earlier form of First Isaiah is to be seriously considered. Sweeney and others have attempted to show that the book of Isaiah is a redactional unity and that the themes of each of the major sections of the book are present throughout the book. This implies that, although the book reflects three distinct historical periods (Assyrian, Babylonian, Persian) and although these historical periods roughly correspond to First, Second and Third Isaiah, nevertheless the growth of the book cannot be conceived as having arisen from the simple juxtaposition of the three major blocks of material. It appears, rather, that at each successive stage in the book's growth the earlier material was reshaped by the concerns of the later material.[1]

specific sense of the post-Ezra period. Finally, we know that the question of membership in the community was of fundamental importance at the time of Ezra and Nehemiah.

1. For a careful and provocative study of the growth of the material in Isa. 56–66 and its relationship to earlier forms of the book of Isaiah, see O.H. Steck, 'Tritojesaja im Jesajabuch', in J. Vermeylen (ed.), *The Book of Isaiah, Le Livre d'Isaïe* (BETL,

The implications of such an approach for Third Isaiah studies are manifold. The most provocative is that the concerns of Third Isaiah, containing as it does the majority of the latest material in the book, ought to be present throughout the book. It has long been noticed that criteria for membership in the restoration community play a large role in Isaiah 56–66. It is my contention that the final shape of the book of Isaiah also reflects this concern, and that an investigation of Third Isaiah that focuses on the question of who is to be *excluded* from the restoration community can significantly contribute to our understanding of the overall message of Isaiah and provide one key to the redactional growth of the book. As a result, it can be argued that attempts to interpret the material in Isaiah 56–66 apart from its relationship to the book as a whole will be at best, inadequate, and at worst, misleading.

As was stated early on in this chapter, the problem of dating the oracles in Isaiah 56–66 is an extremely difficult one because there are few explicit historical references. I regard Isa. 64.10 as the single concrete historical reference, referring as it does to the burning of the temple: בית קדשינו ותפארתנו אשר הללוך אבתינו היה לשרפת אש וכל מחמדינו היה לחרפה ('Our holy and glorious house where our fathers worshipped you has been burned with fire, and everything precious to us has come to ruin'). This paucity of concrete historical evidence led McCullough to date all of Isaiah 56–66 to the period running from 587 BCE to 562 BCE, the latter date coinciding with the death of Nebuchadnezzar.[1] But such a position is only possible if one reads Isaiah 56–66 independently of 40–55, an approach that has become highly problematic in the light of more recent research.

In spite of this paucity of historical evidence, most scholars today would date Isaiah 56–66 to the early restoration period in Palestine. A post-exilic dating for these oracles is necessitated by their dependence on chs. 40–55. In addition, the overriding motif of Isaiah 56–66 is the restoration and glorification of Zion. The only attempt to date the oracles

---

81; Leuven: University Press, 1989), pp. 361-406. Steck argues that 'der Begriff "Tritojesaja" ist nichts anderes als Exponent schriftgelehrter Prophetie, die sich primär an vorgegebenen literarischen Corpora orientiert und diese als ganze aktualisierend weiterschreibt', p. 405. See also Steck, 'Beobachtungen zu Jesaja 56–59', *BZ* 31 (1987), pp. 228-46; *idem*, 'Beobachtungen zur Anlage von Jes 65–66', *Biblische Notizen* 38/39 (1987), pp. 103-16; *idem*, 'Jahwes Feinde in Jesaja 59', *Biblische Notizen* 36 (1987), pp. 51-56.

1. W.S. McCullough, 'A Re-Examination of Isaiah 56–66', *JBL* 67 (1948), pp. 27-36.

sequentially that does not rely on questionable or circular argumentation is Hanson's. His schema, based on a combination of prosodic analysis and a typology of prophetic genres, is provocative, but it is dependent upon the contention that Isa. 66.1-2 is a reference to the building of the second temple in 520–515 BCE. The question is whether Isa. 66.1-2 can carry this kind of historical weight. Hanson and others who interpret the passage in this way may be correct, but they could just as easily be wrong.

Given the almost total lack of historical references in Isaiah 56–66, a good measure of restraint is in order. It may be that anything approaching a precise dating of this material will forever remain an impossibility.[1] At the risk of being overly cautious, my proposal is to place the oracles of Isaiah 56–66 in the period from approximately 538 to approximately 400 BCE.[2] The result is that studies that wish to extrapolate historical and sociological conditions in restoration Judah from the oracles of Isaiah 56–66 ought to limit themselves to making relatively general statements. Such an approach is appropriate to and consistent with the nature of the sources.

1. The very same problems are encountered in the interpretation of Second Zechariah, Malachi and Joel. See E.M. Meyers, 'The Persian Period and the Judean Restoration: From Zerubbabel to Nehemiah', in P.D. Miller, Jr, P.D. Hanson and S.D. McBride (eds.), *Ancient Israelite Religion: Essays in Honor of Frank Moore Cross* (Philadelphia: Fortress Press, 1987), pp. 509-21; J. Blenkinsopp, *A History of Prophecy in Israel* (Philadelphia: Westminster Press, 1983), pp. 225-80.

2. This does not exclude the possibility of a narrower time frame, but it is a reminder that overly specific dating of the material is a precarious enterprise. The choice of 400 BCE as a *terminus ad quem* is based upon Sweeney's sober arguments for the dating of the final redaction of the book of Isaiah. See Sweeney, *Isaiah 1–4*, p. 99.

Chapter 2

THE HISTORICAL BACKGROUND OF THE SOCIETY
OF RESTORATION JUDAH

The Babylonian Exile

Any description of the restoration period is dependent upon how the exile[1] is conceived. In fact, the term 'restoration' is itself dependent upon the prior term 'exile'. There are at least four basic questions relating to the exile that must be answered satisfactorily. Who were the people who were exiled to Babylon? Who were the people who remained behind in Judah? Who were the people who returned from Babylon? Who were the people whom those who returned from Babylon encountered in Judah?

The Hebrew Bible records three separate deportations: the first in 597, the second in 587, and the third in 582 BCE. For the initial deportation, which took place during the reign of King Jehoiachin, 2 Kgs 24.14 records the number of deportees as 10,000, 2 Kgs 24.16 records 8000, while Jer. 52.28 records 3023.[2] For the second deportation, under King Zedekiah, Jer. 52.29 records 832 deportees, and for the final deportation in 582 BCE Jer. 52.30 records 745. Scholars have long struggled to make sense of these numbers in an attempt to sketch a general demographic picture of exilic Judah. John Bright has pointed out that in addition to deportees, one would also have to reckon with battle casualties, starvation, disease, execution, refugees and so forth. According to Bright, when all of these factors are coupled together with the deportations, one is led to the conclusion that 'the population of the land [of Judah] was drained away'.[3] Given the strong probability that the biblical

---

1. I will use the terms 'Babylonian exile' and 'exile' interchangeably.
2. See M. Brettler, '2 Kings 24.13-14 as History', *CBQ* 53 (1991), pp. 541-52.
3. J. Bright, *A History of Israel* (Philadelphia: Westminster Press, 2nd edn, 1972), p. 344 (parentheses mine).

deportation figures refer only to males, Bright asserts that the total number of people exiled could have been as high as 20,000 and that these people would have constituted Judah's upper class.[1] According to Bright, the nucleus of what had constituted the nation of Judah, its 'political, ecclesiastical, and intellectual leadership', was exiled to Babylonia, while those remaining behind in Judah are to be viewed as 'leaderless and helpless'.[2]

Bright's reconstruction of the picture of exilic Judah was intended as a strong modification of that of Martin Noth. Noth had argued that it was the groups that were not exiled to Babylonia but remained behind in Judah who 'continued to be the centre of Israelite history and Israelite life'.[3] Bright, however, countered with the claim that the exiles 'were the ones who would shape Israel's future, both giving to her faith its new direction and providing the impulse for the ultimate restoration of the Jewish community in Palestine'.[4]

An adequate resolution of the debate between Bright and Noth is difficult because the historical information relating to exilic Judah that is presently available to us is quite sparse. And not only is the information sparse, it is also ambiguous. We know from archaeology, for example, that, in addition to Jerusalem, the Babylonians also destroyed 'Lachish, Tell Zakariya (Azekah), Eglon, Tell Beth Mirsim, Tell el-Ful, Beth Zur, Ramat Rachel, Beth-Shemesh, Bethel, Arad, Ein Gedi and others'.[5] This

---

1. Bright, *A History of Israel*, p. 345. The figure of 20,000 deportees is the maximum number estimated by K. Galling, *Studien zur Geschichte Israels im persischen Zeitalter* (Tübingen: Mohr, 1964), pp. 51-52. That the exiles would have represented the upper class of Judean society is consistent with ancient deportation practices and with the biblical record which lists princes (השׂרים), warriors (גבורי חיל), craftsmen (החרשׁ), smiths (המסגר), and men of property (אנשׁי חיל) as those who were deported. See 2 Kgs 24.14, 16. For the translation 'men of property', see J. Gray, *I and II Kings* (OTL; Philadelphia: Westminster Press, 2nd edn, 1970), p. 761. Another biblical witness to this practice is the prophet Ezekiel.

2. Bright, *A History of Israel*, p. 345.

3. M. Noth, *The History of Israel* (trans. P.R. Ackroyd; New York: Harper & Row, 2nd edn, 1960), p. 292. Noth was moved to this position because of his conviction that the Deuteronomistic History was written in the land of Palestine, and that Deuteronomic law would have remained in effect during the exilic period. I will argue that a Palestinian provenance for DtrH is doubtful. See below.

4. Bright, *A History of Israel*, p. 345. The argument here is not over numbers. Bright agrees with Noth that the exiles were numerically smaller.

5. B. Oded, 'Judah and the Exile', in J.H. Hayes and J.M. Miller (eds.), *Israelite and Judean History* (Philadelphia: Westminster Press), p. 475.

is, to be sure, a widespread pattern of destruction, and it led W.F. Albright to argue for 'a complete devastation of Judah'.[1] Many scholars also assumed that, with such a massive destruction, Judah would have ceased to exist as a political entity.[2] But there is other evidence supporting Noth's contention that exilic Judah would have remained as a thriving religious community: Ezek. 33.23-29 speaks of a group of Judaites who use their having survived the fate of deportation as grounds for making land claims; Zech. 7.1-7 reports that the people of the land and the priests have been fasting and mourning in the fifth month and the seventh month throughout the period of exile; the deportation numbers supplied by the Bible are relatively small; and archaeology has confirmed that all of the villages of northern Judah and Benjamin were in existence during the exile.[3]

In the final analysis, both Noth and Bright have evidence on their side, but not enough to be decisive. If one wants to make a reliable historical statement about the condition of exilic Judah, one is hard pressed to do better than Oded who writes,

> Unfortunately, there is no clear information concerning the population of Judah during the period under discussion and it is hard to know the extent of the devastation in the towns, the precise size of the deportations, and what kind of Judaean community continued to live in Judah during the exilic period.[4]

In other words, the question as to where one is to look for the 'center' or the 'nucleus' of the Judaite community during the exilic period remains unresolved.

In spite of Oded's argument, however, there is another avenue open to us, and that is to inquire into what the biblical texts themselves want us to believe about the condition of exilic Judah. That is to say, we can inquire into the *Tendenz* of the biblical texts and then draw some conclusions based upon this.

The reports of the deportations in 2 Kings 24–25 are undoubtedly formulaic, hyperbolic and tendentious. For example, 2 Kgs 24.14 states that 'all Jerusalem' (כל ירושלם) was deported in 597 BCE, and the only

1. Oded, 'Judah and the Exile', p. 478.
2. The main beneficiaries of the Babylonian destruction appear to have been the Edomites. Cf. 1 Esd. 4.50 and Obadiah.
3. E. Stern, *The Material Culture of the Land of the Bible in the Persian Period 538–332 BCE* (Jerusalem: Bialik Institute/Israel Exploration Society, 1982), p. 229.
4. Oded, 'Judah and the Exile', p. 477.

ones who remained in the land were the 'poor' (דלת עם הארץ).[1] Such a description of the events of 597 BCE makes little historical sense, but it is common to all of the biblical texts which describe the various deportations. In 2 Kings 25 we learn that in 589–587 BCE, contrary to the report of 2 Kgs 24.14, the city was far from depopulated because a two-year siege was required in order to bring it to its knees! After the fall of the city in 587 BCE another deportation ensued, and again it is recorded that the only people who remained behind in the land were 'some of the poor' (מדלת הארץ). What is one to make of this? I contend that 2 Kings 24–25 wants to make the theological point that there did not remain in Judah and Jerusalem any people of importance. This position is unequivocally stated in 2 Kgs 25.21: ויגל יהודה מעל אדמתו ('Judah was taken into exile out of its land'). According to 2 Kings, whoever the people were who remained behind in the land, they were not 'Judah'.

The position of 2 Kings 24–25 with respect to exilic Judah is shared by Jeremiah 39–44 and 52. Jer. 39.9-10 claims that the only people who remained behind in the land after the deportation in 587 BCE were 'the poor who owned nothing' (העם הדלים אשר אין להם מאומה).[2] And Jer. 44.22 describes the land of Judah as having become 'a desolation and a waste and a curse, without inhabitant' (ותהי ארצכם לחרבה ולשמה ולקללה מאין יושב). The general picture of exilic Judah presented in Jeremiah 39–44 is that no person of any importance was left behind in the land. This picture is supported by ch. 52 as well.[3]

2 Chronicles 36 is even more schematic than either 2 Kings or Jeremiah. The impression created by 2 Chron. 36.17-21 is that the land of Judah was completely depopulated during the exile, or at least the text (deliberately?) makes no mention of anyone remaining behind. As was the case with 2 Kings and Jeremiah, the author of 2 Chronicles has no interest whatsoever in the people who continued to live in Judah during the exile. All three works assert that the totality of Judah's life and culture had shifted to Babylonia.

On the purely historical level, Noth was surely correct in arguing against the Hebrew Bible's picture of a Judah devoid of its native inhabitants. That a substantial number of people did in fact remain behind in

1.   See Brettler, '2 Kings 24.13-14 as History'.
2.   That the historical reality of the situation was significantly more complex than this is witnessed to by the events recorded in Jer. 40–44, namely the brief tenure of Gedaliah at Mizpah and the subsequent flight of Judeans to Egypt.
3.   See especially Jer. 52.15-16.

Judah after the Babylonian destruction is a logical and highly probable
inference. In addition, we must reckon with incursions by Edomites
from the South, Ammonites and Moabites from the East, Phoenicians
from the West, and Samaritans from the North.[1] But the main conclusion to be drawn from the Hebrew Bible's own description of the
destruction and deportations under the Babylonians is that the texts in
question undoubtedly represent the perspective of the Babylonian גולה
('exiles'). All three documents surveyed would have been excellent
ammunition in the hands of those who returned from exile with a claim
to the land of Judah. Conversely, if there were groups, and there surely
were, who remained in Judah during the exile and continued to practice
their religion and, thus, claimed to have a legitimate right to the land and
its traditions, it would have been suicidal for them to have appealed to
any of these three documents for support.[2] The historical books of the
Hebrew Bible[3] are interested only in the exiles[4] and not in those who

1.   G.W. Ahlström, *Who Were the Israelites?* (Winona Lake: Eisenbrauns,
1986), pp. 104-105.
2.   This makes it highly unlikely that the Deuteronomistic History was composed
in Palestine, as Noth claimed. Cross has argued that there were two editions of the
Deuteronomistic History, DtrH1 and DtrH2. The first edition was a piece of propaganda for Josiah's reform and was composed at that time, whereas the second edition
was an exilic edition, composed around 550 BCE, that took into account the destruction of Judah and Jerusalem by the Babylonians in spite of Josiah's reform. See
F.M. Cross, 'The Themes of the Book of Kings and the Structure of the
Deuteronomistic History', in *Canaanite Myth and Hebrew Epic* (Cambridge, MA:
Harvard University Press, 1973), pp. 274-89. If Cross is correct, then Noth's
assertion of Palestinian provenance would obviously be right with regard to the first
edition of the work. But the position of DtrH in its final form supports my contention.
3.   It is really a misnomer to refer to these books as 'historical' books. Kings,
Chronicles and Jeremiah are self-consciously theological treatises. 'History' is
written from a theological perspective with the purpose of making theological claims.
For example, the entire reign of a king can be glossed over in one or two sentences
with the claim that he either did or did not remain faithful to the LORD. Even more
illustrative is the great confession of Ezra that is recorded in Neh. 9. Ezra recounts the
'history' of the people, beginning with creation and continuing to his own day. Here,
however, it is not the reign of one king that is glossed over in one or two sentences,
but rather the reigns of all of the kings of the nation! The entire 'history' of the
monarchy is recounted and evaluated in one verse, Neh. 9.30!
4.   Specifically, the Babylonian exiles.

remained behind in the land, and the purpose of these books is to make the polemically charged theological statement that 'God's people' were taken into exile.[1]

Return from Babylon

According to the books of Ezra and Nehemiah, just as 'God's people' were taken into exile, so also 'God's people' returned from exile and rebuilt the temple.[2] This return was made possible by an edict of King Cyrus of Persia, the conqueror of Babylon.[3] Although there is a great deal of ambiguity surrounding the relationship between Sheshbazzar, called הנשיא ליהודה ('prince of/to Judah') in Ezra 1.8 and פחה ('governor') in Ezra 5.14,[4] and Zerubbabel, called פחת יהודה ('governor of Judah') in Hag. 1.2, Ezra and Nehemiah speak of a single, massive return shortly after the edict of Cyrus, consisting of approximately 50,000 people.

Ezra and Nehemiah present a schematic and stereotyped picture of the peoples involved in the exile and return. Those who return from exile are called בני הגולה ('exiles') and those whom they encounter in

---

1. For this reason I would argue that the debate between Noth and Bright is somewhat misguided. Both attempt to make historically reliable statements about the 'nucleus' of the people Israel during the exile. But whatever the actual historical reality was, the theological perspective which comes to expression in 2 Kings, 2 Chronicles and Jeremiah is decidedly pro-גולה.

2. Ezra's term for 'God's people' is בני הגולה (literally, 'the children of the exile').

3. The edict is recorded in Ezra 1 (in Hebrew) and Ezra 6 (in Aramaic). For a recent discussion of the authenticity of this edict and its relationship to the Cyrus Cylinder, see J. Blenkinsopp, *Ezra–Nehemiah: A Commentary* (OTL; Philadelphia: Westminster Press, 1988), pp. 73-76, 123-25.

4. Sheshbazzar is a shadowy figure known only from Ezra 1.8, 11, 5.14, 16. It has been common to identify him with the 'Shenazzar' of 1 Chron. 3.18, and thus to regard him as a son of King Jehoiachin and an uncle of Zerubbabel. Others have argued that Sheshbazzar and Zerubbabel are the same person, based upon the fact that descriptions of the two men in Ezra, Haggai and Zechariah so often overlap. For a summary of the evidence supporting both of these possibilities, see B.T. Dahlberg, 'Sheshbazzar', in *IDB*, IV, pp. 325-26. The possibility that Sheshbazzar was neither a Judaite nor, much less, a Davidide, but rather a Babylonian political official, has recently been argued by G.W. Ahlström, 'Some Aspects of Historical Problems of the Early Persian Period', *Proceedings of Eastern Great Lakes and Mid West Biblical Societies* 4 (1984), pp. 54-56; *idem, Who Were the Israelites?* (Winona Lake: Eisenbrauns, 1986), p. 113.

Judah are called עם הארץ ('the people of the land'). In Ezra–Nehemiah the term עם הארץ is a decidedly pejorative technical term. Everyone who is not considered to be a part of בני הגולה is lumped into the category of עם הארץ. Gunneweg has demonstrated that the term (עם הארץ) has undergone a substantial change in meaning since pre-exilic times. Originally, the term may have referred to the 'state supporting upper class', but in Ezra–Nehemiah עם הארץ and its various plural forms (עמי הארץ ['the peoples of the land'], עמי הארצות ['the peoples of the lands']) refer to the exact opposite of the state-supporting upper class, namely 'the hostile foreign people and pagans'.[1] Gunneweg's goal in describing this 'semantic revolution' is to show that the term עם הארץ and its plural forms are primarily theological terms in Ezra–Nehemiah, as opposed to political or sociological terms.[2]

Ezra 2 and Nehemiah 7 record a list of those who returned from Babylon under the leadership of Zerubbabel and Joshua and who then took part in the rebuilding of the temple.[3] Chapters 1–6 of Ezra are devoted to this subject, whereas Ezra 7 begins the story of the mission of Ezra himself. The case has repeatedly been made that Ezra 1–6 contains a substantial amount of telescoped material; that is to say, the experiences of Ezra that are described in Ezra 7–10 and in Nehemiah 8–9 have shaped the description of events in Ezra 1–6.[4] The result of this

---

1. A.H.J. Gunneweg, 'עם הארץ—A Semantic Revolution', *ZAW* 95 (1983), pp. 437-38. That the עם הארץ were people of stature is clear from Ezek. 22.23-31, where they are included in a list of the leaders of the community and are savaged by the prophet for social abuses. Ezek. 22.29 records the specific accusations against the עם הארץ עשקו עשק וגזלו גזל ועני ואביון הונו ואת הגר עשקו בלא משפט :עם הארץ ('The people of the land have practiced fraud and committed robbery; they have wronged the poor and needy, have defrauded the stranger without redress'). The translation is that of the new JPSV. See also Ezek. 46.3, 9.

2. Ahlström has argued for a similar semantic revolution with respect to the meaning of the name 'Israel' in Ezra. See his chapter, 'Israel: An Ideological Term', in Ahlström, *Who Were the Israelites?*, pp. 101-18. See also Williamson, 'The Concept of Israel in Transition'.

3. On the origin and function of this list, see K. Galling, 'The "Gola List" according to Ezra 2/Nehemiah 7', *JBL* 70 (1951), pp. 149-58.

4. The book of Ezra jumps immediately from the rebuilding of the temple in 515 BCE to the mission of Ezra. This substantial period of time is linked together in 7.1 by the simple temporal clause, 'after these things' (ואחר הדברים האלה). As a result, the description of return and restoration in Ezra 7–10 and Nehemiah 8–9 mirrors the description of return and restoration in Ezra 1–6, so much so that it is difficult to distinguish between the two. For example, just as those who returned under Zerubbabel

telescoping is that Ezra and Nehemiah present a unified picture of conflict between בני הגולה and עם הארץ, that is, between 'God's people' and 'foreigners', a conflict which had its beginnings under Zerubbabel and Joshua and continued under Ezra and Nehemiah.

As was the case with 2 Kings 24–25, Jeremiah 39–44, 52 and 2 Chronicles 36, whose purpose it was to make the polemically charged theological statement that 'God's people' were taken into exile, so Ezra and Nehemiah identify 'God's people' with those who returned from exile, either under the leadership of Zerubbabel and Joshua, or later, under the leadership of Ezra himself. So strong is the dichotomy between בני הגולה and עם הארץ that the return from Babylon is presented as analogous to the conquest under Joshua![1] Like Joshua, the בני הגולה have the task of ridding the land of its 'foreign' pollutions and establishing the proper, orthodox cult of YHWH. The dominant theological claim of Ezra and Nehemiah is that the 'holy seed' (זרע הקדש) must not become 'mixed' (התערב) with foreign elements (Ezra 9.2). The conflict that ensues takes the form of opposition to 'mixed' marriages, with mixed marriages being defined primarily as the marriage of a male member of בני הגולה to a female member of עם הארץ.[2]

are called בני הגולה, so those who returned with Ezra are called בני הגולה; see Ezra 8.35. In Neh. 8.17, after Ezra reads 'the book of the law of Moses' (ספר תורת משה), we are told that 'all the assembly of those who had returned from the captivity' (כל הקהל השבים מן השבי) celebrated Succoth.

Perhaps the clearest evidence of telescoping can be seen in Ezra 6.14, where it is stated that the temple had been rebuilt under the authority and 'by the decree of Cyrus and Darius and Artaxerxes the king of Persia' (מטעם כורש ודריוש וארתחששתא מלך פרס). The inclusion of the name of Artaxerxes serves to link Ezra temporally with the rebuilding of the temple.

For a good treatment of the phenomenon of telescoping in Ezra–Nehemiah, see P.R. Ackroyd, 'The Jewish Community in Palestine in the Persian Period', in Davies and Finkelstein (eds.), *The Cambridge History of Judaism*, I, pp. 130-61; Blenkinsopp, *Ezra–Nehemiah*.

1.   See Ezra 9.1 which describes the inhabitants of the land as Canaanites, Hittites, Perizzites, Jebusites, Ammonites, Moabites, Egyptians and Amorites. Canaanites, Hittites, Perizzites, Jebusites and Amorites are the familiar names of the ancient inhabitants of the land who were driven out by Joshua. The thematic parallels between the conquest under Joshua and the 'conquest' under Ezra have led Ahlström to argue that 'the Wilderness-Conquest theme and the Ezra writings originated in the same circles'. Ahlström, *Who Were the Israelites?*, p. 107.

2.   See Deut. 7.3; Exod. 34.10; Josh. 23.12. Also J. Milgrom, 'Religious Conversion and the Revolt Model for the Formation of Israel', *JBL* 101 (1982),

In spite of the seeming clarity and consistency with which Ezra presents his case, however, the definition of the term בני הגולה is somewhat maleable. Ezra 6.19-22 reports the celebration of the first Passover after the rebuilding and dedication of the temple in 515 BCE. According to Ezra 6.21 this Passover was eaten by בני ישראל השבים מהגולה ('the Israelites who had returned from exile'), but it is also stated, surprisingly, that another group of people participated as well: כל הנבדל מטמאת גוי הארץ אלהם לדרש ליהוה אלהי ישראל ('all who had joined them and separated themselves from the pollutions of the nations of the land to worship YHWH, the God of Israel'). The implication of this passage is that it was possible to *join* בני הגולה even if one had not actually returned from exile or been a descendent of someone who had. Ezra 9 shows that the converse was true as well, that is, that it was possible for people to *forfeit* their status as בני הגולה by participating in mixed marriages. Thus, the real distinction between the terms בני הגולה and עם הארץ is one of religious affiliation.[1] The former applies to those who accepted Ezra's תורה (law) and the latter to those who did not. Those who accepted Ezra's תורה assumed the identity of people who had returned from exile. Whether they had actually done so was not the issue.[2]

pp. 169-76. As Ezra 9.12 shows, however, the issue was not limited to male members of בני הגולה marrying female members of עם הארץ. Ezra 9.12 also prohibits female members of בני הגולה from marrying male members of עם הארץ. See also the proposal made by Hamor in Gen. 34.8-12.

The prohibition against mixed marriages is consistent with the conquest ideology so evident throughout the book of Joshua. Although the specific term, 'mixing' (התערב), does not occur, Josh. 23.1-13 directly prohibits intermarriage with the native people of the land. It must not be overlooked, however, that both Ezra and Nehemiah were agents of the Persian government whose missions were authorized by that same government; Ezra the scribe is sent from Babylon with an official letter from King Artaxerxes, and Nehemiah, the king's cupbearer, is sent from Susa. The prohibition against mixed marriages may have had roots in the Persian administration. Williamson has stated the case as follows: 'The requirement of an external power to be able to define who it was dealing with administratively has had more effect on the history of Judaism than has perhaps been previously appreciated'. Williamson, 'The Concept of Israel in Transition', p. 155.

1.   By using this term I do not mean to imply that it is somehow analogous to modern, voluntary, religious associations. The question of religious affiliation in Ezra and Nehemiah is intimately linked with genealogy and family affiliation.

2.   On this point Ezra and Nehemiah differ significantly from Joshua. In Joshua nationality and religious affiliation are inseparable concepts, and as a result prose-lytism is largely unthinkable. In Ezra and Nehemiah, however, it is plainly asserted

When 2 Kings 24–25, Jeremiah 39–44, 52, 2 Chronicles 36, and Ezra–Nehemiah are viewed together, the following picture results: God's people were taken into exile by the Babylonians; subsequently, God's people returned to the land of Judah with Persian permission and rebuilt the temple in Jerusalem; later, under Ezra, the community in Judah was purified of its 'foreign' elements and defined as those people who had accepted Ezra's תורה.

The picture of the restoration that emerges in Ezra and Nehemiah is dominated by the scheme of conflict between בני הגולה (returning exiles) and עם הארץ (the foreign people in the land of Judah who had not gone into exile). On the historical level, this scheme is surely an artificial one, constructed in the interests of the Chronicler's own perspective. It is not, however, a perspective that was developed *de novo* by the Chronicler but is consistent with 2 Kings, Jeremiah and even Ezekiel.[1] But the problem with this perspective is that it is not shared by Haggai and Zechariah 1–8. If one did not have the books of Ezra and Nehemiah, one would be hard pressed to demonstrate that Haggai and Zechariah 1–8 presuppose a massive return of Babylonian exiles.[2] In fact, it is even

---

that it is possible to 'overcome' one's nationality by changing one's religious affiliation. That is to say, it is possible to join the group known as בני הגולה or בני ישראל.

Contrary to almost everything written on the subject, the position of Ezra and Nehemiah is echoed in the roughly contemporary text Isa. 56.1-8, a text which is usually described as 'universalistic' because it grants access to the temple to both the 'foreigner' (בן הנכר) and the 'eunuch' (הסריס). It is consistently overlooked, however, that it is not foreigners and eunuchs as such who are granted access to the temple, but only those foreigners and eunuchs 'who have joined themselves to YHWH' (הנלוים אל/על יהוה). Isa. 56.1-8, like Ezra and Nehemiah, sets up criteria by which a foreigner may be allowed to participate in the cult. This, however, is something very different from 'universalism'. See Milgrom, 'Religious Conversion'. For an excellent discussion of the phenomenon of proselytism in the ancient world, see A.D. Nock, *Conversion* (London: Oxford University Press, 1933).

1.   Seitz has recently demonstrated that the final shape of Jeremiah, and Ezekiel in all of its stages, agree that restoration is reserved for the exiles alone. Being exiled was viewed as a prerequisite for participating in the restoration. C.R. Seitz, *Theology in Conflict* (BZAW, 176; Berlin: de Gruyter, 1989), pp. 158-63.

2.   The only reference to any return from Babylon in these two books is Zech. 6.10: לקוח מאת הגולה מחלדי ומאת טוביה ומאת ידעיה ובאת אתה ביום ההוא ובאת בית יאשיה בן צפניה אשר באו מבבל ('Take from the exiles Heldai, Tobijah and Jedaiah, who have arrived from Babylon; and go the same day to the house of Josiah, the son of Zephaniah'). Neither Haggai nor Zechariah know Sheshbazzar; neither knows of any previous attempt to rebuild the temple before their time, nor do they know of any

unclear whether Haggai was himself a returned exile.[1] But the main difference between Haggai, Zechariah 1–8 and Ezra–Nehemiah is that the first two do not speak of any conflict between גולה and עם הארץ. Contrary to its meaning in Ezra–Nehemiah, the term עם הארץ is neither polemical nor pejorative in Haggai and Zechariah 1–8.[2] In short, the conflict scheme, so in evidence in Ezra–Nehemiah is lacking in Haggai and Zechariah 1–8.[3] When one compares biblical material from the early restoration period, namely Haggai and Zechariah 1–8, with material from the later restoration period, namely Ezra–Nehemiah, it becomes clear that the scheme of a massive return from Babylon and subsequent conflict between the returning exiles and the people of the land is a theological construct of the Chronicler that reflects the concerns and problems of his own day.[4] Ironically, the book of Ezra itself confirms this when it states that prior to Ezra's arrival in Jerusalem 'the people of

previous foundation laying. See Blenkinsopp, *Ezra–Nehemiah*, pp. 100, 104.

1.   See the discussion in D.L. Petersen, *Haggai and Zechariah 1–8* (OTL; Philadelphia: Westminster Press, 1984), pp. 17-19.

2.   See Hag. 2.4 and Zech 7.5. In Hag. 2.4 the עם הארץ are ordered by Haggai to participate in the rebuilding of the temple! This position is in direct contradiction to that of Ezra 1–6 which makes it clear that the עם הארץ were prohibited from participating in the rebuilding. See Ezra 4.3 where the returned exiles say, כי אנחנו יחד נבנה ליהוה אלהי ישראל ('We alone will build to YHWH, the God of Israel'). Gunneweg has argued that the reason for this discrepancy is that in Haggai/Zech. 1–8 עם הארץ still retains its traditional meaning of 'the upper class of land owners', and has not yet taken on the technical, polemical sense that it has in Ezra. A.H.J. Gunneweg, 'עם הארץ—A Semantic Revolution', *ZAW* 95 (1983), p. 439.

3.   Haggai's addressees are as follows: Zerubbabel the governor of Judah (פחת יהודה), Joshua the high priest (הכהן הגדול), the priests (הכהנים), the remnant of the people (שארית העם), and the people of the land (עם הארץ). In Hag. 2.1-4 שארית העם and עם הארץ are used interchangeably; along with Zerubbabel and Joshua they are called on to participate in the rebuilding of the temple. Zech. 1–8 speaks of Zerubbabel, Joshua, the exiles (הגולה), those who are far off (רחוקים), the priests of the house of the Lord of hosts and the prophets (הכהנים אשר לבית יהוה צבאות והנביאים), the people of the land (עם הארץ), the remnant of this people (שארית העם הזה), the house of Judah and the house of Israel (בית יהודה ובית ישראל). Just as in Haggai, the שארית העם הזה and the עם הארץ appear to be synonomous terms.

4.   This was argued long ago by C.C. Torrey, *The Chronicler's History of Israel* (New Haven: Yale University Press, 1954). On the question of the authorship of Chronicles and Ezra–Nehemiah, see Blenkinsopp, *Ezra–Nehemiah*; S. Japhet, 'The Supposed Common Authorship of Chronicles and Ezra–Nehemiah Investigated Anew', *VT* 18 (1969), pp. 330-71; H.G.M. Williamson, 'The Composition of Ezra i–vi', *JTS* 34 (1983), pp. 1-30.

Israel, the priests, and the Levites' were accustomed to participating in mixed marriages (Ezra 9.1). Prior to Ezra's coming the people themselves were unaware of any conflict between גולה and עם הארץ; Ezra had to 'make' them aware of the conflict!

According to Williamson, the evidence of the biblical texts leads to the conclusion that for the early restoration period 'there may not have been so many immediate points of tension between the exilic and Palestinian communities as often supposed'.[1] I would add that there is a reason that this is so: texts from the early restoration period do not speak of a conflict between גולה and עם הארץ, that is, between the exilic and Palestinian communities, because these terms as definitions of these two groups reflect the theological definition of 'Israel' as those people who have accepted the תורה, and in the early restoration period this specific definition had not yet been promulgated.

The question must now be asked: does the description of events in Haggai and Zechariah 1–8 compromise what was stated above, that the historical books of the Hebrew Bible claim that 'God's people' were taken into exile and 'God's people' returned from exile to rebuild the temple? The answer is 'No'. The scheme of exile and return is perfectly consistent with the message of Haggai and Zechariah, but those prophets are simply not aware of any conflict between a Palestinian group and a Babylonian group. Therein lies the only real difference. The 'conflict' scheme was a product of the later Persian period, not the earlier.

The Persian Period in Judah[2]

There is general agreement among scholars that after the fall of Babylon to Cyrus the Great in 538 BCE, exiled Judaites began to return to their homeland. There is little agreement, however, in regard to both the number of people and the number of 'returns' involved. It is now common to posit several small returns over a long period of time.[3]

Although Persian period Judah was a demographically complex

1.   Williamson, 'The Concept of Israel in Transition', p. 152.
2.   Commonly, the period from Cyrus II's conquest of Babylon in 538 until Alexander's defeat of Darius III at Issus in 333 BCE.
3.   As was stated above, it is the Hebrew Bible itself, that is, the evidence of Haggai and Zech. 1–8, that forces scholars to qualify the stylized picture of exile and return described by the Chronicler.

area, it was geographically small,[1] and numerically and economically impoverished.[2] But as was the case throughout its entire previous history, the area in and around Judah continued to be of immense importance to the great military powers of the ancient Near East, located as it was on the land-bridge to Egypt.

Modern biblical scholars who are interested in the theology and religion of ancient Israel and Judah are drawn to the Persian period because it appears to have been the seminal time in the shaping of the Hebrew Bible as we have it today.[3] As was argued in Chapter 1, Persian period Judah also forms the background for the oracles of Isaiah 56–66 and for the final redaction of the book of Isaiah as a whole.[4] The purpose of the next three sections will be to highlight some specific historical aspects of Persian period Judah that directly impact the interpretation of Isaiah 56–66.

The Persian Empire

Achaemenid Persia was the first true 'empire' in world history.[5] Its greatness is recalled in Est. 1.1 where it is recorded that the empire

1.   Attempts to draw the borders of Judah in the Persian period have not succeeded. What we do know is that after the campaign of Sennacherib in 701 BCE, Judah was, for all practical purposes, reduced to Jerusalem and its immediate environs.

2.   Persian period archaeological remains, occupying as they do the upper levels at most sites, are meager due to erosion. What archaeological evidence we do possess supports such an assessment. See Stern, *Material Culture*. The results of the new investigations into the 'socio-economic history' of Persian period Judah are tightly summarized by Petersen, *Haggai and Zechariah 1–8*, pp. 28-31. Drawing on the work of H. Kippenberg, H. Kreissig and J. Weinberg, he points to three characteristics of life in this period: (1) the period was marked by the evolution of the social unit called 'the fathers' house' (בית אבות); (2) the economy of Persian period Judah had little productive capability; and (3) the temple was of major importance.

3.   See Appendix 1.

4.   Of all the books in the Hebrew Bible, only Isaiah can approach the redactional complexity of the Pentateuch. Like the Pentateuch, Isaiah, in its final form, is a Persian period document containing material from virtually the entire history of Israel and Judah. But when, how and why these materials were combined is hotly debated. As is the case in Pentateuchal studies, the position one takes on the redactional growth of Isaiah has major ramifications for one's reconstruction of the history of the religion of Israel and Judah.

5.   The administrative capital of the empire was located in Susa, while the capital

stretched 'from India to Ethiopia' (מהדו ועד כוש). Judah, or 'Yehud' (יהוד)[1] as it was officially known in Aramaic, was located on the western fringe of the empire and was a sub-province of the huge satrapy 'Beyond the River' (עבר נהרא).[2] Judah was strategically important to the Achaemenids because of its proximity to Egypt and to the maritime cities of Phoenicia, and also because this western fringe of the empire was politically unstable.[3]

It would be safe to argue that the political history of Judah during the Persian period was closely linked with the instability in Egypt and its continuous revolts. Darius I conquered Egypt in 525 BCE, but the Achaemenids had a constant struggle to maintain control of that nation. Egyptian revolts are known from 518, 486, 459 and 411 BCE. From 401 until 343 BCE Egypt was independent. During this time it advanced into the coastal plain of Palestine and was in constant conflict with Persian armies.[4] In 343 BCE Artaxerxes III restored Egypt to Persian

---

of Persia itself was Persepolis. The administrative language of the empire was Aramaic. See M. Dandamayev, 'Babylonia in the Persian Age', in Davies and Finkelstein (eds.), *The Cambridge History of Judaism*, I, p. 333. The Persians are often described as having been enlightened and lenient toward their subjugated people. This may be true in regard to their attitude toward native cults and with respect to their administrative practices, but this leniency was more than balanced by an aggressive taxation policy. See E. Stern, 'The Archeology of Persian Palestine', in Davies and Finkelstein (eds.), *The Cambridge History of Judaism*, I, pp. 112-13.

1.　The Aramaic name 'Yehud', known from post-exilic biblical texts (Dan. 2.25; 5.13; 6.14; Ezra 5.1, 8; 7.14), also occurs on Persian period coins, seals and stamps. What the exact boundaries of Yehud were is unclear. A common view is that the northern border would have been somewhere between Jerusalem and Bethel, the western border in the transition area between the hill country and the Shephelah, and the southern border at Beth-zur or, perhaps, farther south at Hebron. Most scholars would concur that the area was very small, very poor, rural and agrarian.

2.　According to Herodotus, Darius I divided the empire into twenty satrapies. In Darius's own inscriptions, though, the satrapy 'Beyond the River' does not appear. Stern has proposed that at the time of Darius (522–486 BCE) 'Beyond the River' was part of the satrapy 'Babylon' and remained so until Xerxes I crushed the Babylonian rebellion in 482 BCE. After this time 'Babylon' and 'Beyond the River' became separate satrapies. See Stern, 'The Persian Empire', p. 78.

3.　The period was marked by a series of revolts throughout the empire which usually coincided with times of succession. These factors help to account for the fact that the rebuilding of Jerusalem and its temple were accomplished with Persian permission and encouragement. See A. Kuhrt, 'The Cyrus Cylinder and Achaemenid Imperial Policy', *JSOT* 25 (1983), p. 94.

4.　Archaeologists point to two waves of destruction in Palestine during the Persian period. The first is dated to c. 480 BCE in which several towns in Benjamin

rule. According to Morton Smith, Palestine 'became the line of com-
munications for the Persians' during these periods of Egyptian revolt,
and during the period of Egyptian independence Palestine served as the
Persians' 'base for repeated attempts to reconquer Egypt', as evidenced
by a series of Persian forts that runs 'for some fifteen miles across
country south of Gaza'.[1] It can also be argued that the periodic
upheavals at the heart of the empire, in Babylon, would have provided
occasions for Judaites to return home.[2]

The Political Status of Judah

What was the political status of Judah in the Persian period? Or more
precisely, what was the political relationship between Judah and Samaria
prior to the arrival of Nehemiah?[3] The books of Ezra and Nehemiah
mention only three Judean governors by name: Sheshbazzar, Zerubbabel
and Nehemiah. Why is there such a long gap between Zerubbabel and
Nehemiah? Some have argued that at the beginning of the Persian
period Judah was independent from Samaria, but because of problems
under Zerubbabel, for example, his possible messianic pretensions, Judah
was then annexed to Samaria and remained so until Nehemiah.[4]
Another solution was proposed by Alt who claimed that Judah achieved
the status of an independent subprovince (מדינה, מדינתא) only at the time
of Nehemiah.[5] But in order to support this claim, Alt had to disregard

were destroyed. The second is dated to c. 380 BCE and was confined to the coastal
area and the Negeb. The latter is probably associated with Egyptian battles for
independence, but, as yet, there is no known cause of the former. See Stern, 'The
Archeology of Persian Palestine', p. 114.

1. Smith, *Palestinian Parties and Politics*, pp. 44-45.
2. See Appendix 2.
3. There is no question of Judah's status subsequent to Nehemiah. Beginning
with the late fifth century 'there is a sudden appearance of large numbers of seal
impressions of various types, all of them bearing the inscription Yehud, the Aramaic
name of Judah...Together with these seal impressions, new small silver coins begin
to appear. These are inscribed with the name of the state (one found is in Aramaic and
all the others are in Hebrew).' Stern, 'The Persian Empire', p. 82. The occurrence of
these Yehud stamps and coins is the surest evidence of Judah's independent status.
4. This is the position of Blenkinsopp, *Ezra–Nehemiah*, pp. 262-65. He views
Ezra 4.7-24 as a story that explains why Judah lost its independence.
5. A. Alt, 'Die Rolle Samarias bei der Entstehung des Judentums', in *Kleine
Schriften zur Geschichte des Volkes Israel* (2 vols.; Munich: C.H. Beck'sche
Verlagsbuchhandlung, 1953), II, pp. 316-37. Alt's thesis has been accepted by Stern,

the clear references to Sheshbazzar and Zerubbabel as 'governor' (פחה).[1] A third alternative is that Judah was never annexed to Samaria during the Persian period but was an independent subprovince of the empire with its own governor and administration. This is clearly what is implied by Neh. 5.15, a passage in which Nehemiah criticizes the practices of the former Judean governors who had ruled prior to him (הפחות הראשנים אשר לפני, 'the former governors who were before me').[2] This third possibility has now received considerable support with the discovery of the actual names of Judean governors; these have been published by Avigad,[3] and he has proposed the following sequence of governors.[4]

Name	Title	Source	Date
Sheshbazzar	פחה	Ezra 5.15[5]	c. 538 BCE
Zerubbabel	פהת יהודה	Hag. 1.1, 14	515 BCE
Elnathan	phw'	bulla and seal	late 6th century BCE
Yeho'ezer	phw'	jar impression	early 5th century BCE
Ahzai	phw'	jar impression	early 5th century BCE
Nehemiah	הפחה	Neh. 5.14; 12.26	445–433 BCE
Bagohi	פחת יהוד	CAP 30[6]	408 BCE
Yehezqiyah	hphh	coins	c. 330 BCE

All three of these possibilities continue to have adherents, but each is somewhat problematic. The first possibility, that Judah originally had independent status, then lost it, then regained it, is based on an argument from silence, that is, that the Bible mentions no Judean governors

'The Persian Empire', pp. 82-86, and Petersen, *Haggai and Zechariah 1–8*. For a brutal critique of Alt's thesis, see Smith, *Palestinian Parties and Politics*, pp. 147-53.

1.   Hag. 1.1, 14; Ezra 5.14.

2.   The logic of Nehemiah's argument is dependent on there having been former governors. A similar passage is Mal 1.8 which speaks of 'your governor' (פחתך).

3.   N. Avigad, *Bullae and Seals from a Post-Exilic Judean Archive* (trans. R. Grafman; Qedem, 4; Jerusalem: 'Ahva' Co-op Press, 1976). Avigad's thesis has been accepted by C.L. Meyers and E.M. Meyers, *Haggai, Zechariah 1–8* (AB, 25B; Garden City, NY: Doubleday, 1987), pp. 13-17.

4.   The names of the governors in this list are followed by the official title, the source of the title and Avigad's proposed date for tenure of office. Avigad, *Bullae and Seals*, pp. 34-35. He qualifies his position with the claim that only Sheshbazzar and Zerubbabel were Davidides. Their successors are to be seen as 'reliable non-entities'.

5.   In Ezra 1.8 he is called הנשיא ליהודה.

6.   A. Cowley, *Aramaic Papyri of the Fifth Century BC* (repr.; Osnabrück: Otto Zellner, 1967), pp. 108-19.

between Zerubbabel and Nehemiah. This silence should not surprise us, however, because the Bible mentions virtually nothing of a specific nature for the time between the rebuilding of the temple and the missions of Ezra and Nehemiah. The second possibility, that Judah gained its independence only at the time of Nehemiah, can support its claim only by rejecting all of the specific references to actual Persian period Judean governors on which the first and third possibilities depend. The third possibility, that Judah was independent throughout the Persian period, appears, at first glance, to present the strongest case because it takes account of both the biblical and the newly discovered archaeological evidence. But its weakness is that there is no way at present to verify Avigad's proposed dates for these governors.

Recently an attempt to resolve the question of Judah's political status in favor of the proposal of Alt has been made by McEvenue. He makes three philological arguments: (1) references to Judah as a 'province' (מדינה, מדינתא) do not prove autonomy because the term is general rather than technical, meaning something like 'region'; (2) the term for 'governor' (פחה) is likewise a non-technical term in Aramaic, and can be used to describe officials who are obviously not on the same level, for example, Sheshbazzar (Ezra 5.14), Zerubbabel (Ezra 6.7) and Tattenai (Ezra 5.3, 6; 6.6, 13), and, thus, cannot be used to prove autonomy either; (3) the term תרשתא, used to describe both Zerubbabel and Nehemiah, is inconclusive. According to McEvenue, we know that Nehemiah was a governor of an independent subprovince, not because of what he was called but because of what he did. This is what separates him from all of the governors (פחות) who preceded him. McEvenue's final argument is that Alt's proposal is the only one that can make sense of the enormous lack of information in the Bible relating to the Persian period. The reason there is so little biblical evidence for this period is that it was suppressed because of Judah's subjugation to Samaria in the period prior to Nehemiah.[1] In spite of McEvenue's claim to have resolved the argument in favor of Alt, he does not succeed. But what he does do is demonstrate that Alt's proposal must still be reckoned with; this he accomplishes by pointing out the genuine weaknesses in Avigad's proposal. We must conclude, therefore, that the problem of the political status of Judah prior to Nehemiah remains unresolved.

1. Sean E. McEvenue, 'The Political Structure in Judah from Cyrus to Nehemiah', *CBQ* 43 (1981), pp. 353-64. This position has been accepted by Petersen, *Haggai and Zechariah 1–8*.

The Samaritan Schism

A related question has to do with what might be called the 'religious' relationship between Judah and Samaria. In other words, when did the so-called 'Samaritan schism' occur?[1] If the schism can be dated to the Persian period, then this would have an obvious impact on the interpretation of Persian-period Judean texts. In this regard, it has been customary to cite Ezra 4.1-3 as evidence of a growing antipathy between Judaites and Samaritans in the early Persian period.[2] It is then argued that this antipathy reached a climax at the time of Nehemiah when he ejected a son of the high priest in Jerusalem on the grounds that the man had married a daughter of Sanballat of Samaria (Neh. 13.28). The argument continues by drawing on the testimony of Josephus who relates, in like manner, that the building of the Samaritan temple on Mt Gerizim resulted from a controversy under Sanballat, governor of Samaria, whose daughter was married to a member of the high priestly family of Jerusalem.[3] It is then concluded that Josephus's account is actually a more complete version of the events described in Neh. 13.28, showing that the Samaritan schism took place at the time of Nehemiah. This conclusion is drawn notwithstanding that the Sanballat spoken of by Josephus is a contemporary of Alexander the Great who lived some one hundred years after Nehemiah! This rather obvious problem is overcome with the claim that Josephus was simply wrong in linking the building of the temple on Mt Gerizim with Alexander.

We now possess extra-biblical evidence from two different sources that calls this popular reconstruction of events into serious question. The

---

1.   'Samaritan schism' is understood to refer to the emergence of the Samaritans as a distinctive sect.

2.   Josephus already interpreted the passage in this way. In his paraphrase of the passage he uses the technical term 'Samaritans' (Σαμαρεῖται) as a description of 'the opponents of Judah and Benjamin' (צרי יהודה ובנימן), *Ant.* 11.84. A modern example of the exact same interpretation of Ezra 4.1-3 is that of Kessler: 'Die Judäer und die Führung der Gola haben den Einfluss der samaritanischen Mischbevölkerung gefürchtet und darum eine Baubeteiligung von dieser Seite abgelehnt'. Kessler, *Gott geht es um das Ganze*, p. 16. Scholars who interpret the passage in this way also tend to understand the designation 'people of the land' (עמי הארצות, עם הארץ) in Ezra–Nehemiah to be a circumlocution for 'Samaritans'. The polemical passages in Persian period texts are then interpreted as anti-Samaritan in character.

3.   *Ant.* 11.302-25.

first is the Elephantine papyrus known as *CAP* 30.[1] This papyrus is a copy of a letter written in Aramaic to a certain Bigvai (בגוהי), the governor of Judah (פחת יהוד), from a Judaite military garrison located at Elephantine (יב) in Egypt. The letter is dated to the seventeenth year of Darius II, that is, 408 BCE. The author of the letter, Yedoniah (ידניה), writes to Bigvai asking for help in rebuilding the colony's 'temple of the god Yahu' (אגורא זי יהו אלהא)[2] which had been destroyed three years earlier by a group of Egyptian priests. The part of the letter, however, that is of pivotal significance for our question is the second last line, line 29: 'Also the whole matter we have set forth in a letter in our name to Delaiah and Shelemiah the sons of Sanballat governor of Samaria' (אף כלא מליא באגרה חדה שלחן בשמן על דליה ושלמיה בני סנאבלט פחת שמרין).[3] As stated by Cowley, 'the fact that the Jews of Elephantine applied also to Delaiah and Shelemiah at Samaria and mention this to the authorities at Jerusalem, shows that (at any rate as far as they knew) no religious schism had as yet taken place'.[4] It is clear that the author of the letter considered the matter of the temple of the god Yahu in Elephantine to be of mutual importance to the authorities in Judah and in Samaria.[5]

The second body of evidence that calls into question the dating of the Samaritan schism to the Persian period is the collection of papyrus fragments, seals and coins discovered in the Wadi Daliyeh, commonly known as the Samaria Papyri.[6] The papyri, all of which are legal/

---

1. Cowley, *Aramaic Papyri*, pp. 108-19. For other collections of texts from Elephantine, see G.R. Driver, *Aramaic Documents of the Fifth Century BC* (Oxford: Clarendon Press, 1957); E.G. Kraeling, *The Brooklyn Museum Aramaic Papyri: New Documents of the Fifth Century BC from the Jewish Colony at Elephantine* (New Haven: Yale University Press, 1953). For an extensive bibliography on works relating to Elephantine, see B. Porten, *Archives from Elephantine* (Berkeley: University of California Press, 1968).

2. In line 15 this god is also referred to as 'Yahu, the lord of heaven' (יהו מרא שמיא).

3. The translation is Cowley's. All three names, Delaiah, Shelemiah and Sanballat occur in the book of Nehemiah.

4. Cowley, *Aramaic Papyri*, p. 110.

5. This has obvious implications as well for our understanding of the issue of cultic centralization in Jerusalem.

6. See F.M. Cross, Jr, 'The Discovery of the Samaria Papyri', *BA* 26 (1963), pp. 110-21; *idem*, 'Aspects of Samaritan and Jewish History in Late Persian and Hellenistic Times', *HTR* 59 (1966), pp. 201-11; *idem*, 'Papyri of the Fourth Century BC from Daliyeh', in D.N. Freedman and J.C. Greenfield (eds.), *New Directions in Biblical Archaeology* (Garden City, NY: Doubleday, 1969), pp. 41-62; *idem*, 'A

administrative documents, have been persuasively dated by Cross to the years 375–335 BCE. Of significance for our question is the occurrence of the name 'Sanballat' who is twice described (once in Hebrew on a bulla or seal[2] and once in Aramaic on a papyrus[3]) as the father of a governor of Samaria but who cannot be identical with the Sanballat of Nehemiah.[4] In other words, we now have three Sanballats to deal with: Sanballat of Nehemiah, Sanballat of the Samaria Papyri and Sanballat of Josephus. Some scholars had previously argued that Nehemiah's Sanballat and Josephus's Sanballat were actually two different people, and thus that Josephus's description of the Samaritan schism was not another version of Neh. 13.28 but rather a description of a completely different event from a later time. This hypothesis, however, was usually dismissed as too speculative.[5] The Samaria Papyri have removed the speculation. There is now concrete evidence to support the claim, not just that there were two Sanballats, but that there were at least three men of this name who served as governor of Samaria. In Cross's words:

Reconstruction of the Judean Restoration', *JBL* 94 (1975), pp. 4-18.

1.   Cross, 'The Discovery of the Samaria Papyri', pp. 112-15. Based upon the date formulae used in the papyri themselves, the proposed dates appear to be firm. The date formula in Papyrus 1 is so exact that Cross is able to give the actual day it was written: 18 March 335 BCE. So also for Papyrus 8: 4 March 354 BCE. We also learn from Cross that approximately 200 human skeletons were discovered together with the papyri. His proposal is that these people deposited the papyri prior to their being massacred by Alexander's troops. See Cross, 'Papyri of the Fourth Century BC from Daliyeh', pp. 47-51.

2.   '...-iah, son of (San)ballat, governor of Samaria', Cross, 'The Discovery of the Samaria Papyri', p. 111.

3.   'Jesus son of Sanballat (and) Hanan, the prefect', Cross, 'The Discovery of the Samaria Papyri', p. 111.

4.   We know from *CAP* 30 that by 408 BCE Delaiah and Shelemiah, the sons of Sanballat, were already ruling in his place in Samaria. This is Sanballat the Horonite, known from the book of Nehemiah. From Samaria Papyrus 8, which dates to 4 March 354 BCE, we learn of a certain 'Hananiah, governor of Samaria'. From a bulla, however, we know Hananiah to be the 'son of Sanballat'. Sanballat the Horonite cannot have been this man's father, but he could have been his grandfather or great grandfather.

5.   For instance, Cowley asserts, 'The view that there were two Sanballats, each governor of Samaria and each with a daughter who married a brother of a High Priest at Jerusalem, is a solution too desperate to be entertained', Cowley, *Aramaic Papyri*, p. 110.

> Once the existence of a second Sanballat, father of governors of Samaria,
> is firmly established, paradoxically it becomes far easier to accept a third
> Sanballat in the age of Alexander. That is to say, with the appearance of
> Sanballat II in the Daliyeh Papyri, most if not all objections to a Sanballat
> III melt away.[1]

What the Samaria Papyri have done is to give credence to Josephus's dating of the building of the Samaritan temple on Mt Gerizim to the Hellenistic period.

Building on the work of Cross and massing all of the available evidence, Purvis has proposed the following sequence of events.[2] The Samaritan temple on Mt Gerizim was built under the aegis of Sanballat III with the permission of Alexander the Great, that is, in the early Hellenistic period. At roughly the same time a Macedonian colony was established in Samaria (the city) in retribution for an insurrection there against Greek rule.[3] Subsequently, Shechem was rebuilt and repopulated by 'the disenfranchised Yahwists of Samaria'.[4] A century and a half later, in 128 BCE, the Hasmonean John Hyrcanus destroyed the temple on Gerizim, and in 107 he destroyed Samaria. According to Purvis, it is these actions on the part of Hyrcanus that mark the 'complete and irreparable break in relations between the Samaritans and the Jews'.[5] The conclusion is, therefore, that the 'Samaritan schism' took place in the Hasmonean period, some 300 years after the time of Nehemiah.

1. Cross, 'Papyri of the Fourth Century BC from Daliyeh', p. 55; *idem*, 'Aspects of Samaritan and Jewish History', p. 203. The recurrence of the name Sanballat points to a Sanballatide hereditary dynasty in Samaria. Cross combines evidence from the Bible, from Elephantine and from the Samaria Papyri to propose the following sequence of Samaritan governors:

> Sanballat I
> Delaiah
> Sanballat II
> (Yeshua')
> Hananiah
> Sanballat III

2. J.D. Purvis, *The Samaritan Pentateuch and the Origin of the Samaritan Sect* (HSM, 2; Cambridge, MA: Harvard University Press, 1968).

3. This insurrection is a possible explanation of what caused the Samaritan nobles to take refuge in the Wadi Daliyeh together with their papyri.

4. Purvis, *The Samaritan Pentateuch*, p. 109. He also notes that recent archaeological digs at Shechem reveal that the city was not inhabited during the Persian period.

5. Purvis, *The Samaritan Pentateuch*, p. 118.

Such a late dating of the schism makes sense of several pieces of evidence. First, the Hebrew Bible knows of no new cult on Gerizim; even the Chronicler is completely silent about the Gerizim temple. Secondly, with the exception of the authorized place of worship, the Samaritan Pentateuch and the Pentateuch of the Hebrew Bible are identical theologically.[1] This implies that the emergence of 'Samaritanism' post-dates the final redaction of the Pentateuch. When this is coupled with the evidence of *CAP* 30, it becomes difficult in the extreme to continue to argue for a 'Samaritan schism' in the Persian period.

In Chapters 4 and 5 I will propose an interpretation of the several polemical passages in Isaiah 56–66, and the dating of the Samaritan schism has a direct impact on this task. In Isaiah 65, for example, an anonymous group of people is showered with vitriolic taunts. Scholars have traditionally viewed this passage and others like it in Third Isaiah as directed against the 'Samaritans' (understood as forming a distinct social and religious group). In this regard, Ezra 4.1-3 has played the major role. But if, as was argued in Chapter 1, the book of Isaiah as a whole most probably dates to the Persian period, then in light of the work of Cross and Purvis on the dating of the 'Samaritan schism', I regard it as most unlikely that the Samaritans are the ones who are being castigated in Third Isaiah.[2] In addition, I will show that the points of contention in Third Isaiah concern issues that Samaritans and Jews would most likely have agreed upon. This I will do by identifying the theological presuppositions inherent in the polemical passages of Third Isaiah.

1. See all of the positive references to Shechem in Genesis and Deuteronomy. See also Judges! It is really only from the New Testament period and from the rabbinic period that we have substantial information on Jewish/Samaritan antipathy. From Josephus, the New Testament and the rabbinic material it is clear that the Samaritans were not pagans, but rather sectarian Jews. Purvis has summarized the issue at stake between the two groups: 'Basically, the distinction between Jews and Samaritans is found in the claim of the latter that Gerizim and not Zion (or Shechem and not Jerusalem) is the legitimate center of Hebrew worship—a claim for which the Samaritans have considerable support in the Pentateuch and the Book of Joshua'. Purvis, *The Samaritan Pentateuch*, p. 121.

2. On the possibility that Ezra 4.2b is best understood as a polemical anachronism, see Smith, *Palestinian Parties and Politics*, pp. 85-86. Smith asserts that the real adversaries of the returning exiles would not have been the 'Samaritans' but rather the local Judean population. A later editor has rewritten the incident in a way that reflects the Judean–Samaritan conflicts of his own day.

The Political and Social Context of Third Isaiah

From Isaiah 56–66 itself we learn little of a 'political' nature other than that Persian hegemony over Judah was taken for granted. Second Isaiah had elevated Cyrus to the status of messiah, as one who ruled and conquered by the will of YHWH, the God of Israel.[1] It would have been a short step to view Cyrus's empire as divinely mandated as well.[2] As I see it, this helps to explain the lack of any anti-Persian polemic in biblical prophetic texts. The Persians receive the credit for liberating the exiled Judaites; the Persians receive the credit for making the rebuilding of the temple of YHWH possible; the Persians receive the credit for thwarting those who opposed the rebuilding of temple and city. In addition, the two main figures of the Persian period, Ezra and Nehemiah, carry out their missions as agents of the Persian government. And finally, the reconstituting of the community under Ezra as one defined by allegiance to the 'law' (תורה or דת) took place with explicit Persian permission and may also have been instigated by them as well.[3]

That Second Isaiah's high estimate of the Persians is adopted by Third Isaiah is evidenced by the fact that in spite of explicit passages in pre-exilic and exilic prophets,[4] Third Isaiah entertains no notions of restoring the Davidic dynasty.[5] The only reference to David in Isaiah 40–66 is Isa. 55.3, but, ironically, this sole mention of David shows that hopes for the restoration of the Davidic dynasty have been abandoned.[6] Isaiah 40–66

---

1.   See Isa. 44.28-45.1; 41.1-4. For a discussion of the claim that the Cyrus material in Second Isaiah is secondary, see the discussion in Chapter 1 dealing with the work of C.C. Torrey.

2.   See Smith, 'II Isaiah and the Persians'.

3.   See Williamson, 'The Concept of Israel in Transition', p. 155.

4.   Isa. 9 and 11; Jer. 23 and 33; Ezek. 34 and 37.

5.   See Blenkinsopp, *A History of Prophecy in Israel*, p. 245.

6.   Perhaps a better word than 'abandoned' might be 'transformed'. Isa. 55.3b reads as follows: ואכרתה לכם ברית עולם חסדי דוד הנאמנים. The new JPSV translation of this difficult passage is 'And I will make with you an everlasting covenant, the enduring loyalty to David'. Taking דוד as an objective genitive, the sense of the passage is that the covenant made with David now passes to the people; in other words, the Davidic covenant has been democratized. See G. von Rad, *Old Testament Theology* (trans. D.M.G. Stalker; 2 vols.; New York: Harper & Row, 1962–65), II, pp. 46, 240, 271, 325; Westermann, *Isaiah 40–66*, pp. 283-86; F.M. Cross, 'The Ideologies of Kingship in the Era of the Empire: Conditional Covenant and Eternal Decree', in *Canaanite Myth and Hebrew Epic*, p. 263; W.A.M. Beuken, 'Isa. 55, 3-5:

envisions a restoration of Israel in which the Davidic dynasty plays no role, a significant difference from the first 39 chapters of the book.

One could argue that the reason the Davidic dynasty is not mentioned is because to do so would have been self-destructive, but in light of the high estimate of the Persians that is so in evidence in Second Isaiah, together with the lack of anti-Persian polemic in the prophets in general,[1] the more probable explanation is that Isaiah 40–66 reflects a situation in which Persian political dominion was accepted as divinely mandated.[2]

This may be the most significant characteristic of chs. 40–66 of Isaiah. The chapters are occupied with the topic of the restoration of the people Israel, the rebuilding of Jerusalem and the temple, and the fulfillment of

The Reinterpretation of David', *Bijdragen* 35 (1974), pp. 49-64; W. Brueggemann, 'Isaiah 55 and Deuteronomic Theology', *ZAW* 80 (1968), pp. 191-203; H.G.M. Williamson, '"The Sure Mercies of David": Subjective or Objective Genitive?', *JSS* 23 (1978), pp. 31-49. Mark S. Smith has recently called attention to Isa. 58.8 as another instance of the democratization of royal ideology. In the ancient Near East it was common for the monarchy to be described with solar terminology. 2 Sam. 23.3-4 and Ps. 72.5-6 are examples of this practice in Israel. But in Isa. 58.8 this traditional language is applied 'not to a royal group, but to Israel as a whole'. M.S. Smith, *The Early History of God: Yahweh and the Other Deities in Ancient Israel* (San Francisco: Harper & Row, 1990), p. 119. One could also add Judg. 5.31 to Smith's list. Isa. 42.1-4 can be understood in similar fashion. In these verses 'Israel's relationship to the nations is somehow analogous to the relationship of the king to the nation within Israel'. P. Wilcox and D. Paton-Williams, 'The Servant Songs in Deutero-Isaiah', *JSOT* 42 (1988), p. 87. The democratization of royal ideology can also be seen in the Bible's very first chapter, where it is said (Gen 1.26) that God created humanity in his own image (צלם) and likeness (דמות). Levenson has argued that in this passage humanity as a whole assumes what are properly royal prerogatives, and thus, in Gen 1.26-27, 'the human race is YHWH's plenipotentiary, his stand-in'. J.D. Levenson, *Creation and the Persistence of Evil* (San Francisco: Harper & Row, 1988), p. 114. Levenson also points out that in the Hebrew Bible democratizing tendencies are evident in the priestly sphere as well. See, for example, Exod 19.6. But, for Levenson, democratization of priestly and royal prerogatives does not have to be understood to imply the abolition of those offices. See J.D. Levenson, *Theology of the Program of Restoration of Ezekiel 40–48* (HSM, 10; Atlanta: Scholars Press, 1976), p. 99.

1. A possible exception is the language about Zerubbabel in Zech. 1–8.

2. The radicality of this position should not be minimized. From the perspective of the Hebrew Bible, native Israelite and Judean kingship was a problematic phenomenon and was often viewed with a certain suspicion and uneasiness. In addition, the Bible's own surveys of the monarchical period emphasize the negative.

ancient prophecy, but all of this is spoken of apart from any discussion of the restoration of native kingship. In this regard, the significance of Isa. 55.3 should not be underestimated. In Isaiah 40–66 God's people have taken the place of the Davidic king, and God's covenantal relationship with his people is no longer mediated through the Davidic line. Such a position is reflective of several things, but it mainly reflects a certain scepticism toward native kingship that is evident in many sections of the Hebrew Bible. The book of Judges, for example, is dedicated to a scathing critique of the phenomenon of hereditary kingship.[1] The position of Judges is continued in 1 Samuel 8. When the people ask Samuel to appoint a king for them like all the nations, God addresses Samuel with the following words: שמע בקל העם לכל אשר יאמרו אליך כי לא אתך מאסו כי אתי מאסו ממלך עליהם ('Do what the people have asked you, because it is not you that they are rejecting; they have rejected me from being their king'.)[2] The Deuteronomistic History takes great delight in pointing out the shortcomings of the kings of Israel and Judah: no northern king receives a positive evaluation; in the south only David, Asa, Jehoshaphat, Hezekiah and Josiah receive positive marks. A few positive words are said about Solomon, Jehoash, Amaziah, Uzziah and Jotham, but the final verdict on their reigns is negative. All of this supports the contention that there is a persistent (but by no means, exclusive) tendency, evident in broad sections of the Hebrew Bible, to

---

1.   The positive figures in Judges are those who are raised up based upon their charismatic gifts, whereas those who rule solely because they belong to a royal family are derided. No positive figure in Judges is described with the root מלך; instead various forms of the roots שפט and ישע are used. The distinction is polemical rather than semantic. Recent research has shown that the root שפט is, for all practical purposes, synonymous with מלך. See W. Richter, 'Zu den "Richtern Israels"', *ZAW* 77 (1965), pp. 40-41; K.D. Schunck, 'Die Richter Israels und ihr Amt', in J.A. Emerton et al. (eds.), *Volume du Congrès, Genève 1965* (VTSup, 15; Leiden: Brill, 1966), pp. 252-62. But although the terms are semantically synonymous in a lexical sense, they are not so for the author of Judges. Only negative figures are called מלך. The author's hostility toward hereditary kingship is most evident in the Gideon-Abimelech cycle. Gideon's glorious career as a deliverer of the people is qualified by his naming one of his sons אבימלך ('my father is king'). The story of Abimelech's brutal accession and rule is told in a way that reinforces the author's conviction that hereditary leadership leads to catastrophe. While one could argue that מלך occurs in Judg. 18.1 and 19.1 in a non-pejorative sense, it still remains true, however, that no positive figure in the book receives this title.
2.   The translation is mine. These are the harshest words in the Hebrew Bible concerning kingship.

speak of kingship in negative and skeptical terms.[1]

When seen in this light, the fact that Isaiah 40–66 envisions the restoration of the people Israel apart from the restoration of the native dynasty is not surprising.[2] The material in these chapters reflects the inherently negative attitude towards kingship that is in evidence in many sections of the Hebrew Bible, and it is also coupled with a highly positive evaluation of the new Persian empire. But there is more to it than this. Isaiah 40–66 is also shaped by the fundamental theological conviction that in the coming restoration of people, temple and city, YHWH will rule his people directly. In other words, what is proclaimed, looked for and expected by the writers of this material is nothing less than the *Endtheophanie*, or παρουσία, of YHWH.[3]

---

1. This is true in spite of the fact that the most basic confessional formula in the Hebrew Bible is: יהוה מלך ('YHWH is king'), Ps. 96.10; 97.1; 99.1; 146.10; 1 Chron. 16.31; Mic. 4.7; Exod. 15.18; etc. The sentiments expressed in these verses will eventually crystallize into one of the more radical petitions of the Shemoneh Esreh: ומלך עלינו אתה יהוה לבדך בחסד וברחמים ('Rule over us, O LORD, you alone, with mercy and compassion'). All of these passages express or long for the unmediated rule of YHWH over his people. Connections with the New Testament and Christian tradition are manifold. Scholars are in almost unanimous agreement that the primary content of the proclamation of Jesus of Nazareth was the 'kingdom' of God.

Levenson sees this skepticism toward kingship as born out of the crisis of the Babylonian exile. He argues that one of the main purposes of the exilic edition of the Deuteronomistic History (DtrH2) was to harmonize the promise of the eternal covenant with David with the Deuteronomic command to keep the statutes and ordinances of the Torah. This harmonization was accomplished in 1 Kgs 8.25 where the Davidic covenant is made conditional upon obedience to the Torah. In Levenson's words, 'the eternal pledge to David had to be harmonised with the promise that Israel would be blessed only if she observed the commandments from Sinai (Deuteronomy 28)'. J.D. Levenson, 'From Temple to Synagogue: 1 Kings 8', in B. Halpern and J.D. Levenson (eds.), *Traditions in Transformation* (Winona Lake: Eisenbrauns, 1981), p. 163.

2. With the exception of the brief Hasmonean interlude, history was to conform to this expectation. In addition, it is surely not accidental that in the foundation document of Judaism, the Pentateuch, the people of Israel have no human king, and, apart from Deut. 17.14-20, there are no provisions for making anyone king. The description of the king that is provided in Deut. 17 is obviously utopian; his task is to sit upon his throne and study Torah.

3. Like Second Isaiah, Third Isaiah announces the imminent παρουσία of YHWH, but Third Isaiah is also concerned with the question of who will be allowed to participate in the fruits of this παρουσία and who will not, and also with the question of what sorts of actions on the part of the people will either hinder or encourage the

Another significant characteristic of Third Isaiah is its lack of almost all historical specificity.[1] When one inquires into the political and social context(s) which formed the background for the oracles of Third Isaiah, what one finds is that those who were responsible for the production of this material either did their best to obscure this kind of information or, at the very least, they had no interest in providing it.[2]

This conscious suppression of virtually all historical specificity differentiates Third Isaiah from the roughly contemporary books of Haggai and Zechariah 1–8, where the prophetic word is tied up with very specific people, places and dates; it is this same historical vagueness, however, that links Third Isaiah to Zechariah 9–14, a collection of texts which, like Isaiah 56–66, has been notoriously difficult to date. Historical allusions are not lacking in Zechariah 9–14, but it has proven virtually impossible to agree upon the referents.[3] But the difference between Zechariah 9–14 and Isaiah 56–66 is the way in which each is related to the previous material in the book in which it is located. Recent work on the redaction of the book of Isaiah by Childs, Ackroyd, Rendtorff, Clements, Sweeney and others has shown that the book should be viewed as a redactional unity, that is to say, the editors of the book intended it to be read as a whole. This does not seem to be the case with Zechariah 1–8 and 9–14, where the kinds of stylistic devices and thematic and theological emphases that bind Isaiah together are not to be found.[4] By suppressing virtually all specific historical references in

arrival of YHWH's rule. See Chapters 3 and 4.

1.   See the discussion in Chapter 1. Brevard Childs has argued that this is of major importance for the interpretation of these texts. According to him, the 'original' historical context of Isa. 40–66 has been consciously and intentionally subordinated to that of the first 39 chapters of the book so that the latter half of the book could serve, what was for the authors, its more important theological function: the completion of the vision of Isaiah ben Amoz. See Childs, *Introduction to the Old Testament as Scripture*, pp. 325-30.

2.   Childs, *Introduction to the Old Testament as Scripture*, p. 78.

3.   The historical concreteness of Haggai and Zech. 1–8 has been an obvious drawback with respect to the usefulness of these texts for subsequent generations. The books have had little impact on either Jewish or Christian history. The opposite of course is true for Isa. 56–66 and Zech. 9–14. The vaguer the 'original' historical context, the more 'maleable' are the texts for subsequent readers.

4.   This does not mean that they are not there, only that they have proven extremely difficult to discover. Whatever the editorial intentions were, it is evident that Zech. 9–14 has much more in common with Malachi than with Zech. 1–8. Zech. 9–14 and Malachi are stylistically linked by the thrice recurring phrase 'Oracle of the word

Isaiah 56–66, the editors of the book of Isaiah encourage those who would interpret chs. 56–66 to read them in the light of the other material in the book.

Third Isaiah and Persian Period Prophecy

Wanke has argued that the matrix of virtually all post-exilic prophecy is located in the mental climate created by Second Isaiah's proclamation that the time of judgment was at an end and the time of Israel's salvation had arrived. So powerful was this proclamation that 'all the prophets after Deutero-Isaiah had to take a position in regard to this expectation of impending salvation'.[1] No prophet is more intimately ∿ linked to this issue than is Third Isaiah, occupied as this material is with the question of who it is who will participate in the fruits of this impending salvation and the question of what sorts of actions on the part of the people will either hinder or encourage the arrival of YHWH's rule. The answers that Third Isaiah gives to these pressing questions will be the subject matter of Chapters 3, 4 and 5.

of YHWH' (משא דבר יהוה), a phrase that occurs only here in the Hebrew Bible. Childs has stated that 'the canonical process which resulted in shaping the book of Zechariah was of a very different order than that which fashioned the Isaianic corpus', Childs, *Introduction to the Old Testament as Scripture*, p. 480.

1. G. Wanke, 'Prophecy and Psalms in the Persian Period', in Davies and Finkelstein (eds.), *The Cambridge History of Judaism*, I, p. 163.

Chapter 3

THE PROPOSAL OF PAUL HANSON

The Problem

As was stated at the end of Chapter 2, chs. 40–55 of Isaiah are characterized by the powerful rhetorical theme that the time of Israel's salvation had arrived.[1] It is my contention that the primary function of the subsequent chapters, chs. 56–66, is to serve to develop and clarify this powerful theme of Second Isaiah. Isa. 56.1 continues Second Isaiah's proclamation that the arrival of God's salvation is at hand: כה אמר יהוה שמרו משפט ועשׂו צדקה כי קרובה ישׁועתי לבוא וצדקתי להגלות ('Thus says the LORD, keep justice and practice righteousness, for my salvation is about to come and my righteousness is about to be revealed'). Isa. 60.1 continues the theme that God is about to restore Zion/Jerusalem to its former glory: קומי אורי כי בא אורך וכבוד יהוה עליך זרח ('Arise and shine, for your light has come and the glory of YHWH has risen upon you'). This theme of the impending salvation of God, however, is not the dominant theme in Third Isaiah; that is to say, Third Isaiah does not simply continue the proclamation of his predecessor. Instead, what is found in Third Isaiah is the provocative juxtaposition of oracles proclaiming the impending salvation of God and oracles dealing with the fact that the arrival of God's salvation has been delayed.[2] It is this theme of delay that characterizes Isaiah 56–66 as a whole. But the chapters are not interested in merely stating that a delay has occurred. The real interest of these chapters is to explain why the delay in the arrival of God's salvation has occurred. Illustrative of this point is Isa. 59.1-2: הן לא קצרה יד יהוה מהושׁיע ולא כבדה אזנו משׁמוע כי אם עונתיכם היו מבדלים בינכם לבין

1. See especially Isa. 40.1-2.
2. See Kraus, 'Die ausgebliebene Endtheophanie'. Kraus interprets Third Isaiah primarily under this rubric of 'delay' and claims that the struggle with the delay in the arrival of God's promised salvation, so in evidence in Third Isaiah, is a major characteristic of post-exilic Judaism.

אלהיכם וחטאותיכם הסתירו פנים מכם משמוע ('The LORD's hand is not too short to save nor is his ear too dull to hear, rather it is your iniquities that have separated you from your God and your sins that have caused him to turn his face away and not listen to you'). Third Isaiah takes the position that the arrival of God's salvation has certain preconditions, and unless these preconditions are met, the promised salvation of the people will not take place.

In addition to positing preconditions for the arrival of God's salvation, Third Isaiah is also occupied with the concern to identify and to define who the people are who will be allowed to participate in this salvation, and conversely, to identify and to define who the people are who will not participate in this salvation. In Second Isaiah the recipients of the proclamation of salvation are consistently identified as either Jacob/ Israel (Isa. 40–48) or Zion/Jerusalem (Isa. 49–55). But for Third Isaiah these terms were no longer sufficient in and of themselves, and, as a result, they had to be modified and clarified. For example, it has long been recognized that the familiar collective designation of the people in Second Isaiah as ישראל עבדי ('Israel, my servant') does not occur in Third Isaiah but is replaced by the plural designation עבדי ('my servants').[1] For some reason the designation of the recipients of the message of salvation as 'Jacob' or 'Israel' or 'my servant' had become problematic for Third Isaiah, and as a result the tendency in Third Isaiah is to avoid collective designations for the recipients of the message of salvation and to use plural designations instead. This development is most obvious in the change from עבדי ('my servant') to עבדי ('my servants').

And so the problem is this. In Isaiah 40–55 the questions, who are 'the saved' and who are 'the condemned', are really no questions at all

---

1.   The first occurrence of the plural of עבד ('servant') is in Isa. 54.17c, which uses the expression, עבדי יהוה ('the servants of the LORD'). This passage is part of what is traditionally ascribed to Second Isaiah. Some authors even see this as evidence that Third Isaiah begins much earlier than originally thought. See for example, J.D.W. Watts, *Isaiah 34–66* (WBC; Waco, TX: Word Books, 1987), p. 244. Watts is not concerned to demonstrate the existence of a Third Isaiah, separate and distinct from Second Isaiah. But he does see Isa. 54.17c as of major structural importance in the book. He argues that the plural use of the term עבד that begins in Isa. 54.17c marks the beginning of the final section of the book, a section that will culminate in Isa. 65.13-16 with the identification of the 'true servants and the false'. It is more likely, in my opinion, that the expression עבדי יהוה was a genuine expression first used by Second Isaiah and was then picked up, emphasized and turned into a *terminus technicus* by Third Isaiah.

because the answers are obvious. Oracles of salvation are spoken to Jacob/Israel and oracles of judgment are spoken against the Chaldeans. It is even possible to describe Isaiah 40–55 as a whole as a single oracle of salvation addressed to Jacob/Israel.[1] The identity of 'God's people' on the one hand, and 'God's enemies' on the other, is perfectly clear. But when we move to Isaiah 56–66 it is precisely the answers to these basic questions that have become unclear.

In Third Isaiah's struggle to explain the delay in the arrival of God's promised salvation, traditional prophetic modes of address came to be seen as incapable of resolving the situation. The traditional prophetic way of viewing the world as divided into two parts, Israel on the one hand and the nations on the other, a view that most certainly characterizes the message of Isaiah 40–55, undergoes a fundamental change in Third Isaiah. For some reason it was no longer possible for Third Isaiah to simply equate 'Israel' with 'God's people'. In my opinion, this was so because Third Isaiah had either adopted or had himself developed a controversial position with regard to the definition of the term 'Israel'. This controversial position of Third Isaiah is echoed by a later Jewish writer, Paul of Tarsus, who wrote, οὐ γὰρ πάντες οἱ ἐξ Ἰσραὴλ οὗτοι Ἰσραήλ ('Not everyone who is from Israel is Israel') (Rom. 9.6). Thus, what we have in Isaiah 56–66 is an early attempt to answer the question: who or what is 'Israel'?[2]

It will be the task of this and the following chapters to elucidate the change in the prophetic world-view that is in evidence in Third Isaiah. And the answer to the question, who or what is 'Israel', can only be answered by first clarifying the identity of 'the saved' and 'the condemned' in Third Isaiah.

Third Isaiah and the Proposal of Paul Hanson

When Third Isaiah is viewed as a whole, the most obvious characteristic of the material is its polemical nature. Second Isaiah was highly polemical as well, but the difference is that the polemic in Third Isaiah is not directed outwardly, that is, toward foreign nations, but rather inwardly,

---

1. This makes Isa. 40–55 the primary counterpart to Isa. 1–39. Chs. 1–39 are made up predominantly of oracles of judgment directed against עמי ישראל ('my people, Israel'). See Isa. 1.3.

2. See Alhström, *Who Were the Israelites?*, especially pp. 101-18; Williamson, 'The Concept of Israel in Transition'.

toward groups or individuals within the restoration community.

In 1975 Paul D. Hanson published a book entitled *The Dawn of Apocalyptic* in which he attempted to pinpoint the historical and socio-logical matrix out of which arose the phenomenon known as apocalyptic eschatology.[1] Hanson developed the elaborate and provocative thesis that apocalyptic eschatology was not a foreign import into Israel but rather was a phenomenon that more or less evolved naturally from traditional Israelite prophecy. This, of course, was not a new argument. What was new was Hanson's contention as to what brought about this evolution. Based upon a rigorous exegesis of two collections of anony-mous prophetic texts, Isaiah 56–66 and Zechariah 9–14, Hanson came to the conclusion that the rise of apocalyptic eschatology in Israel was the result of a bitter, intra-community struggle for control of the temple between visionary and hierocratic groups in early, post-exilic Judah, and that it is this bitter intra-community struggle that lies behind the polemics of Third Isaiah. He has described a situation in which a group of 'visionaries', those who were proponents of the program of restora-tion described in Isaiah 60–62,[2] and a group of 'hierocrats', those who were devoted to the program of restoration described in Ezekiel 40–48, engaged in theological combat over the question of which group would lead the restoration community. As the visionary group grew more and more powerless and the hierocratic group grew more and more power-ful, the visionaries lost confidence in the 'historical realm as a suitable context for divine activity' and, as a result, they began to disclose

---

1.   Hanson argues that biblical prophetic texts exhibit two distinct kinds of escha-tological thought: classical prophetic eschatology and apocalyptic eschatology. The distinction between these two forms of eschatology consists in the fact that in the former the divine vision/word is translated by the prophet 'into the terms of plain history, real politics, and human instrumentality', whereas in the latter the vision/word is not translated 'into the terms of plain history, real politics, and human instrumentality', *Dawn*, p. 11. Hanson goes to great lengths to distinguish 'apocalyptic eschatology' from two other terms, 'apocalypse' and 'apocalypticism'. He defines 'apocalypse' as a literary genre, and 'apocalypticism' as a socio-religious movement. 'Apocalyptic eschatology', on the other hand, is not to be confused with either of these, but is to be viewed as 'a religious perspective which views divine plans in rela-tion to historical realities in a particular way', *Dawn*, p. 431. His work provides some much needed controls for dealing with the wealth of material that is often lumped under the single confusing category of 'apocalyptic'.

2.   Hanson names this group of visionaries as 'the visionary disciples of Second Isaiah'.

their vision in a manner of growing indifference to and independence from
the contingencies of the politico-historical realm, thereby leaving the
language increasingly in the idiom of the cosmic realm of the divine
warrior and his council.[1]

The record of the losing battle that the visionaries fought with the
hierocrats and the subsequent flight of the visionaries into the realm of
apocalyptic speculation are reflected in the oracles of Isaiah 56–66.[2]

Hanson's interest, as is reflected in the title of his book, is to explore
the roots of apocalyptic eschatology in Israel, and he has forcefully
argued that Third Isaiah is the linchpin in the transition from classical
prophetic eschatology to apocalyptic eschatology. What I propose to do
is to challenge one significant aspect of Hanson's thesis, namely, the
identity of the group that is singled out for condemnation in Third
Isaiah.[3] Hanson's provocative contention is that the polemics of Third
Isaiah are directed against the Zadokite priesthood and, more specifically, against the priestly, Pentateuchal theology that it espouses. In other
words, Hanson reads Third Isaiah as an attack on the Jerusalem temple
cult, a cult whose foundation document is the Pentateuch!

I will proceed by first explaining how Hanson arrived at this surprising

1. *Dawn*, p. 12.
2. As was stated in Chapter 1, Hanson's thesis involves a reordering of the
oracles of Isa. 56–66 into what he considers to have been the original chronological
order. Hanson's methodology for dealing with this problem involves a combination
of prosodic analysis and a typology of prophetic genres. See Chapter 1 for further
explanation.
3. There have been numerous reviews of the book and also several criticisms of
the various theses of the book, but none of these have confined themselves specifically
to Hanson's exegesis and interpretation of Third Isaiah. Reviews: P.R. Ackroyd, *Int*
30 (1976), pp. 412-15; R.E. Brown, *CBQ* 38 (1976), pp. 389-90; M. Delcor, *Bib* 57
(1976), pp. 577-79; J. Eaton, *ExpTim* 87 (1975–76), pp. 119-20; J.G. Gammie, *JBL*
95 (1976), pp. 651-54; R. Tournay, *RB* 83 (1976), pp. 150-53; I. Willi-Plein, *VT* 29
(1979), pp. 122-27. For criticisms of Hanson, see J. Barton, *Oracles of God* (New
York: Oxford University Press, 1986), pp. 111-13, 167, 220, 288; R.P. Carroll,
'Twilight of Prophecy or Dawn of Apocalyptic?', *JSOT* 14 (1979), pp. 3-35;
P.R. Davies, 'The Social World of Apocalyptic Writings', in R.E. Clements (ed.),
The World of Ancient Israel (Cambridge: Cambridge University Press, 1989),
pp. 251-71; M.A. Knibb, 'Prophecy and the Emergence of the Jewish Apocalypses',
in R. Coggins, A. Phillips and M. Knibb (eds.), *Israel's Prophetic Tradition: Essays
in Honour of Peter R. Ackroyd* (Cambridge: Cambridge University Press, 1982),
pp. 155-80; R. Mason, 'The Prophets of the Restoration', in Coggins, Phillips and
Knibb (eds.), *Israel's Prophetic Tradition*, pp. 137-54.

conclusion. Then, in the following chapter, I will seek to demonstrate exegetically why such a conclusion is untenable. And finally, by describing the theological trajectory of the oracles of Third Isaiah, I will propose a more satisfactory reading of these texts, one that will clarify what really is at issue in the polemics of Third Isaiah, and thus, hopefully, make a contribution to our understanding of early restoration Judah.

Visionaries and Hierocrats[1]

I argued in Chapter 1 that Hanson has moved the study of Third Isaiah in a new direction, and that he has done so by incorporating all of the best insights from the history of scholarship on Third Isaiah. Hanson has moved us away from the almost obsessive focus on the question of authorship and has helped us to see in Isaiah 56–66 the growth of a 'common tradition' arising out of 'a common community situation'.[2]

Hanson's exegetical approach to Third Isaiah involves a combination of prosodic analysis and a typology of prophetic genres. In the prosodic analysis aspect of his exegesis, he argues that classical Hebrew poetry was undergoing fundamental changes in the sixth and fifth centuries BCE; simply stated, 'poetry' was being corrupted by 'prosaic' elements. This development is important for Hanson because it helps him date the oracles in Third Isaiah: the more poetic, the earlier; the more prosaic, the later. This approach places Hanson into what Kugel has described as 'the Syllable-Counting Text-Rewriting school of biblical prosody'.[3] Kugel has forcefully challenged all of the traditional habits of categorizing biblical Hebrew as either poetry or prose based upon systems of metrical

---

1. Indispensable for understanding Hanson's work on Third Isaiah are the following books: K. Mannheim, *Ideology and Utopia* (trans. L. Wirth and E.A. Shils; New York: Harcourt, Brace & Co., 1949); O. Plöger, *Theocracy and Eschatology* (trans. S. Rudman; Richmond, VA: John Knox Press, 1968); E. Troeltsch, *The Social Teaching of the Christian Churches* (trans. O. Wyon; 2 vols.; New York: Harper & Row, 1960); M. Weber, *The Sociology of Religion* (trans. E. Fischoff; Boston: Beacon Press, 1963). Although Hanson refers to Plöger only in one footnote, the influence of Plöger on Hanson is obvious.

2. *Dawn*, p. 41. The common tradition is the tradition of Second Isaiah, and the common community situation is the struggle for control of the temple in Jerusalem in the early restoration period.

3. Kugel, *The Idea of Biblical Poetry*, p. 296; *idem*, 'Some Thoughts on Future Research into Biblical Style: Addenda to *The Idea of Biblical Poetry*', *JSOT* 28 (1984), pp. 107-17.

analysis. His claim is that 'meter' (in any sort of traditional sense) is non-existent in biblical Hebrew, and that, therefore, categories such as 'poetry' or 'prose' are not only inappropriate ways of describing biblical Hebrew, they are also highly misleading and distorting. Kugel's work is of importance for us because it raises the question of whether the entire prosodic analysis aspect of Hanson's book is of any value at all. But it should be stated in Hanson's favor that even if the results of this type of exegetical approach are highly questionable, his overall thesis is not significantly affected. This is so because the thesis is much more dependent on his description of the typology of prophetic genres that occurs in Isaiah 56–66.[1]

Hanson has made a major contribution to Third Isaiah studies in particular, and to the study of the prophets in general, with his identification and explication of the 'salvation-judgment oracle' in Third Isaiah. In his exegesis of Isa. 56.9–57.13, 58.1-12, 59.1-20, 65.1-25, 66.1-16, Hanson shows how words of salvation and judgment are no longer delivered along national lines (e.g., salvation for Israel and judgment for the nations, or vice versa), 'rather the line cuts through one nation, and thus in an oracle delivered to that nation, salvation and judgment words' occur side by side.[2] It is this juxtaposition of salvation and judgment words within a single oracle that Hanson refers to as a 'salvation-judgment oracle'.[3] Although this juxtaposition does not occur in every oracle of Third Isaiah, it is evident in several places and is, therefore, a major stylistic characteristic of Third Isaiah.

Hanson contends that the salvation-judgment oracle in Third Isaiah, which pits one part of the restoration community over against another, is reflective of a theological battle that was going on within this same restoration community. He then goes on to explicate this battle and attempts to identify the protagonists. Those who are addressed with the message of salvation are identified as the visionary disciples of Second Isaiah together with their followers, and those who receive words of judgment are identified as the Zadokite priesthood. How was Hanson able to arrive at such a conclusion? To answer this question, we must

1. For this reason, I will not treat this particular aspect of Hanson's exegesis beyond what was already stated in Chapter 1.

2. *Dawn*, p. 150.

3. This is a rather obvious advance over traditional form-critical studies that used the occurrence of judgment and salvation words in a single oracle as evidence that such an oracle is not original.

look first at his assumptions regarding the origins of the early, post-exilic priesthood.[1]

Hanson's book is divided into five chapters: (1) 'The Phenomenon of Apocalyptic in Israel: Its Background and Setting'; (2) 'Isaiah 56–66 and the Visionary Disciples of Second Isaiah'; (3) 'The Origins of the Post-Exilic Hierocracy'; (4) 'Zechariah 9–14 and the Development of the Apocalyptic Eschatology of the Visionaries'; (5) 'An Allegory and its Explication'. It is curious that the third chapter, which is a historical reconstruction of priesthood in Israel, comes after the exegesis of Isaiah 56–66 rather than before it. It is curious because this third chapter contains all of the historical presuppositions that inform the exegesis. Hanson brings key presuppositions about priesthood in Israel to his exegesis of Isaiah 56–66; these presuppositions then lead him to draw certain conclusions from the material in question; he then uses these conclusions to justify his presuppositions. If chapters 3 and 2 were reversed, it would be clearer what he has actually done. But the problem would still be the same: it is a classical case of circular argumentation. This is one of my fundamental criticisms of the book, because the book gives the impression, when first read, that the exegesis in chapter 2 has led to the conclusions drawn in chapter 3. It appears, however, to be the other way around. The material in Isaiah 56–66 has been interpreted in such a way so as to make it conform with the historical reconstruction provided in chapter 3. It is for these reasons that this third chapter is the real heart of the book.

Hanson begins chapter 3 with the assertion that the Zadokite priests 'controlled the high priesthood from the first years of the Solomonic temple down to the second century BC'.[2] He evidently assumes this to be a self-evident assertion, because he gives no justification for making it. He also sees this control as uninterrupted.[3] The Zadokites controlled the temple of Solomon and the Zadokites also controlled the Persian-period temple.

It is at this point that Hanson brings the sociological analyses of Mannheim, Troeltsch and Weber to bear. He has correctly stated that a

---

1. Hanson refers to this priesthood as a 'Hierocracy'.
2. *Dawn*, p. 210.
3. This is an especially problematic assertion. The evidence from Malachi would seem to suggest that in the period from 515 to 458 BCE the cult had fallen into general disuse. If the Zadokites were 'in control' of the temple during this period, it is very difficult to account for the description of the temple cultus provided by Malachi.

trauma such as occurred in 597 and 587 BCE would have led to major
sociological problems, especially when it comes to the question of how a
destroyed community is to be reconstituted. In such a situation

> a profound need is created to find models upon which to pattern the
> reconstruction of the community, but the result is often a bitter struggle
> between groups each claiming that its particular model offers the legitimate
> basis for reconstruction. The reason for that struggle is clear; the catas-
> trophe has not created the divergent views but has merely destroyed the
> hegemony of the controlling party thereby releasing latent dissent.[1] The
> disaster has suddenly made peers of ruler and subject, *clerus major* and
> *clerus minor*, and an abrupt end comes to the peace imposed by the domi-
> nant party, for its loss of power undermines its ability to minimize the
> tension between the divergent forces in the society. The result is rivalry
> and struggle which tend to polarize and throw into bold relief the divergent
> forces lying at the heart of the society in question.[2]

Of importance for this study is the fact that these problems are not
restricted to the political sphere but encompass the religious as well:

> In the realm of religious institutions, as in the realm of politics, the polari-
> zation tends to develop primarily between two forces, the one embodied in
> the ruling classes and devoted to preservation of the former institutional
> structures, the other found among the alienated and oppressed and bent on
> revolution leading to change of the status quo. The models to which each
> turns in the search for a basis for restoration is intimately related to the
> social status of each group. The ruling classes, because of their vested
> interest in the institutional structures of the immediate past, construct a
> program for restoration on the basis of those recently disrupted structures
> so as to preserve their position of supremacy. The alienated and oppressed
> classes look to the more distant past for models which call into question
> the position of power claimed by the ruling classes, and readily adhere to
> prophetic figures calling for revolutionary change on the basis of such
> archaic models.[3]

According to Hanson, given the profound nature of the national disaster
of 587 BCE, one should expect to find all of the following elements present in the society of the restoration period: the visionary and the
realistic, the prophetic and the priestly, the alienated and the ruling class,
the oppressed and the oppressors, proponents of revolution and

1.   This is evident in our own day in the events surrounding the breakup of the
Soviet Union. The divergent political voices that are now being heard are not new.

2.   *Dawn*, pp. 211-12.

3.   *Dawn*, p. 212.

proponents of the status quo, utopian thinkers and ideological thinkers, anti-establishment people and pro-establishment people, lower class and upper class, sectarian and worldly, poor and rich, democrats and exclusivists. But it is not just that all of these elements existed at various points in the society. Hanson's claim is that all of these elements fell into two basic groups and constituted two basic mentalities which were at war with one another. The visionary, the prophetic, the alienated, the oppressed, the proponents of revolution, utopian thinkers, anti-establishment people, the lower class, sectarians, the poor and the democrats all belonged to a single group, and this group was opposed by another group made up of the realistic, the priestly, the ruling class, the oppressors, the proponents of the status quo, ideological thinkers, pro-establishment people, the upper class, the rich and the exclusivists.[1]

It is against the background of these sociological presuppositions that Hanson attempts to describe the historical situation of restoration Judah. Operating with the concept that there are 'two basic types of religious parties',[2] he categorizes the literature from the early restoration period accordingly. The literature of the ruling, priestly party is primarily to be seen in Ezekiel 40–48, where the prerogatives of the Zadokite priests are carefully delineated. Ezekiel was the spiritual heir of the pre-exilic Zadokite tradition and was keenly aware of the struggles that had taken place between the various priestly houses in pre-exilic Israel and Judah. Hanson sees these pre-exilic battles, primarily between the Zadokites and the disenfranchised Abiatharite Levites, as the single most important key to understanding the polemics of the restoration period.[3] The destruction

---

1. *Dawn*, pp. 211-17. Note especially his statement on p. 217 that the 'social position of each group determined the models upon which they drew in setting forth their restoration programs'.

2. *Dawn*, p. 225.

3. *Dawn*, p. 220. There is no question that the Bible records several instances of controversy between the descendants of Zadok and the more generic Levites: Deut. 14.25-29; 18.6-7; 2 Kgs 23.9; Num. 18.6-7; Exod. 29.9, 44; 32; 40.12-15; 1 Sam. 2.27-36; Jer. 7; 26. See F.M. Cross, 'The Priestly Houses of Early Israel', in *Canaanite Myth and Hebrew Epic*, pp. 195-215. There is also no question that these controversies had roots in King David's having chosen not one chief priest but two. There is also no question that there came to be two distinct kinds of priests, 'the priests, the sons of Zadok' and 'the Levites'. The problem, however, is when to date these controversies. Simply stated, we do not know whether or to what extent post-exilic controversies were read back into the pre-exilic period. The history of priest-hood in Israel is one of the major unsolved riddles in scholarship on the Hebrew

of Jerusalem and its temple in 587 BCE called into question the hard-fought, pre-exilic Zadokite hegemony over the priesthood, and the result was that many of the battles that had already been fought had to be fought all over again in the restoration period. Ezekiel 40–48 represents the Zadokite manifesto for the restoration of Judah.[1] Among those who returned with the Zadokite-dominated Babylonian גולה were the prophets Haggai and Zechariah. These prophets served as propagandists for Ezekiel's Zadokite manifesto and they gave prophetic legitimation to the program.

Hanson's reconstruction of events to this point reflects a general scholarly consensus. But he adds an additional ingredient to the mix. He argues that the material in Isaiah 56–66 represents a direct challenge to the program of restoration adhered to by Ezekiel, Haggai and Zechariah. Even more provocative, however, is the claim that the group behind the oracles of Isaiah 56–66 is made up of a combination of visionary disciples of Second Isaiah and disenfranchised Abiatharite[2] Levites. What distinguishes these two programs of restoration is that one may be characterized as 'hierocratic' and the other as 'visionary'.[3] The hierocratic group was made up primarily of members of the Babylonian גולה, while the visionary group consisted of disciples of Second Isaiah, disenfranchised

Bible. For an admirable attempt to solve the problem, see A. Cody, *A History of Old Testament Priesthood* (AnBib, 35; Rome: Pontifical Biblical Institute, 1969).

1. Hanson follows many in seeing Ezek. 40.46b, 43.19a, 44.6-31, 45.13-15, 48.11 as forming part of a 'Zadokite revision' of Ezekiel. Hanson dates this revision to the late sixth/early fifth century BCE. The purpose of the revision was to grant 'the Zadokites sole access to the actual priesthood', *Dawn*, p. 267.

2. He sometimes refers to them as 'Ithamarides'.

3. Hanson is often at pains to resist describing the competing groups in terms of a prophet–priest dichotomy. He claims that such a distinction is far too simplistic and does not take into account the history of intra-priestly conflict in Israel and Judah. See *Dawn*, pp. 220-21. Hanson's claims notwithstanding, his tendency is, in fact, to align the visionaries with the prophets and the realists with the priests. An illustration of this is the way in which he treats Ezekiel, Haggai and Zechariah. One gets the strong impression from Hanson that, because of the commitment to the temple and temple theology of Ezekiel, Haggai and Zechariah, they were not 'prophets' in the true sense. They were, rather, a kind of hybrid. See his discussion on pp. 240-62. This tendency to 'dichotomize' is prominent throughout the book and is understandable, given his reliance upon Weber. Both Weber and Hanson see post-exilic Judaism as having been characterized by two basic 'ideological tendencies', the visionary and the realist. Prophets, in the true sense of the term, tended to align themselves with the visionaries. See *Dawn*, pp. 71-72.

Levites, and other dissident groups who did not go into exile.[1]

What is the evidence for the alliance involved in this latter group? Hanson sees striking parallels between the polemics of Third Isaiah, Ezekiel, Haggai and Zechariah on the one hand, and the intra-priestly polemics evident in passages such as Numbers 16–18.[2] Then, based on his exegesis of Isaiah 56–66, he is led to the conclusion that the polemics of Third Isaiah actually represent another instance of this intra-priestly polemic. If Isaiah 56–66 does represent intra-priestly polemic, then the implication is that the visionary disciples of Second Isaiah and a group of disenfranchised Levites had joined forces.[3] Whereas Ezekiel 40–48 represents propaganda for the Zadokites, Isaiah 56–66 is anti-Zadokite propaganda produced by disenfranchised Levites.[4] A continuation of this

1. *Dawn*, pp. 263-69.
2. Compare, for example, the attack on the Levites in Num. 16.8-11 with Ezek. 44.
3. That such a union would have occurred is a logical and natural inference for Hanson to make because, according to his reconstruction, the two groups shared a common social location. But in addition, Hanson also operates with the fundamental presupposition that disenfranchised, dissident groups are naturally drawn together. The significance of this assumption, an assumption based on a particular style of sociological analysis, cannot be overestimated. It is this assumption that enables Hanson to set up the visionary–hierocrat dichotomy that dominates his book. And it is this assumption that enables him to posit that the visionary group would, naturally, have consisted of the prophetic, the alienated, the oppressed, the proponents of revolution, utopian thinkers, anti-establishment people, the lower class, sectarians and the poor.
4. Pointing out and explicating competing theologies within the Hebrew Bible is a common thread running through many of Hanson's writings. In fact, demonstrating that the Hebrew Bible is not theologically monolithic but contains marked tension is a driving force behind his work. Hanson is a man of faith who is involved in the attempt to describe how the Bible is relevant to contemporary theology. Any interpretation or evaluation of his work that does not take this into account does not understand him. Two quotes make this clear: 'For a community or an individual who takes the Bible seriously as the word of God, the theological questions raised by our interpretation of the early post-exilic community are serious. The preponderant emphasis upon Israel's historical confessions in works dealing with biblical theology has helped establish the impression in the minds of many that the Old Testament comprises one normative theological current recording a smooth, uninterrupted disclosure of God's will to his community, an impression which is rudely shattered by the discordant voices of the late seventh, sixth, and fifth centuries delivering irreconcilable messages in the name of the same Yahweh. What interpretation can one offer, in the face of conflicting messages from Haggai and the visionary of Isaiah 66, one proclaiming God's will that the temple be built, the other rejecting the temple plan and condemning

anti-Zadokite propaganda is to be found in the somewhat later oracles recorded in Zechariah 9–14. A summary of Hanson's exegesis of Isaiah 56–66 and his provocative identification of Third Isaiah's opponents as the Zadokite priests is now in order.[1]

The exegesis begins with Isaiah 60–62, passages that Hanson regards as the earliest phase in the Third Isaiah tradition. He describes these chapters as a 'program of restoration'. Isa. 61.1-3 is of importance because it shows that the prophetic office has come to be understood in collective terms;[2] it is also an attempt to legitimate the new message by stating that 'the mission of the servant [of Second Isaiah] was living on in this post-exilic community'.[3] The point is to emphasize that the group that is producing this material stands in and carries on the tradition of Second Isaiah. Isa. 61.6 states: ואתם כהני יהוה תקראו משרתי אלהינו יאמר לכם ('You will be named the priests of Yahweh, ministers of our God').[4] This passage is a major interpretive key for Hanson because it 'represents an astonishing democratization of the formerly exclusive sacerdotal office'.[5] And 62.3 shows that this democratization is not limited to the sacerdotal sphere but extends even into the royal sphere: והיית עטרת תפארת ביד יהוה וצניף מלוכה בכף אלהיך ('You will be a beautiful crown in Yahweh's hand,

---

the practices and leaders of the temple cult?' 'Revelation in the Bible is not the announcement of immutable truths, but is a record of Yahweh's involvement in the crises and struggles of his human community... Revelation thus is found not in an unbroken progression stemming from the creation to the eschaton, but occurs in a dialectical movement often marked by tension and dissention, frequently tottering between the extremes of desperate escape into the repose of the cosmic vision and myopic preoccupation with the day-to-day control of cult and community', *Dawn*, pp. 410-11. I share many of these very same concerns. It is my contention, however, that Hanson has misunderstood what is really at stake in biblical polemics. In identifying competing theologies and the groups that produced these theologies, Hanson consistently overlooks the question of what these groups and theologies have in common. By overlooking or minimizing this crucial aspect of the literature of the Hebrew Bible and the groups that produced it, Hanson is unable to see intra-biblical polemic for what it really is. The remainder of this chapter will attempt to clarify this assertion.

1.   I will treat Hanson's exegesis of Isa. 56–66 according to his reconstructed chronological order of the passages.

2.   Compare Isa. 49.3.

3.   *Dawn*, p. 66 (parentheses mine).

4.   For the sake of simplicity, all of the translations in this section will be those of Hanson.

5.   *Dawn*, p. 68.

a royal diadem in the hand of your God'). It is well-nigh impossible to overstate the significance for Hanson of this concept of 'democratization'. It represents one of the defining characteristics of the visionary tradition.[1] In 62.6-7 the group producing this material designates themselves as YHWH's 'watchmen' (שׁמרים), whose task it is to witness 'on behalf of the people before Yahweh until the restoration plan developed in chapters 60-62 is fulfilled'.[2]

Hanson's primary claim for this section is not just that these three chapters represent a program of restoration, but that they were written in conscious opposition to the program of restoration of Ezekiel 40–48. The difference between the two programs is that the former is a prophetic, visionary one, while the latter is the program of 'hierocratic realists or pragmatists'.[3] These programs of restoration represent 'two sharply contrasting mentalities'.[4] One is pragmatic and mundane, the other is idealistic. This claim is so important for Hanson's overall thesis that it is necessary to quote him in full:

> These contrasting mentalities are brought into sharp focus when one compares the corresponding details within the two programs: (1) The leaders of the prophetic community are Peace and Righteousness (Isa. 60.17b), those of the hierocracy are the various officials of the priestly and civil hierarchies, headed by the high priest and the prince. (2) The promise of the visionary is that the whole nation 'will be named the priests of Yahweh, the ministers of our God' (Isa. 61.6); the realist carefully regulates: '...mark well those who may be admitted to the temple and all those who are to be excluded from the sanctuary...; [the Levites] shall not come near to me, to serve me as priest...' (Ezek. 44.5, 13); '...the sons of Zadok... alone among the sons of Levi may come near to the Lord to minister to him' (Ezek. 40.46; cf. 44.15). (3) The visionary exults, 'Your people shall all be righteous...' (Isa. 60.21); 'They will be called "The Holy People"...' (Isa. 62.12); the realist meticulously explains that holiness is reserved for the few and that it must be safeguarded by ordinances: when

---

1. Isa. 61.6 and Exod. 19.6 are passages that Hanson returns to over and over again. For him, these passages not only imply an astonishing democratizing tendency, they also show that the visionary tradition was committed to 'inclusivity'. Like democratization, inclusivity is a major concept for Hanson because it enables him to portray the visionary tradition as the polar opposite of the 'exclusivistic' Zadokite priests.

2. *Dawn*, p. 68-69.

3. *Dawn*, p. 71.

4. *Dawn*, p. 72.

the Zadokites leave the inner court, 'they shall put off the garments in which they have been ministering, and lay them in the holy chambers; and they shall put on other garments, lest they communicate holiness to the people with their garment...They shall teach my people the difference between the holy and the common...' (Ezek. 44.19, 23). A special place is designated where the priests are to boil the offerings, 'in order not to bring them out into the outer court and so communicate holiness to the people' (Ezek. 46.20). (4) The visionary announces: 'The glory of Lebanon will come to you, the cypress, the plane, and the pine together, to adorn the site of my sanctuary, that I may glorify the resting place of my feet' (Isa. 60.13); the realist draws up architectural plans, exact in every detail, for the new temple, and lays it before the people to build it (Ezek. 43.10-12). (5) The visionary proclaims, 'Foreigners will rebuild your walls, and their kings will serve you', whereas the attitude of the realist could be summarized in the old maxim: 'God helps those who help themselves'.[1]

Because these two programs deal with the very same issues, 'rebuilding of walls and sanctuary, the officials of the community, membership in the priesthood, the problem of holiness', Hanson concludes that Isaiah 60–62 was intentionally written as a rival program to that of Ezekiel 40–48.[2] With the promulgation by the visionary disciples of Second Isaiah of a rival program of restoration, the battle lines are drawn. The remainder of the oracles of Third Isaiah witness to the subsequent course of the battle between the visionaries and the hierocrats that was fought in early restoration Judah. As the visionaries were systematically excluded from participation in the life of the cult, their vision of restoration became transformed more and more into the idiom of apocalyptic eschatology. The realities of everyday life in Judah and the monopolization of power by the Zadokite priesthood forced the visionaries to take refuge in ancient hymns to the divine warrior and led them to plead for divine intervention on their behalf. It is this battle between visionaries and

---

1. *Dawn*, pp. 72-73. In the scriptural references in this quote, I have inserted the abbreviations for Ezekiel (Ezek.) and Isaiah (Isa.) for the sake of clarity. These do not appear in the original text.

To get a sense of where Hanson's sympathy lies, it should be understood that when a Lutheran describes someone else's theology as a 'God-helps-those-who-help-themselves-theology', he or she is making the most scathing statement possible. Hanson's descriptions of the hierocratic tradition are consistently pejorative throughout the book. A typical example is when he evaluates the explicit detail of Ezek. 40-48 as evidence of an 'obsession'. See *Dawn*, p. 73.

2. *Dawn*, p. 74.

hierocrats in early restoration Judah that led to what Hanson calls, 'The Dawn of Apocalyptic'.[1]

The next step in the exegesis is Isa. 63.7–64.11, a section that Hanson entitles: 'The Ideal Undermined By Opposition'.[2] The passage is a communal lament and deals with the discrepancy between YHWH's glorious saving acts in the past and the present situation which is characterized by YHWH's absence. According to Hanson, the lament form is the traditional refuge of 'oppressed sectarian groups'.[3] When an oppressed group's hopes for the future are dashed by present reality, these groups often take refuge in a longing for an idyllic past era. Such is the case here. The interpretation of Isa. 63.15-17 is key. The thrice repeated phrase 'You are our Father' indicates to Hanson that 'someone is contesting this claim'.[4] This someone is 'Abraham' and 'Israel'. 'The referent of the designations Abraham and Israel can be taken most naturally as the central Israelite community of this period, that is, the group returning from exile under the leadership of the Zadokite priests'.[5] It is crucial for Hanson's exegesis that he interpret the phrase כי אברהם לא ידענו וישראל לא יכירנו ('though Abraham does not acknowledge us, and Israel does not regard us') in terms of 'rejection'. The group that calls God 'our Father' is being 'rejected' by the group that goes by the names of 'Abraham' and 'Israel'.[6]

When it comes to the question of identifying the group behind the lament, Hanson points to the prominent role played by the figure of

---

1. This historical/sociological reconstruction of the early restoration period makes clear one of Hanson's fundamental tenets, that apocalyptic eschatology is the product of oppressed, out-of-power groups.

2. *Dawn*, p. 92. Cf. Isa. 40.4-5; 40.25-26; 41.21ff.; 41.28-29.

3. *Dawn*, p. 90.

4. *Dawn*, p. 92. The Hebrew of each of these three phrases is slightly different. 63.16a: ועתה יהוה אבינו אתה; 63.16c: אתה יהוה אבינו; 64.7: כי אתה אבינו.

5. *Dawn*, pp. 92-93.

6. Here Hanson makes the significant point that the group behind the oracles of Third Isaiah tends to use non-traditional names for the purpose of self-designation. His examples are 63.17: עבדיך ('your servants'); 65.8-9, 13-15: עבדי ('my servants'); 66.14: עבדיו ('his servants'); 65.9, 15, 22: בחירי ('my chosen'); 61.6: כהני יהוה ('the priests of YHWH'); 62;4: חפצי בה ('my delight is in her'); בעולה ('married'). The self-designation עבדיך ('your, i.e., YHWH's, servants') in 63.17 is especially revealing, because as 66.14 shows, it comes to be the self-designation of those who oppose God's enemies. Isa. 66.14: ונודעה יד יהוה את עבדיו וזעם את איביו ('The power of the LORD shall be revealed in behalf of His servants; but He shall rage against his foes'). The translation of Isa. 66.14 is that of the new JPSV.

Moses. The group sees Moses as the central figure in Israel's past. According to Hanson, because many Levites traced themselves back to the figure of Moses, it is logical to assume that it is a Levitical group that stands behind this lament. It is this group that would have been in charge of the cultic activities that were carried on in the temple ruins during the period of exile, and, along with the disciples of Second Isaiah, they would naturally have been opposed to the Zadokite-led גולה group and their exclusivist restoration program.[1] In support of this assumption is the fact that 'the central concern of the Third Isaiah material is the priestly concern of possession of Zion'.[2]

Hanson argues that such an interpretation makes Isa. 63.18 understandable. The reference in this verse to עם קדשך ('your holy people') is a Levitical self-reference, while the designation צרינו ('our adversaries') is a description of the Zadokites. Hanson's translation of the verse is 'For a brief time your holy people held possession, but our adversaries have desecrated your sanctuary'. The passage thus confirms the claims of the above paragraph, that a group of Levitical priests, עם קדשך, were in charge of the cultic activities that went on in the temple ruins during the exile, but they were evicted in the early restoration period by the returning Zadokite priests: צרינו בוססו מקדשך.

The actual battle for control of the temple would have been short-lived because of the fact that the Zadokites had in hand a Persian mandate to take charge. Isa. 63.7–64.11 already reflects a situation when the Zadokites have taken over. Thus, with the exception of Isaiah 60–62, the oracles of Third Isaiah were produced by a prophetic Levitical group that was out of power. This is crucial for Hanson because it enables him to read Third Isaiah as 'protest literature' produced by an oppressed group in the face of 'crushing opposition'.[3]

---

1. The supposed union of Palestinian Levitical priests and the disciples of Second Isaiah is an integral part of Hanson's thesis. This union enables him to read the polemics of Third Isaiah against the background of a Babylonian–Palestinian dichotomy. It is highly problematic, however, not least of all because Second Isaiah was a primary character in the Babylonian גולה and his prophecy was the driving force behind the decision of exiled Babylonian Judaites to return to Judah. If the material in Third Isaiah is as closely related to the tradition of Second Isaiah as Hanson himself argues, it becomes a rather large task to make Third Isaiah into a piece of propaganda written against the Babylonian גולה! This criticism will be developed further below.

2. *Dawn*, p. 95.

3. *Dawn*, p. 97. As the possibilities dwindle for the oppressed to realize their dreams within the context of ordinary political structures, their vision becomes more

The next section, which deals with Isa. 58.1-12[1] and 59.1-20, is entitled 'Tension within the Community Grows'. Isa. 58.1-12 represents an oracular form that is in transition between the classical judgment oracle and the salvation-judgment oracle. The theme of the oracle is the traditional one: 'obedience is better than sacrifice'.[2] Hanson sees in this oracle further evidence of a dichotomy in the restoration community. Judgment is pronounced in 58.2-5 against the cultic observances of a particular group, and in 58.6-12 words of salvation are spoken to another group that fasts in the proper way. This oracle represents the beginning of a process that will eventually result in a new oracular genre, the salvation-judgment oracle. In 58.1-12 it is obvious that there is no Israel-versus-the-nations dichotomy. Rather, the problem is intra-communal.[3]

The affinities that this passage has with Isa. 63.7–64.11 and with all of Second Isaiah show that Isa. 58.1-12 is part of the same tradition. But who or what is being attacked in 58.2-5? Hanson again claims that it is the Zadokite priests. His main evidence for this contention is the occurrence of two *termini technici*: דרש ('to inquire') and קרב ('to draw near').[4] This is priestly terminology, and especially the latter 'is a central concept in the language of P and Ezekiel'. He follows this by saying that 'the entire enterprise described in verse 2 is the priestly activity around the cult, betraying the same obsessions with statutes and ordinances which characterize the hierocratic tradition'. In Hanson's words, the claim is being made that this group has 'turned their backs on true religion in their self-righteous obsession with the particulars of cultic observance'.[5] The obvious implication of Hanson's description is that the P source in the Pentateuch and Ezekiel are self-righteous and obsessive.

In Isa. 58.3a the Zadokites cry out: למה צמנו ולא ראית ענינו נפשנו ולא תדע ('Why do we fast, but you do not see, afflict ourselves, but you do not

and more detached from real history and evolves into an apocalyptic rather than a prophetic eschatology. The driving force behind this evolution is social oppression.

1. Isa. 58.13-14 is considered to be part of a later redaction because it deals with the issue of Sabbath, whereas the rest of the chapter is concerned with fasting.

2. *Dawn*, p. 106.

3. The reason Hanson does not regard this as a true salvation-judgment oracle is that it leaves 'the *possibility* of salvation open to the whole nation while categorically promising it to no one group', *Dawn*, p. 108.

4. Isa. 58.2. Cf. Num. 17.5; Ezek. 44.15-16.

5. *Dawn*, p. 109.

know it?'). For Hanson, this cry exposes the fundamental flaw in the
theology of P and Ezekiel: it is an attempt to manipulate the deity
through cultic observance, and can best be characterized as pagan
superstition.[1] Over against this cult, the visionaries pose an alternative
cult, a cult 'of meekness and mercy'.[2]

Isa. 59.1-20 is close thematically to 58.1-12. The difference between the
two is that 59.1-20 is the 'first fully developed example of a salvation-
judgment oracle'.[3] Hanson reads ch. 59, like ch. 58, as an attack on 'the
defiled (Zadokite) cult'[4] by the out-of-power prophetic-visionary group.
The claim of the oracle is that it is because of the defilement of the cult
that the promises of Second Isaiah have proven to be total failures. In
Isa. 59.9-10 the restoration promised by Second Isaiah and reiterated in
Isaiah 60–62 'is turned inside out into the corresponding curse to
describe the existing conditions'.[5] The situation has become so bleak for
the visionaries that they now begin to take refuge in the ancient myth of
the divine warrior.[6] This move on the part of the visionaries indicates
that they have begun to give up 'interpreting divine activity within the
context of plain history', and the end result of this move into the realm
of myth will eventually be 'the death of prophecy and the birth of
apocalyptic eschatology'.[7]

Various kinds of social abuses are catalogued in Isa. 59.3-8, and
Hanson sees these verses as close parallels to 58.3b-4. Standing behind
both chapters is the complaint that YHWH has failed to act, and in each

---

1. *Dawn*, p. 110.
2. *Dawn*, p. 110. One would have to ask what sort of 'cult' this would be! The
assertion is highly problematic, even on Hanson's own terms. On the one hand,
Hanson wants to assert that the point at issue with the program of restoration of Ezek.
40–48 is that it excludes the Levites from participation as full priests. But, on the
other, he asserts that Isa. 58.3a is an attack on cultic theology as such. It goes without
saying that Levitical groups would have been opposed to the claims made in Ezek. 44.
This, however, is a relatively superficial kind of criticism, a disagreement over questions of leadership. But can one envision the Levites contesting the validity of cultic
theology as such? This contradiction runs throughout Hanson's interpretation of
Third Isaiah. For a further discussion of this problem, see Carroll, 'Twilight of
Prophecy'.
3. *Dawn*, p. 120.
4. *Dawn*, p. 120 (parentheses mine).
5. *Dawn*, p. 132.
6. See Isa. 59.15b-20.
7. *Dawn*, p. 132.

case the prophetic group responds by claiming that it is the defilement
of the Zadokite cult that is at fault and not YHWH. Hanson's primary
evidence for identifying the Zadokites as the ones attacked in this oracle
is the occurrence in Isa. 59.2 of another priestly *terminus technicus*, פנים
('presence'). His interpretation, however, of וחטאותיכם הסתירו פנים מכם משמוע
('your sins have hidden the Presence so that you are not heard by the
Lord') as a condemnation of the Zadokite priests is strained. Such an
interpretation requires him to claim that the prophetic speaker is making
use of a priestly *terminus technicus* in order to condemn the priests.
Viewed in isolation, this is an interesting possiblility, and if true, the
accusation would certainly have been a sharp one. But the problem here
is that Hanson has interpreted the occurrence of a priestly *terminus
technicus*, פנים, in a way exactly opposite from his interpretation in
ch. 58. There it was the *termini technici*, דרש and קרב, as such that were
regarded as the problem. It was the typical priestly functions of
'inquiring' and 'drawing near' that were used by Hanson as evidence of
the 'obsession with statutes and ordinances' that is characteristic of
Zadokite cultic theology as such. But in Isa. 59.3 the speaker is obviously using Zadokite priestly terminology in a positive sense: the sins of
the people have caused YHWH's פנים to be hidden. If Hanson were to be
true to his own line of argument, that the occurrence of priestly *termini
technici* points directly at the Zadokite priesthood, then he would have
to claim that the most probable interpretation of Isa. 59.3 is that it is the
Zadokite priests who are the ones doing the condemning here. But such
an interpretation is an impossiblity for Hanson.

The next step in the exegesis is Isa. 65.1-25, entitled 'The Schism
Widens, Vindictiveness Increases, Hope is Deferred, and the Seeds of
Apocalyptic Eschatology are Sown'. The chapter is characterized by
alternating words of salvation for עמי אשר דרשוני ('my people who seek
me')[1] and words of judgment for עם סורר ('a stubborn people').[2] Indeed,
the most striking thing about this particular oracle is that 'the sentence
of judgment to one group and the promise of salvation to the other are
offered unconditionally and categorically'.[3] This is evidence that the
schism between the two groups has widened. The evidence for identifying the group being attacked consists again in the fact that Isa. 65.1-7

1. Isa. 65.10.
2. Isa. 65.2.
3. *Dawn*, p. 144.

is 'saturated with the technical language of the cult'.[1] The key verse is 65.3a: העם המכעיסים אותי על פני תמיד ('a people who provoke me to anger before my very Presence continually'). The entire section charges the group in question with defiled cultic practices, and here once more we find the use of the priestly *terminus technicus*, פנים. According to Hanson, this term is the specific designation of the Jerusalem temple where YHWH's 'presence' tabernacled,[2] and it indicates that it is the activities going on in this very same temple that are being condemned.

Isa. 65.3b-4 lists the abuses with which the accused group is charged: זבחים בגנות ומקטרים על הלבנים הישבים בקברים ובנצורים ילינו האכלים בשר החזיר ופרק פגלים כליהם ('who offer sacrifices in the gardens, burning incense upon altars, who sit in tombs and spend the night in secret places, who eat the flesh of swine, a polluted soup in their dishes'). Hanson is understandably perplexed as to what to do with these accusations, because according to his own schema they are being leveled against the Zadokite temple priests. But even he is unwilling to saddle the Zadokites with such practices. His solution is to argue that the accusations are 'symbolical'. But symbolical of what? From elsewhere in the Hebrew Bible we know that practices such as the ones that are described in Isa. 65.3b-4 were characteristic of various Canaanite religions. Hanson thus argues that charging the group in question with utilizing Canaanite religious practices is the writer's way of 'equating' the Zadokite cult with various Canaanite cults. In other words the writer is claiming, in hyperbolic fashion, that the Zadokite cult is thoroughly defiled. But the accusations are not to be taken literally.[3]

1. *Dawn*, p. 146.
2. The interpretation that Hanson gives to this term is subject to the same criticism as in the previous exegetical unit. Just as in Isa. 59.3, the speaker is using 'Zadokite' priestly terminology in a positive sense. The speaker is intensely concerned with the defilement of YHWH's פנים. Cf. Isa. 1.12.
3. Such reasoning on Hanson's part betrays a prejudice common to numerous biblical scholars. It is the assumption that the religion of Israel and Judah, from its very origins, was fundamentally different from the neighboring Canaanite religions. Once this assumption is accepted, then all offensive and aberrant religious practices to which the Bible refers are labeled as either Canaanite or pagan. It is for this reason that Hanson has to interpret the accusations against the group in question in a symbolic or metaphorical fashion. He has to do this because taking the accusations at face value would implicate the central Judaite community in these practices and would, thus, call into question the common scholarly prejudice that the religion of Israel and Judah, from its very origins, was fundamentally different from the

Isa. 65.5a is another key in identifying the group being attacked: האמרים קרב אליך אל תגש בי כי קדשתיך ('who say, "keep your distance, approach me not, or I will communicate holiness to you"'). In this verse, three more Zadokite *termini technici* occur: קרב, נגש and קדש (*piel*). All three of these terms are familiar from P and Ezekiel,[1] and because they are used here in accusations against a certain group, that is to say, because the group being attacked is characterized by its use of these terms, Hanson argues that this is inescapable evidence for identifying the group in question as the Zadokite temple priesthood.

After the condemnations of Isa. 65.1-7 comes the proclamation of salvation in 65.8-10, a proclamation that utilizes the image of an אשכול ('grape cluster'). The writer uses the אשכול as a metaphor for the nation as a whole; the nation is like a grape cluster that includes both good and bad grapes. It is for the sake of the good grapes, identified as עבדי ('YHWH's servants'), that YHWH will not destroy the entire cluster: כה אמר יהוה כאשר ימצא התירוש באשכול ואמר אל תשחיתהו כי ברכה בו כן אעשה למען עבדי לבלתי השחית הכל ('Thus Yahweh says: Just as, when new wine is found in the cluster, they say, "Destroy it not, for it contains blessing"; so I will act for the sake of my servants in order not to destroy the whole'). This reveals just exactly what is going on with this new phenomenon called the salvation-judgment oracle. The recipients of the messages of salvation and judgment can no longer be divided along national lines. Instead, what we are witnessing in Third Isaiah in general, and in Isa. 65.1-25 in particular, is a situation in which the traditional 'historical boundary demarcating Israel from the nations is replaced by the spiritual boundary setting Israel off from Israel'.[2] YHWH's judgment is proclaimed against the wicked in Israel, and YHWH's salvation is promised to the righteous in Israel. This is a major difference from the message of Second Isaiah. Second Isaiah proclaimed salvation to

neighboring Canaanite religions. But this is just the question. It is certainly the case that the Hebrew Bible, in its final form, describes a religion fundamentally different from the neighboring Canaanite religions. But the prophetic books in general, and Third Isaiah in particular, are full of accusations against the kings, priests and prophets of Israel and Judah that would seem to indicate that the nations of Israel and Judah practiced, for a very long time, a form of religion that was not so different from the various religions of their neighbors. On this whole issue, see Wellhausen, *Prolegomena to the History of Ancient Israel*; M. Smith, 'The Common Theology of the Ancient Near East', *JBL* 71 (1952), pp. 135-47.

1.   See the list of biblical references in *Dawn*, p. 149.
2.   *Dawn*, p. 151. This is a penetrating insight.

Jacob/Israel as a whole. In fact, the entire proclamation of Second Isaiah is grounded in the belief that the time of judgment against Israel was at an end.[1] But what we find in Third Isaiah is the positing of a new time of judgment against various elements in the restoration society.[2] This goes beyond anything envisioned by Second Isaiah.

In Isa. 65.9 the group singled out as the recipients of the promise of salvation are identified as בחירי ועבדי ('my chosen ones and my servants'). The terms obviously derive from Second Isaiah, with the exception that they are used here in the plural rather than the singular. Immediately following, condemnation is pronounced against הערכים לגד שלחן והממלאים למני ממסך ('you who set a table for Gad, and who fill cups of mixed drink for Meni'). Again, Hanson sees this accusation as hyperbolic, the intention of which is to assert that the Zadokite cult is symbolically equivalent to pagan cults.

Isa. 65.17-25, the final section of the oracle, describes the new era of peace and prosperity that will ensue after YHWH's judgment purges the community of its defiled cult, an era that is reserved solely for YHWH's faithful people. Hanson finds 'in this passage one of the cardinal doctrines of the apocalyptic literature', namely, the 'earliest clear formulation' of 'the doctrine of world epochs'.[3] This doctrine has its roots in the proclamation of Second Isaiah, particularly Second Isaiah's use of the 'former things–new things' dichotomy, but here the dichotomy has developed much further. Whereas Second Isaiah always linked mythological language to concrete historical and political reality, in this passage from Third Isaiah we see mythological language being utilized in literal fashion. The judgment to be visited upon YHWH's enemies (the Zadokite priests) will be followed by nothing less than a new creation: כי הנני בורא שמים חדשים וארץ חדשה ('for now I create new heavens and a new earth').[4] The transition in prophetic eschatology that is evident in this oracle

---

1. See Isa. 40.1-2.

2. This new judgment is most clearly expressed in Isa. 65.13-15, a passage that posits a kind of eschatological reversal.

3. *Dawn*, p. 155.

4. Isa. 65.17. Hanson's description of this major evolution in prophetic eschatology shows that, already in the early restoration period, we are not all that far removed from the world-view of rabbinic Judaism which speaks of העולם הזה and העולם הבא ('this world' and 'the world to come') or from that of Paul in Gal. 1.4 who longs to be delivered ἐκ τοῦ αἰῶνος τοῦ ἐνεστῶτος πονηροῦ ('from this present evil age').

'heralds the death of prophecy and the birth of apocalyptic eschatology'.[1]

The next step in the exegesis is Isa. 66.1-16,[2] entitled 'Controversy over the Building of the Temple and Expulsion from the Cult'. As regards Hanson's identification of the group being attacked in Third Isaiah as the Zadokite priests, this passage is his *sine qua non*. Isa. 66.1b reads as follows: אי זה בית אשר תבנו לי ואי זה מקום מנוחתי. Hanson's translation is: 'What is this house which you would build for me, and what is this throne dais?' Prior to Hanson, interpretation of this passage fell into four general categories: (1) the passage is from the time of Ezra and constitutes an attack against the Samaritans who are attempting to build their own temple as a rival to the Jerusalem temple, c. 450 BCE; (2) the passage dates to c. 520 BCE and is an attack by the prophet against the עם הארץ ('the people of the land') who desire to participate in the rebuilding of the Jerusalem temple; (3) the passage is an attack against an attempt to rebuild the temple during the exile; (4) the passage is a repudiation of temple building as such and cannot be related to any concrete historical situation.[3] Hanson's solution is to combine elements from numbers 2 and 4, but he also reworks them according to his overall thesis. He argues that the situation in question is, indeed, the rebuilding of the Jerusalem temple in 520 BCE,[4] but the difference is that the passage is not an attack on the עם הארץ who are attempting to participate in the rebuilding, but an attack against the Zadokite temple as such! The Zadokite priests who are rebuilding the temple are condemned in 66.1, while in 66.2 the group that opposes them receives blessings. This group is made up of עני ('the humble'), נכה רוח ('the broken in spirit') and חרד על דברי ('those who tremble at my word'). For Hanson, the distinction between the two groups here described is a distinction between 'two religious stances, the one centered around the formal worship of the temple, the other based on an attitude of humility and fear before Yahweh'.[5] It is important to realize that this is the very same dichotomy that Hanson sees running throughout the salvation-judgment

1. *Dawn*, p. 161.
2. Hanson does not treat 66.17-24 because he regards these concluding verses as part of the redactional framework of Third Isaiah, along with 56.1-8.
3. *Dawn*, pp. 169-70.
4. This oracle is the only one for which Hanson offers a concrete date. His contextual-typological method yields only relative dates. This one concrete date enables him to date the other oracles forward or backward, depending on their relationship to 66.1-16.
5. *Dawn*, p. 170.

oracles of Third Isaiah: salvation for the pious, prophetic minority, and judgment for the priestly majority. His description of the priestly religious stance as one that is 'centered around the formal worship of the temple' definitely implies that it is temple religion as such that is being attacked.

It was Haggai who commanded, בנו הבית ('build the house!').[1] Hanson sees Isa. 66.1-2 as a 'direct repudiation' of this command.[2] According to Hanson, the problem with Haggai's proclamation and the theology that undergirds it is that it was 'an attempt to force Yahweh's hand', it was an attempt to force YHWH to act. This is the very same problem that Hanson sees with all priestly theology. For him, all priestly theology is in essence *ex opere operato* theology. The polemic of Isa. 66.1-2 represents the climax of 'a century-long struggle between two concepts of salvation'.[3] The visionary group depends on the direct intervention of YHWH, while the hierocratic group depends on 'cultic orthopraxy'.

The condemnation of the hierocratic program of restoration continues in Isa. 66.3: שוחט השור מכה איש זובח השה ערף כלב מעלה מנחה דם חזיר מזכיר לבונה מברך און. Hanson's translation: 'Who slaughters an ox and kills a man, who sacrifices a lamb and breaks a dog's neck, who presents an offering and (offers) swine's blood, who burns incense and blesses an idol'. The passage is characterized by the juxtaposition of typical Zadokite cultic activities and various pagan abominations. The intention of this juxtaposition is to make the bold statement that 'sacrifice of an ox is no better than murder', and so on. Here again Hanson interprets the polemical accusations in symbolical or metaphorical fashion. The meaning of the passage is not that actual pagan sacrificial practices are being conducted in the temple, but rather the visionary group is stating, in symbolical fashion, that 'the practices of the temple party are no less abominable than the most shocking pagan rites'.[4]

After the thoroughgoing condemnation of the temple party in Isa. 66.3-4, the oracle turns again in 66.5 to the visionaries, החרדים אל דברו

1. Hag. 1.8.
2. *Dawn*, pp. 173-74, 178. Hanson regards Ezek. 40–48, Haggai and Zech. 1–8 as standing in the same line of tradition. In fact, the temple-building program of Zerubbabel and Joshua was an attempt to apply 'carefully the details of Ezekiel 40–48', p. 174. Thus, for Hanson, a repudiation of Haggai is a repudiation of Ezek. 40–48.
3. *Dawn*, p. 178.
4. *Dawn*, p. 180. Hanson is surely correct when he says that this passage is the most polemical one in the Hebrew Bible.

('you who tremble at his [i.e., YHWH's] word'), and states that they (the visionaries) have been thrown out of the cult by their very brethren: אחיכם שׂנאיכם מנדיכם למען שׁמי ('your brethren who hate you, and thrust you out for the sake of my name').[1] Whether or not one accepts Hanson's identification of אחיכם ('your brothers') as the Zadokite priests, it is clear that he makes a major point by claiming that the polemics of this passage are intra-community polemics. Those being attacked are, in some sense, 'the brothers' of those doing the attacking.

Just as in ch. 65, so now in ch. 66 the oracle moves on to a description of a new era of peace and prosperity that is to follow YHWH's judgment on his enemies, an era that will be enjoyed only by YHWH's faithful remnant. This faithful remnant will consist of those who survive the fiery judgment: כי באשׁ יהוה נשׁפט ובחרבו את כל בשׂר ורבו חללי יהוה ('for Yahweh will execute judgment with fire, and with his sword against all flesh, and those slain by Yahweh will be many') (Isa. 66.16). That the judgment here described is a universal one, that is, that it will be executed against כל בשׂר ('all flesh'), shows how far the eschatology of Third Isaiah has moved in the direction of apocalyptic. YHWH's judgment can no longer be related to historical reality. Instead it is conceived as a purely spiritual phenomenon; it is a judgment that will separate the 'righteous' from the 'wicked'.[2]

The final section of Hanson's exegesis of Third Isaiah is Isa. 56.9–57.13,[3] entitled 'The Conflict Grows Acrimonious'.[4] This oracle is an example of the salvation-judgment oracle at its fully developed stage. This can be clearly seen in the first section of the oracle, 56.9–57.2. Here the leaders of the community come in for condemnation, but an innocent group, the אנשׁי חסד ('pious'), receives the proclamation of deliverance. The leaders of the community who are singled out for condemnation are

---

1. In Tannaitic Hebrew the word נדה came to be used in the technical sense of 'excommunication'. Hanson does not think the word has this specific sense here, but it may refer to an actual historical event when the visionaries were excluded from participation in the temple.

2. *Dawn*, p. 185.

3. Hanson thinks the original unit was 56.9–57.2 and that this unit was subsequently expanded by adding 57.3-13. As it now stands it is a single, unified oracle.

4. Actually, the final oracle treated by Hanson is 63.1-6. He is, however, unsure of what to do with this oracle, or where to place it on his trajectory. At any rate, 63.1-6 is not directly related to the question of the opponents of Third Isaiah, therefore it can be left out of consideration for the time being.

identified as the צפים, the חזים[1] and the רעים. Hanson takes these as generic designations of priests, prophets and political leaders, respectively. In Isa. 56.12 these community leaders are pictured singing a drinking song: אתיו אקחה יין ונסבאה שכר והיה כזה יום מחר גדול יתר מאד ('Come, let me fetch wine, and let us guzzle beer; tomorrow will be like today, even far more glorious'). This drinking song is, according to Hanson, reflective of the 'anti-eschatological' attitude of the community's leaders. It is the same anti-eschatological attitude reflected by the group singled out for condemnation in 66.5: יכבד יהוה ונראה ('Let Yahweh display his glory that we may see!'). This is evidence that we are once again dealing with the leaders of the restoration community, the core of which was the Zadokite priesthood. On the other hand, the description of the suffering righteous man in 57.1-2 evokes memories of the suffering servant of Second Isaiah and shows that it is the visionary disciples of Second Isaiah who stand behind this oracle.

Isa. 57.3-6 goes on to make further accusations against the leaders of the community and to condemn their cultic practices. They are accused, among other things, of participating in pagan fertility rites and offering child sacrifice: הנחמים באלים תחת כל עץ רענן שחטי הילדים בנחלים תחת סעפי הסלעים ('growing passionate with the Els under every leafy tree, slaughtering children in the valley among the rocky crags'). Hanson emphasizes that all of the polemical accusations made in this section are couched in the traditional language of the pre-exilic prophets. And once again he argues that the purpose of these accusations is not to state what is actually being practiced, but rather to say in a symbolical or metaphorical way that the Zadokite cultus is thoroughly defiled.

Isa. 57.7 describes a whore who has set up her bed on a high and lofty mountain: על הר גבה ונשא שמת משכבך. Going against virtually all traditional scholarship which has regarded this משכב ('bed' or 'couch') as a reference to a pagan במה ('high place'), Hanson understands it as a symbolical reference to the Jerusalem temple that the Zadokites are building. In bold and shocking fashion the visionaries describe the new temple as a 'gigantic bed of prostitution, a brothel upon Mt Zion'.[2] The description in 57.9 of a treaty entered into by the whore and a foreign nation is actually a not-so-subtle condemnation of the alliance between the hierocratic party and the Persian government.

Isa. 56.9–57.13 thus represents the final stage of the battle fought

---

1. Emended from the MT הוים.
2. *Dawn*, p. 200.

between visionaries and hierocrats in the early restoration period.[1] It shows how bitter the battle had become, how disillusioned the visionaries had become, and how far apart these two religious mentalities had grown. The program of restoration of Ezekiel 40–48 had won the day, while the program of restoration described in Isaiah 60–62 underwent radical change as the visionaries transformed this vision into the idiom of apocalyptic eschatology.

An Alternative to Hanson

It must be stated at the outset that Hanson's work in *The Dawn of Apocalyptic* is most ingenious. It is one of a mere handful of books written by a modern, critical biblical scholar that could be described not only as interesting but also as exciting. My argument with Hanson is not over the general question of the origins of apocalyptic in Israel, the question that has dominated most discussions and criticisms of his book. Instead, I am interested in a few basic exegetical questions concerning Third Isaiah. For example, is it legitimate to describe Third Isaiah, as Hanson does, as dissident literature? That is to say, is Third Isaiah best understood as having been written by an out-of-power, disenfranchised group? This is a major question, because Hanson ultimately wants us to see Third Isaiah as literature produced by none other than the עם הארץ ('the people of the land') and written against those who returned from the Babylonian גולה. Secondly, does Third Isaiah represent, as Hanson has argued, an attack on Pentateuchal cultic theology? That is to say, are those who are attacked in Third Isaiah really to be identified as the Zadokite priests, the very group responsible for the production of the Pentateuch?

As regards the first question, whether Third Isaiah ought to be viewed as dissident literature written more or less by the עם הארץ, there are certain facts that directly contradict several of Hanson's basic assumptions. Modern scholarship has established beyond a shadow of a doubt that there is an intimate relationship between the oracles of Isaiah 56–66 and those of Isaiah 40–55. It is also clear that Isaiah 40–55 is literature of the Babylonian גולה, by the Babylonian גולה, and for the Babylonian גולה. Second Isaiah is to be credited with announcing the

---

1. This battle between visionaries and hierocrats is not at an end. It will carry on into the later restoration period, and the record of this stage of the conflict is recorded in Zech. 9–14.

re-establishment of the people Israel, an event that he described as a new act of redemption on the part of YHWH, a new Exodus. If, as Hanson himself claims, the oracles of Isaiah 56–66 are best described as the product of 'the visionary disciples of Second Isaiah', what possible sense can it make to simultaneously claim that 56–66 is anti-גולה in outlook? If there is an intimate relationship between the oracles of 40–55 and those of 56–66, and if 40–55 is a kind of foundational document for the restoration community that had its origins in the Babylonian גולה, then the most obvious deduction is that 56–66 would be pro-גולה literature as well. If this is the case, then Hanson's thesis is turned on its head, and 56–66 is best viewed as having been written by the very people that Hanson claims it was written against!

A similar objection can be raised with respect to Hanson's exegesis of Isa. 57.9. The treaty described there between a whore and a foreign nation is for Hanson a condemnation of the alliance between the Zadokites and the Persians. This is a recurring theme in the exegesis, that the Zadokite temple was defiled because it was built under Persian aegis. But when one recalls Second Isaiah's attitude toward the Persians in general and Cyrus in particular, it becomes difficult to criticize the hierocrats for working together with the Persian administration.[1]

In addition, much recent scholarship has attempted to demonstrate that the book of Isaiah as a whole reflects an intentional, redactional unity.[2] In other words, not only is there an intimate relationship between Isaiah 40–55 and 56–66, but there is also an intimate relationship between the second half of the book and the first. When this insight is coupled with the fact that many of the concerns of 56–66 are reflected in the very first chapter of the book of Isaiah, then one is led to the conclusion that 56–66 and the final redaction of the book of Isaiah are somehow related. If this is the case, then it becomes difficult in the extreme to see 56–66 as dissident literature produced by an out-of-power, disenfranchised group. This is because the production of the unified book of Isaiah was one of the major accomplishments of post-exilic Judaism. The compositional complexity of the unified book of Isaiah is rivaled only by that of the Pentateuch itself, and such a massive undertaking would have required close access to the religious power structures of the day. When one asks the question of who could have had the resources to accomplish such a

---

1. See my discussion of this issue in Chapter 2, and especially my claim that Second Isaiah viewed Cyrus's empire as having been mandated by YHWH himself.

2. See Chapter 1.

task, one is led to the same central Israelite community that produced the Pentateuch, namely, the Babylonian גולה.

The second question, whether Third Isaiah represents an attack on Pentateuchal cultic theology, is a more complicated one. Quite obviously, someone or something is being attacked in Third Isaiah. The group in question is charged with child sacrifice, eating swine, participating in Canaanite fertility rites, necromancy, offering sacrifice to Gad and Meni, and a host of other things. As was shown in the summary of Hanson's exegesis, he regards all of these charges as symbolic or metaphorical. This is a convenient and necessary maneuver on his part because it allows him to escape from those who would point out the obvious fact that all of the accusations made against the group in question are consistently and repeatedly condemned in the Pentateuch. Hanson's solution, though possible, reveals a significant prejudice on his part. It is the prejudice that only the Canaanites were guilty of participation in these kinds of religious rites. Whenever the Canaanites are charged with child sacrifice, necromancy, and so on, Hanson finds no need to understand the accusations in symbolical or metaphorical ways; he is willing to take the charges simply at face value. But when members of the Israelite or Judaite community are charged with the very same practices, then the solution is either to posit a corrupting Canaanite influence or to read the accusations symbolically or metaphorically. Hanson's work on the salvation-judgment oracle in Third Isaiah makes the strong case that the polemics of the book are intra-community polemics. Therefore, in order to uphold his thesis that it is the Zadokites who are being attacked, he is forced to read the accusations symbolically. In my view, it is this interpretive move on Hanson's part that constitutes the major weakness in his thesis. No one would deny that in the realm of polemics the 'combatants' often caricature the position of their opponents, and hyperbolic speech tends to be the rule rather than the exception. The Hebrew Bible is full of examples of this. It also true, however, that the twin phenomena of caricature and hyperbole are rhetorically effective only because they have some basis in reality. A caricature takes certain basic features of a person or of a group of people and exaggerates them. But in the exaggeration, one is still able to perceive the basic features that make the person or the group identifiable. The same holds true for the phenomenon of stereotyping. The reason that stereotypes provoke such hostility in the people who are described by them, that is to say, the reason that stereotyping is such an effective rhetorical device, is that the stereotype always 'plays on' a certain real tendency or real characteristic of the person or group in question. Caricature, hyperbole and stereotype are almost always used for comic or polemical purposes, or both, and they are effective rhetorical devices precisely because of the basic facts that they exploit. On the other hand, a caricature loses its edge if it has no basis in reality or fact. To use a modern example, an American political candidate would gain nothing by calling Ted Kennedy a 'John Bircher'. But, in effect, this is how Hanson has interpreted the polemics of Third Isaiah. Labeling the Zadokite priests, the very people who produced the Pentateuch, as 'child sacrificers' and 'swine eaters' would have been as rhetorically effective then as calling Ted Kennedy a 'John Bircher' would be today.

But what if the accusations in Third Isaiah are taken more at face value? If so, then we are led to the conclusion that a group within the restoration community is actually being charged with such practices. This conclusion would then have manifold ramifications, not the least important of which is that Third Isaiah would be a witness that the type of religion that was so often condemned by the pre-exilic prophets persisted into the restoration period and continued to be practiced by leading members of the restoration community.

I will now attempt to demonstrate that this is the best way to understand the polemics of Third Isaiah. In so doing, I will show that Third Isaiah and the Pentateuch would most likely have had a common opponent, namely, traditional pre-exilic Israelite religion, and that in this respect 'the visionary disciples of Second Isaiah' and the Zadokite temple priests would have been allies.

Chapter 4

CONFLICT IN THE COMMUNITY

Introduction

It was pointed out at the beginning of Chapter 1 that the Third Isaiah
hypothesis is to be attributed to Bernhard Duhm. Fundamental to
Duhm's hypothesis was the demonstration that there were enough
significant differences between Isaiah 40–55 and 56–66 to make it
necessary to posit different authors for the two collections of oracles.
Both collections deal with the issue of the restoration of God's people,
Israel, but whereas Second Isaiah is primarily concerned with the sweep
of world history and Israel's role in that history, Third Isaiah has the
more narrow concern of the intra-community life of the people in view.[1]
For our purposes, the following words of Duhm are important for
explicating the nature of Third Isaiah and the overall tradition to which
the oracles belong.

> In more than one way our writing proves itself to be a counterpart to the
> book of Malachi and a forerunner of the priestly document. The author
> belongs to the line which was established by Ezekiel, promoted by Haggai
> and Zechariah, and came to power as a result of the work of Ezra. He is a
> theocrat of the purest kind; he regards the temple, the sacrificial cult, the
> law, the Sabbath, etc., as the most important things. Concepts such as
> Mal'ak and Panim, the holy spirit, the miraculous sign that prompts the
> Gentiles to bring back the Diaspora, and expectations such as the new
> heaven, in which the sun and moon are absent, and the new earth, upon
> which people will attain the life-span of the pre-flood patriarchs of the
> priestly document, characterize the post-exilic theologian and apocalyptist.[2]

---

1. Von Rad has described the difference between these two collections as
essentially a thematic one. He argues that in Second Isaiah 'Zion is the climax of the
prediction', whereas for Third Isaiah 'Zion is the starting-point for the prophet's
thoughts', von Rad, *Old Testament Theology*, II, pp. 280-81.
2. Duhm, *Das Buch Jesaia*, p. 418 (translation mine).

Duhm's unfavorable description of Third Isaiah ('he is a theocrat of the purest kind') makes clear how little he valued Third Isaiah as a prophet, and his negative evaluation is understandable when one considers the climate of biblical studies in nineteenth-century Germany. That is a separate issue. But what is important for us is the actual evidence upon which Duhm's negative evaluation is based. It is the evidence that Third Isaiah 'regards the temple, the sacrificial cult, the law, the Sabbath, etc., as the most important things'. This, then, is what led Duhm to conclude that Third Isaiah stands in the same line of tradition that runs from Ezekiel, through Haggai and Zechariah, and finally to Ezra. In other words, Third Isaiah is 'a forerunner of the priestly document'. Duhm's position directly and irreconcilably contradicts the thesis of Hanson. The very thing about Isaiah 56–66 that led Duhm to separate it from Isaiah 40–55 in the first place, that is, the 'theocratic' nature of Isaiah 56–66, is the very thing that Hanson now claims is being attacked in Third Isaiah!

Duhm's initial description of Third Isaiah as standing in the line of tradition that leads directly to Ezra and the 'Priesterkodex' has received recent support from the work of Blenkinsopp.[1] Blenkinsopp draws a connection in Third Isaiah between the עבדי יהוה ('servants of YHWH') and the חרדים ('those who tremble') (Isa. 66.2, 5) by claiming that these are two descriptions of the same group. He then points out that this uncommon participial form of the root חרד also occurs in Ezra 9.4 and 10.3, where it is used as a description of Ezra's support group.[2] His conclusion is that there is a definite connection between the חרדים of Isaiah 66 and those of Ezra 9 and 10. This, of course, would be an impossibility in Hanson's scheme, but it confirms one of Duhm's initial and fundamental insights. To be sure, Blenkinsopp does not push the argument in the same direction that Duhm did. For Blenkinsopp, Third Isaiah and Ezra are moving in the direction of sectarianism. I would

1. See J. Blenkinsopp, 'The "Servants of the Lord" in Third Isaiah: Profile of a Pietistic Group in the Persian Epoch', *Proceedings of the Irish Biblical Association* 7 (1983), pp. 1-23.

2. The only other occurrence is 1 Sam. 4.13. The descriptions of these 'tremblers' in Isaiah and Ezra are strikingly similar. Isa. 66.2: חרד על דברי ('he who trembles at my word'); Isa. 66.5: החרדים אל דברו ('those who tremble at his word'); Ezra 9.4: כל חרד בדברי אלהי ישראל ('everyone who trembles at the words of the God of Israel'); Ezra 10.3: והחרדים במצות אלהינו ('those who tremble at the command of our God'). Blenkinsopp states, 'While in none of these cases is it a title like Pharisee or Essene, it is arguable that it presupposes a certain fixity of usage in the contexts in which it occurs'. Blenkinsopp, 'The "Servants of the Lord" in Third Isaiah', p. 7.

argue, in contrast, that establishing a link between Third Isaiah and Ezra simultaneously establishes a link between Third Isaiah and the line of tradition that will eventually be involved in the promulgation of the Pentateuch.[1] Like the books of Ezra and Nehemiah, Third Isaiah describes a conflict within the restoration community, however it does not do so with the language of גולה ('Babylonian exiles') and עם הארץ ('the people of the land'). Third Isaiah does not give one specific name to its opponents. Instead, it refers to them by describing their cultic practices.

I will now proceed to an exegesis of Third Isaiah, with special emphasis on the polemical passages, and I will show that the theological trajectory reflected in these oracles contains the seeds for the definition of 'Israel' as 'those who have accepted the Torah'. In other words, I will show that Third Isaiah is indeed a true forerunner of Ezra and that the theological positions of these two books are complementary. This, then, will show that Hanson's explication of the nature of Third Isaiah is untenable.

---

1.   When I speak of the 'promulgation' of the Pentateuch, I refer to that point in time when the Pentateuch became the officially recognized foundation of the religion of Judah, that is to say, the point in time when we can begin to call this religion, 'Judaism'. The person of Ezra is inseparably tied to this development. By taking this position, I realize that I am asserting something that has not been proven; indeed it is probably something that cannot be proven. But I also must clarify what I am not saying. I am not saying that the religion described in the Pentateuch is a 'late' phenomenon, only that the promulgation of the Pentateuch as the official religion is 'late'. Secondly, I do not accept the extremely negative evaluation of Pentateuchal religion that is so characteristic of Wellhausen and his followers. For Wellhausen, 'earlier' is always better and 'lateness' is a damning characteristic. On this whole issue, see K. Koch, 'Ezra and the Origins of Judaism', *JSS* 19 (1974), pp. 173-97. Koch points out that the 'transition from Judaeans to Jews has not been sufficiently marked in the Hebrew language'. As a result, 'it is not forbidden to speak of David as a Jew, just as it is possible to range Johanan ben Zakkai among the Israelites, or Maimonides too, for both these rabbis certainly looked on themselves as members of Israel. So the differentiation between (ancient) Israel and Judaism is a matter of convenience among historians, carried out in order better to arrange the different epochs of the Old Testament people and its successors.' (pp. 196-97). However, this should not obscure the fact that the person and work of Ezra mark a major transition in the development of the religion of Israel and Judah.

Isaiah 56.1-8

General Observations

It is common for scholars to view Isa. 56.1-8 as forming part of the redactional framework for Third Isaiah.[1] The assumption is that the passage belongs to the final stage of the growth of the oracles and is, therefore, not truly an integral part of the other oracles.[2] On the other

1. I will treat the oracles of Third Isaiah in the order in which they occur in the unified book of Isaiah. In so doing, I do not intend to imply a complete rejection of Hanson's meticulously detailed attempt at dating the oracles. I do, however, propose that a good deal of restraint is called for. I am highly skeptical of the value of the prosodic analysis aspect of Hanson's work because it involves many unsubstantiated assumptions regarding the nature of the Hebrew language. This has already been discussed in Chapter 3. His typology of prophetic genres, however, has much more to commend it. But it, too, suffers from some of the same flaws as the prosodic analysis. The most problematic is the assumption that life, history, religion and language all follow a kind of rigorous linear progression and can be categorized accordingly. Thus, according to his scheme, the more polemical a passage is, the later it must fall on the trajectory. This may indeed have been the case, but my assumption is that historical developments tend to be much more complicated than this. We must not forget that in the case of Third Isaiah we are dealing with an anonymous collection of texts that are removed from us by some 2500 years, and that these texts are virtually lacking in any concrete historical detail. Hanson, to be sure, recognized this, and this accounts for his need to develop such a meticulous method for dating the oracles. But even he is able to propose relatively absolute dates for the oracles only because he reads Isa. 66.1-4 as an explicit reference to the rebuilding of the temple in 520–515 BCE, a position that is certainly open to dispute. Hanson himself has effectively critiqued previous Third Isaiah scholarship for its attempts to date the oracles based upon vague or supposed historical references. But in my view he ends up doing the very same thing, only in a more sophisticated way. In the final analysis, when it comes to the case of Third Isaiah we are simply left without any tangible historical hooks on which to hang our scholarly hats. The most that I am willing to say with assurance is that Third Isaiah is later than Second Isaiah and earlier than Ezra and Nehemiah. Treating the oracles in the order in which they occur in the unified book of Isaiah emphasizes that the present location of the oracles is a historical fact that cannot be ignored. We have access to these texts only as a part of the unified book of Isaiah, and this was the intention of those who edited the book. While not denying that the texts have a rich and complex prehistory, it acknowledges that the editors have provided the readers of this material with a context for interpretation. Not to take this seriously is to miss a fundamental aspect of the nature of these texts.

2. See Westermann, *Isaiah 40–66*; Volz, *Jesaja II*; Elliger, *Die Einheit des Tritojesaja*. For Elliger, 56.1-2 is to be ascribed to Third Isaiah, but 56.3-8, along

The Opponents of Third Isaiah

hand, there are scholars who interpret 56.1-8 in the opposite fashion, that is, there are those who see 56.1-8 as the key to understanding the entire Third Isaiah collection.[1] Hanson is one of those who regards 56.1-8 as a part of the latest stage of the collection, and he gives the passage only cursory treatment.[2] In a certain sense, it is surprising that Hanson does not make more of 56.1-8 to support his overall thesis. To be sure, Hanson does express the sentiment that this passage breaths the spirit of 'inclusiveness' and 'tolerance', and on these grounds he opposes it to the 'narrow exclusiveness of the hierocratic group'. Uncharacteristically, however, he does not push the argument any further. But when one carefully examines what is being said in 56.1-8, it becomes much clearer why Hanson dealt with the passage in the way he did. Taken as whole, 56.1-8 demonstrates that the various dichotomies set up by Hanson to describe the two groups that are in conflict in Third Isaiah do not stand up to closer scrutiny. Hanson sees two distinct religious mentalities at work in Third Isaiah and argues extensively that the positions held by each are mutually exclusive. But what we find in 56.1-8 is a passage that combines into a unified whole several of Hanson's supposedly mutually contradictory positions. Any honest reader would have to admit that this oracle reveals an extremely high estimate of the temple, so much so that the oracle takes upon itself the task of stating who is to be admitted to the temple. The unqualified position of the oracle is that the temple (and there is absolutely no

with 66.18-22, 57.13c, 57.20-21, 58.13-14, 59.21, belong to the redactor; for Volz, it is 56.1-2 that shows the hand of the redactor.

1. This is the thesis of Pauritsch. Like his predecessors, Pauritsch sees 56.1-8 as redactional. He, however, is primarily interested in understanding Isa. 56–66 as a whole, and for him, therefore, ascribing a passage to the redactor is not a pejorative act. On the contrary, his argument is that Isa. 56–66 is a unified, redactional whole and that it can be described theologically as a 'prophetisches Erweckungsbuch', a prophetic revival-book. In this unified redactional and theological whole, 56.1-8 plays the major role. '56.1-8 gibt das Motto an, unter dem die folgenden Stücke zu betrachten sind', Pauritsch, *Die neue Gemeinde*, p. 243. The motto is the proclamation that God is gathering the outcasts and the poor. Thus, the subtitle of Pauritsch's book: *Gott sammelt Ausgestossene und Arme*. Behind the references to 'foreigners' and 'eunuchs', Pauritsch posits a community of YHWHists in Babylon to whom the book is addressed.

2. Hanson sees 56.1-8 and 66.17-24 as very close thematically to Zech. 14, and he dates all three of these passages together, between 475–425 BCE. See *Dawn*, pp. 162, 388-89.

reason to assume that the reference is to anything other than the new
Persian-period temple) is YHWH's holy house built upon YHWH's holy
mountain.[1] This conception runs unwaveringly throughout Third Isaiah.[2]
The temple is simultaneously a 'house of prayer' and a house of
sacrifice.[3] All of this is impossible according to Hanson's schema
whereby the group who produced this oracle had been thrown out of
the temple community some 50 to 75 years earlier.

The oracle is concerned with the question of the status of two groups
of people in the restoration community: בן הנכר ('the foreigner') and
הסריס ('the eunuch'). The position espoused is that the foreigner and the
eunuch who שמר שבת ('keep Sabbath') are to be granted access to the
temple and to the sacrificial cult. The particular role played by Sabbath
observance in this oracle is unique in the Hebrew Bible, for in this
passage Sabbath observance appears to be the primary criterion by

---

1. Beuken has argued that the function of 56.1-8 is to identify YHWH's holy
mountain with 'the place where Israel can find life (Ch. 55)' and to declare that this
place is 'accessible to all the peoples (56.7)'. W.A.M. Beuken, 'Isa. 56.9–57.13—
An Example of the Isaianic Legacy of Trito-Isaiah', in J.W. van Henten, H.J. De
Jonge, P.T. Van Rooden and J.W. Wesselius (eds.), *Tradition and Re-Interpretation
in Jewish and Early Christian Literature: Essays in Honor of Jürgen C.H. Lebram*
(Leiden: Brill, 1986), pp. 48-64 (56).

2. See 56.5, 7; 57.13; 62.9; 64.10; 65.11, 25; 66.20. See also Isa. 11.9; 27.13;
Ps. 99.9.

3. This is evidently to be seen as a reversal of the prophecy of Isa. 1.15. In spite
of the fact that many have argued to the contrary, there is no suggestion in this passage that prayer and sacrifice were in any way opposed to one another. The concepts
are used almost synonomously. It is only much later, that is, in Talmudic times that
prayer comes to be understood as a substitute for, or even the equivalent of, sacrifice.
See *b. Ber.* 15a-b; 33a; *b. Suk.* 45a; *b. Ta'an.* 26a-27b; *b. Meg.* 31a. This conception
is also reflected in the fact that the daily worship services came to be named for the
daily oblations: מוסף, מנחה, שחרית.

Undoubtedly, there is a thematic connection between Isa. 56.3-8 and 1 Kgs 8. Both
passages speak of foreigners praying in or toward the Jerusalem temple, and both
refer to the temple as a house of prayer. See Weinfeld, *Deuteronomy and the
Deuteronomic School*, p. 42. Levenson points out that referring to the temple as a
house of prayer is not intended as polemic against sacrifice, but rather 'is implicitly a
polemic against the idea that God is literally, even physically present' in the temple.
Levenson, 'From Temple to Synagogue', p. 159. In rabbinic Judaism the fact that
prayer comes to take the place of sacrifice is a function of historical circumstance, not
one of theological evolution as it is in Christianity. The rabbis held firmly to the belief
that the inauguration of the Kingdom of God will bring with it the rebuilding of the
temple and the resumption of the sacrificial liturgy.

which membership in the community is defined, and in that sense, it functions in a manner similar to that of circumcision in Genesis 17.[1] The argument can also be made that Isa. 56.1-8 reflects the extremely high estimation of Sabbath observance that comes to expression in the Priestly creation story, Gen. 1.1-2.4a, where resting on the Sabbath is portrayed as the climax of creation and the means by which faithful Israelites proclaim their allegiance to the creator God.[2]

Exegesis

56.1. The verse picks up directly on the promise of Isa. 46.13 and 51.5,[3] and it is to be seen as the direct application of the message of Second Isaiah to the new community situation.[4] What is being proclaimed is nothing less than the coming of the *Endtheophanie* of YHWH.[5] Duhm understood the command to שמרו משפט ועשו צדקה ('keep justice and practice righteousness')[6] as an expression of 'works righteousness', and

1. See also Isa. 52.1.
2. Other passages that are of importance with regard to the exalted status of שבת are Jer. 17.19-27 and Neh. 13.15-22, both of which interpret the destruction of Jerusalem at the hands of the Babylonians as the result of the failure of the inhabitants of Jerusalem and its environs to obey Jeremiah's command not to carry 'burdens' or 'merchandise' (משא) on the Sabbath. See also Ezek. 20. On the relationship between Jer. 17.19-27, Neh. 13.15-22 and the Deuteronomic decalogue, see M. Fishbane, *Biblical Interpretation in Ancient Israel* (Oxford: Clarendon Press, 1985), pp. 131-34.
3. Isa. 46.13: קרבתי צדקתי לא תרחק ותשועתי לא תאחר ('I bring my righteousness near, it is not far off; my salvation will not tarry'). Isa. 51.5: קרוב צדקי יצא ישעי ('my righteousness is near, my salvation is coming').
4. Steck has argued that 56.1-8 was composed in conscious dialog with Isa. 55.1-13. Isa. 56.1-8 'ist von vornherein in Anknüpfung an Jes 55 formuliert'. Compare 56.1-2 with 55.6-7; 56.3-8 with 55.5; 56.5 with 55.13. Steck, 'Beobachtungen zu Jesaja 56–59', p. 229.
5. See Pauritsch, *Die neue Gemeinde*, p. 238.
6. Cf. Isa. 1.27: ציון במשפט תפדה ושביה בצדקה. The actual phrase 'keep justice' occurs also in Ps. 106.3; Hos. 12.7. There are many instances where שמר is used with the plural form, משפטים. See, for example, Deut. 12.1; 26.16-17; 30.16; 1 Kgs 8.58; 9.4; 2 Chron. 7.17; Ps. 119.106; Ezek. 11.20; 18.9; 20.18-19, 21; 36.27. The combination of עשה and צדקה occurs in Gen. 18.19; Deut. 33.21; Isa. 58.2; Ps. 99.4; 103.6; 106.3; Prov. 21.3; 1 Kgs 10.9; Jer. 9.23; 22.3, 15; 23.5; 33.15; Ezek. 18.5, 19, 21, 22, 27; 33.14, 16, 19; 45.9; 1 Chron. 18.14. There is one instance of עשה and צדק: Ps. 119.121. Only Ps. 106.3 contains both 'keep justice' and 'practice righteousness'. The point in all of this is that the command issued at the beginning of Third Isaiah is one that is at home across a broad spectrum of the Hebrew Bible.

he viewed this as an example of a major difference between Second and Third Isaiah: 'a different intellect is at work here'.[1] Duhm's reading, however, is fundamentally flawed and represents a complete misconstruing of the sense of the passage. The conjunction כי that begins the second half of v. 1 is not to be understood in a conditional but rather in a causative sense. The community is commanded to keep justice and practice righteousness because (i.e., in light of the fact that) קרובה ישועתי לבוא וצדקתי להגלות ('my salvation and my righteousness are about to be revealed').[2] Isa. 56.1 expresses the conviction that ethical conduct is determined by eschatological expectation.[3]

56.2. This verse serves to define what is meant by the command in v. 1 to שמרו משפט ועשׂו צדקה. The answer is: שמר שבת מחללו ושמר ידו מעשׂות כל רע ('he who keeps Sabbath by not defiling it and he who keeps his hand from doing any evil'). This is a radical exaltation of Sabbath-keeping as the primary criterion by which one becomes (or remains) a member of the community.[4]

---

1. Duhm, *Das Buch Jesaia*, p. 419 (translation mine). Because of the subject matter of this oracle, dealing as it does with the temple, sacrifice and Sabbath observance, it presents major difficulties for interpreters who have certain preconceived notions of what 'genuine' prophets are permitted to talk about, and especially for those who see prophetic religion as the true forerunner of Christianity, opposed to the Jewish legalism of the Torah. One approach is to disparage the oracle as Duhm did and try to show that the theological conceptions inherent in it are a corruption of the 'pure' evangelical theology of Second Isaiah. This was Duhm's attitude toward Third Isaiah as a whole. Another approach is for the interpreter to take all of the legal or 'Jewish' sections of Third Isaiah and assign them to a Judaizing redactor. This approach can be clearly seen in the work of Smart. Although Smart assigns Isa. 56–66 to Second Isaiah, he reveals his bias by assigning Isa. 56.1-7 (and 58.13-14) to a 'late', 'orthodox' and 'legalistic' editor. He is forced to do this because of his curious assumption that Second Isaiah was anti-sacrifice and anti-temple. Smart, *History and Theology in Second Isaiah*, pp. 228-30.

2. See Kraus, 'Die ausgebliebene Endtheophanie', p. 328. See also Isa. 60.1. Contrast this interpretation with Smart who translates כי in the sense of 'in order that', *History and Theology in Second Isaiah*, p. 229.

3. See also Zech. 8.16-17. The position of 56.1-2 is strikingly consistent with Zech. 1–8. There is no hint that there has been any delay in the realization of Second Isaiah's promises concerning the restoration. The idea that ethical conduct is determined by eschatological expectation pervades both the New Testament and the Qumran texts.

4. In Neh. 9.12-15 the Sabbath has a similarly exalted status. There it is

56.3-8. The status of two questionable groups of people, בן הנכר and
הסריס, is addressed here.[1] According to Blenkinsopp, the phrase הנלוה
אל[2] יהוה 'means to embrace the YHWH-cult, to become a proselyte'.[3] Isa.
14.1, Zech. 2.15[4] and perhaps Est. 9.27 show that the joining of
foreigners to the cult of YHWH was one of the expected signs of the
time of salvation. The reference to הסריס is best understood as referring
to 'those Jews or proselytes who had been sexually mutilated to qualify
them for certain positions in the imperial service, especially the harem'.[5]

considered to be the pre-eminent example of the laws that were given on Mt. Sinai.

1.   Regarding the phrase in 56.3b, הבדל יבדילני יהוה מעל עמו, see E. Sehmsdorf,
'Studien zur Redaktionsgeschichte von Jesaja 56–66', *ZAW* 84 (1972), p. 553. The
idea is the priestly concept expressed in Exod. 26.33; Lev. 10.10; 11.47; 20.24-25,
36; Num. 8.14; 16.9; Ezek. 22.26; 42.20. See also Neh. 9.2.

2.   הנלוה, as pointed, is a mixed form. Read as a *niphal* masculine singular
participle. See *GKC* §138k.

3.   J. Blenkinsopp, 'Second Isaiah—Prophet of Universalism', *JSOT* 41 (1988),
p. 95. Blenkinsopp translates 56.3a as follows: 'Let not the foreigner, the convert to
YHWH, say…' So also Westermann, *Isaiah 40–66*, p. 312. Sehmsdorf thinks these
'foreigners' were most probably 'fremde Händler und Handwerker'. Sehmsdorf,
'Studien zur Redaktionsgeschichte von Jesaja 56–66', p. 557. See also Milgrom,
'Religious Conversion', pp. 173-76.

4.   ונלוו גוים רבים אל יהוה ביום ההוא והיו לי לעם ('many nations will join themselves to YHWH on that day and they will become my people'). This is very much the
same conception expressed in Isa. 56.3-8, in spite of the fact that it comes from one
of the primary spokesmen for the exclusivistic hierocratic tradition! In addition, see
Zech. 8.20-23: כה אמר יהוה צבאות עד אשר יבאו עמים וישבי ערים רבות והלכו ישבי אחת
אל אחת לאמר נלכה הלוך לחלות את פני יהוה ולבקש את יהוה צבאות אלכה גם אני ובאו
עמים רבים וגוים עצומים לבקש את יהוה צבאות בירושלם ולחלות את פני יהוה כה אמר
יהוה צבאות בימים ההמה אשר יחזיקו עשרה אנשים מכל לשנות הגוים והחזיקו בכנף איש
יהודי לאמר נלכה עמכם כי שמענו אלהים עמכם ('Thus says YHWH of hosts, people and
inhabitants of many cities are yet to come. The inhabitants of one will go and say to
the inhabitants of another, "Let us go and entreat the favor of the presence of YHWH
and seek YHWH of hosts, for I am going". Many peoples and mighty nations will
come to seek YHWH of hosts in Jerusalem and to entreat the favor of the presence of
YHWH. Thus says YHWH of hosts, in those days ten men from nations of every
tongue will take hold of the skirt of a Judaite and say, "Let us go with you because
we have heard that God is with you"').

5.   Blenkinsopp, 'Second Isaiah', p. 95. Sehmsdorf refers to this group as
'hochgestellte Beamte', 'Studien zur Redaktionsgeschichte von Jesaja 56–66', p. 557.
See Isa. 39.7; Jer. 29.2; 34.19; Est. 1.12. See also A.D. Nock, 'Eunuchs in Ancient
Religion', *ARW* 23 (1925), pp. 25-33. On the possibility that Nehemiah was a
eunuch, see Smith, *Palestinian Parties and Politics*, pp. 137-38, 214. For a contrary
position, see Blenkinsopp, *Ezra–Nehemiah*, pp. 210-13, 351.

As a whole, the passage takes the position that, under certain specific conditions,[1] the foreigner and the eunuch are allowed to participate[2] in the temple cult.

Of particular importance for our purposes is the occurrence in 56.4 of the phrase, אשר ישמרו את שבתותי ('who keep my Sabbaths'). Levenson has called attention to the thematic parallel with Lev. 19.30 and 26.2, both of which state: את שבתתי תשמרו ומקדשי תיראו אני יהוה ('my Sabbaths you shall keep, and my Sanctuary you shall revere, I am YHWH').[3] When we recall that what is at issue in Isa. 56.1-8 is access to the temple, then it is clear that what is being stated is exactly what is said in Leviticus, namely, that 'the Sabbath provides access to the sanctuary'.[4] Levenson also points out that, apart from this passage, the phrase שבתותי ('my Sabbaths') only occurs in Ezekiel and P.[5]

Both Blenkinsopp and Fishbane have called attention to the fact that the position of Isa. 56.3-8 with regard to the question of foreigners contradicts the position of Ezek. 44.4-16, and that both of these texts are related to Num. 18.1-7.[6] Ezekiel 44 prohibits foreigners as such from

1. Keeping Sabbath, clinging to the covenant, and so on. Notice that the criteria laid down in 56.3-7 with regard to foreigners and eunuchs are the very same criteria that were applied to the restoration community itself in 56.1-2. In other words, nothing more is required of foreigners and eunuchs than is required of the Judaite community as a whole.

Westermann has pointed out that the word ברית comes to take on the meaning of law or Torah. Once this semantic shift took place, Isa. 56.3-8 could be read as prescribing Sabbath observance and the keeping of Torah as the stipulations for membership in the community. The passage is moving in the direction of what will become rabbinic Judaism. See Westermann, *Isaiah 40–66*, p. 313.

2. Isa. 56.6 uses the verb שרת ('to serve' or 'minister'), a word commonly used of priestly service in the temple. This is clearly seen in 61.6: ואתם כהני יהוה תקראו משרתי אלהינו יאמר לכם ('you will be called "priests of YHWH" and "ministers of our God"'). See also Deut. 10.8; Jer. 33.21.

3. J.D. Levenson, 'The Temple and the World', *JR* 64 (1984), pp. 275-98.

4. Levenson, 'The Temple and the World', p. 292.

5. Exod. 31.13; Lev. 19.3, 30; 26.2; Ezek. 20.12, 13, 16, 20, 21, 24; 22.8, 26; 23.38; 44.24.

6. For Fishbane, Isa. 56.3-8 and Ezek. 44.4-16 are an example of 'contesting exegesis of one common Scripture: Num. 18'. Fishbane, *Biblical Interpretation in Ancient Israel*, p. 144. Blenkinsopp rejects this, but claims that Num. 18.1-7 does appear to be the text from which Isa. 56.1-8 and Ezek. 44.4-14 'take off'. Blenkinsopp, 'Second Isaiah', p. 96.

having access to the temple,[1] whereas Isa. 56.3-8 allows foreign proselytes to serve in the temple. Fishbane has erroneously stated that 56.3-8 'permits all strangers, בני הנכר, to serve in the shrine'.[2] According to this reading, 56.3-8 would be the diametric opposite of Ezekiel 44. But the debate between these two passages is not to be simplified into a pro-foreigner–anti-foreigner debate. Isa. 56.3-8 deals only with a very specific group of foreigners, namely, the ones who have 'joined themselves to YHWH'. This is a significant point and it is important that we be clear about what is being stated in the Isaiah text. Isaiah 56 has no intention of granting membership in the community and participation in the temple cultus to foreigners in general. On this point Isaiah 56 and Ezekiel 44 are in agreement. The issue being debated by Ezek. 44.4-14 and Isa. 56.3-8 is the issue of proselytism, and it is this that is the point of contention. Isa. 56.3-8 accepts proselytes under certain conditions, while it would appear that the very concept of proselytism is an impossibility for Ezekiel.[3] With respect to the question of foreigners in general, it must be said that, when taken together, the end result is that Ezek. 44.4-14 prohibits access to the temple to all foreigners, while Isa. 56.3-8 prohibits access to the temple to most foreigners.[4]

It is important to distinguish between a position that is open to proselytes and the modern theological concept of 'universalism'. Because

---

1. In Ezek. 44.7-9 access to the temple is expressly denied to anyone who is not circumcised. The passage makes clear that the concept of circumcision is not to be 'spiritualized'. Those forbidden to enter the temple are described as: ערלי לב וערלי בשׂר ('those uncircumcised in heart or in flesh'). See Sehmsdorf, 'Studien zur Redaktionsgeschichte von Jesaja 56–66', esp. pp. 545-47. He argues that 56.1-8 represents a complete denial of the fundamental tenet of priestly piety.

2. Fishbane, *Biblical Interpretation in Ancient Israel*, p. 138.

3. Sehmsdorf summarizes the position of Isa. 56.3 nicely: 'Nicht das Stehen in einer ununterbrochenen Geschlechtskette, sondern die freie Entscheidung für Jahwe begründen hier...die Zugehörigkeit zum Gottesvolk'. Sehmsdorf, 'Studien zur Redaktionsgeschichte von Jesaja 56–66', pp. 555-56. Also Blenkinsopp: 'Incorporation and membership [in the community] are determined not on ethnic or national considerations but on a profession of faith and a level of moral performance compatible with it', 'Second Isaiah', p. 95.

4. This is the basic position of the Hebrew Bible as a whole with respect to foreigners, that is, it is one of general hostility. Cf. Isa. 14.1-2; 60.10; 61.5; 62.8. See now the newly published 'Testament of Kohath' and the 'War Prayer' from Qumran, both of which reflect ongoing hostility to foreigners. The texts are published by R.H. Eisenman in *BAR* 17 (1991), pp. 64-65. The word for 'foreigners' in the 'Testament of Kohath' is נכר and in the 'War Prayer' it is בני נכר.

these terms are often not adequately distinguished, it is common for scholars to view Isa. 56.3-8 as the diametric opposite of the position of Ezra–Nehemiah and the anti-intermarriage policy expressed there.[1] Sehmsdorf, for example, regards Isa. 56.3 as a direct attack on the position of Ezra 9.2.[2] This view is shared by Hanson who argues that the oracle 'is a frontal attack on the narrow exclusiveness of the hierocratic tradition with its teaching that the temple priesthood was limited to the sons of Zadok, and that membership in the community was limited to the sons of Israel'.[3] By stating the issue in this way he is able to describe this passage as representing the 'tolerant spirit' of the visionary group, a spirit that was opposed to the 'narrow exclusiveness' of the hierocrats. But such a dichotomy is highly misleading,[4] because Isa. 56.3-8 is not nearly so 'tolerant', nor is Ezra–Nehemiah nearly so 'exclusive' as Hanson would like to think. As I argued in Chapter 2, Ezra 6.21 shows that Ezra's distinction between בני הגולה ('Babylonian exiles') and עם הארץ ('the people of the land') is one of religious affiliation; in other words, it was possible to join oneself to the group called בני הגולה. According to Ezra 6.21, one does this by 'separating oneself' (נבדל) 'from the pollution of the nations of the land' (מטמאת גוי הארץ). Those who accepted Ezra's תורה were members of בני הגולה and those who did not were not.[5] When seen in this light, the criteria for becoming a proselyte that are laid out in Isa. 56.3-8 (keeping Sabbath and covenant) are not at all inconsistent with the position of Ezra–Nehemiah.[6]

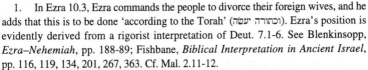

1. In Ezra 10.3, Ezra commands the people to divorce their foreign wives, and he adds that this is to be done 'according to the Torah' (וכתורה יעשה). Ezra's position is evidently derived from a rigorist interpretation of Deut. 7.1-6. See Blenkinsopp, *Ezra–Nehemiah*, pp. 188-89; Fishbane, *Biblical Interpretation in Ancient Israel*, pp. 116, 119, 134, 201, 267, 363. Cf. Mal. 2.11-12.
2. Sehmsdorf, 'Studien zur Redaktionsgeschichte von Jesaja 56–66', pp. 555-56.
3. *Dawn*, p. 389.
4. On this whole issue, see J. Blenkinsopp, 'Yahweh and Other Deities: Conflict and Accomodation in the Religion of Israel', *Int* 40 (1986), pp. 354-66.
5. This is against Morton Smith who claims that the people spoken about in Ezra 6.21 are not proselytes but 'Judeans won to the Yahweh-alone party from the syncretistic cult of Yahweh'. Smith, *Palestinian Parties and Politics*, pp. 137, 214. This seems to me to be an overly subtle distinction and it misses what is perhaps the most fundamental point of the theology of Ezra, which is that 'syncretistic' Judeans and foreigners are lumped into the very same category: עם הארץ.
6. It is not beside the point that Isa. 56.3-8 is concerned with the issue of foreign men, while Ezra–Nehemiah is primarily concerned with the issue of foreign women. Isa. 56.3-8 offers criteria by which foreign men may become members of the

The question of the status of הסרים deals with an issue not treated in Ezekiel 44; Ezekiel is concerned only with the question of ethnicity. The issue of the status of הסרים is the issue of what Blenkinsopp has referred to as 'physical integrity'.[1] Deut. 23.2-9 lists groups of people who are to be denied membership in the קהל יהוה ('the community of YHWH'), and like Ezekiel 44 it debars certain groups based upon ethnicity.[2] But it also raises the issue of physical integrity when it excludes as well those people who have some form of sexual mutilation: the פצוע דכא ('he whose testicles are crushed') and the כרות שפכה ('he whose penis has been cut off').[3] This combination of the issues of ethnicity and physical integrity makes Deut. 23.2-9 and Isa. 56.3-8 close parallels, much more so than Ezek. 44.4-16 and Isa. 56.3-8. The oracular formula in Isa. 56.4 signals the announcement of a new word of YHWH, a word that annuls the legal stipulations of Deut. 23.2-9.[4]

Isa. 56.4-5 explains the role that הסרים will play in the restoration community, and 56.6-7 does the same for בני הנכר. הסרים, a person who is biologically unable to have offspring, is promised יד ושם ('a monument[5] and a name') within the temple and within the walls of Jerusalem. When it is further stated, שם עולם אתן לו אשר לא יכרת ('I will give him an everlasting name that shall not be cut off'), it is clear that the writer is having some fun at the expense of the eunuchs.[6] Proselytes also will be

restoration community. Ezra–Nehemiah, on the other hand, is concerned with the issue of foreign women seducing their Judaite husbands into worshiping other gods. Morton Smith has a helpful discussion of these issues in which he argues that the doctrine of proselytism and the problem of intermarriage are intimately related and that the former was developed in order to solve the latter. Smith, *Palestinian Parties and Politics*, pp. 137-39. He sees Isa. 56 as an early stage in the development of the concept of the proselyte or גר. Cf. Exod. 12.43-50; Num. 9.14; 15.1-31; 19.10; 35.15; Deut. 29.10; Josh. 20.9, all of which presuppose the position of Isa. 56.3-8. The doctrine of proselytism and the problem of intermarriage (specifically, the marriage of a native Judean to a foreign woman) are effectively dealt with in the book of Ruth.

  1.   Blenkinsopp, 'Second Isaiah', p. 96.
  2.   Ammonites and Moabites are debarred forever; Edomites and Egyptians who are third generation may enter the community.
  3.   Also denied membership is the ממזר. This word is traditionally rendered as 'bastard' or 'child of an incestuous union'. It is possible, though, that it may refer to a child resulting from a mixed marriage. See Blenkinsopp, 'Second Isaiah', p. 96.
  4.   See Sekine, *Die Tritojesajanische Sammlung*, pp. 66-67.
  5.   See 2 Sam. 18.18. יד is a traditional euphemism for 'penis'.
  6.   Many commentators have pointed to the phrase לא יכרת as a link with Isa. 55.13, and have argued that this catch-phrase explains the juxtaposition of these two

allowed into the temple precincts and will be permitted to offer sacrifice.[1]
The point of 56.4-7 is that eunuchs and proselytes are to be granted the
status of full members of the community.[2] Isa. 56.8 concludes with the
statement that YHWH has still more 'outcasts' to gather into the
community.[3]

Isaiah 56.9–57.13; 57.14-21

General Observations
The transition from 56.8 to 56.9 is harsh. Beuken has proposed that
both 56.1-8 and 56.9–57.13 serve as commentaries on ch. 55, that is,
they serve to clarify several things that were left unclear in Isaiah 55,
and it is this that accounts for the present location of these two oracles.[4]
Sekine sees 56.9–57.13 as the other side of the universalistic theology of
56.1-8.[5] But all in all, the logic behind the juxtaposition of this oracle
with the previous one is elusive.[6]

As a whole, the passage is an attack on the leaders of the restoration

---

oracles. This may well be. But it is surprising how few commentators notice or
choose to mention the obvious and humorous sexual pun in 56.5. See Blenkinsopp,
'Second Isaiah', p. 102.

1. Cf. Isa. 19.19-22.

2. In 56.6 the בני נכר are given the name עבדים ('servants'). Because this term
plays such an important role in Third Isaiah, it is helpful to determine exactly what it
means here. Those who are given this name are people who can be identified by
certain specific actions on their part. They are those who 'join themselves to YHWH
(הנלוים על יהוה) in order to minister to him (לשרתו) and to love the name of YHWH
(ולאהבה את שם יהוה), to become YHWH's servants (להיות לו לעבדים)'.
The statement that the sacrifices of foreigners are 'acceptable' (לרצון) is a strong
one. Westermann has stated, 'The acceptance of foreigners' sacrifice means that,
properly speaking, they cease to be foreigners', *Isaiah 40–66*, p. 315.

3. On the phrase מקבץ נדחי ישראל, see Isa. 11.12, Zeph. 3.19, Ps. 147.2. The
Targum renders עוד אקריב גלוותהון לכנשא יתהון with עוד אקבץ עליו לניקבציו ('I will yet
bring near their exiles, gather them in').

4. Beuken, 'The Isaianic Legacy of Trito-Isaiah', pp. 48-64.

5. Sekine, *Die Tritojesajanische Sammlung*, p. 228.

6. Long ago Luther called attention to the problems that arise when an attempt is
made to read a prophetic book continuously. He stated that prophetic books 'maintain
no kind of order but leap from one matter to another so that a man can neither
understand nor endure it'. Quoted in K. Koch, *The Prophets* (trans. M. Kohl; 2 vols.;
Philadelphia: Fortress Press, 1983–84), I, p. 165. Luther's comment is certainly to the
point with respect to the transition from 56.8 to 56.9.

community and a diatribe against various cultic acts. The accusations are general enough to accommodate a wide variety of historical dates, and for this reason there has been no consensus regarding the literary unity of the passage. As Hanson has stated, 'the difficulty naturally stems from the fact that one finds Hosea, Amos, Isaiah, Jeremiah, Ezekiel, and Ezra all facing the problems of corrupt leaders and defiled cults similar to those depicted in this oracle'.[1] Hanson's point is to emphasize that attempts to date this oracle based upon the kinds of religious practices that it describes is futile. This is correct. But there is something else to be gleaned from Hanson's argument, something that he himself has failed to recognize. This is the fact that since there is nothing peculiar or unique about the accusations made in this oracle, what we have here is an example of traditional prophetic polemic, polemic that can be found throughout the prophetic corpus. In Hanson's own words, the passage could just as easily have been written by Ezekiel as by Third Isaiah. But I would push this argument still further. Isa. 56.9–57.13 is not just traditional 'prophetic' polemic; it is representative of the generic polemic of the Hebrew Bible as a whole. There is not a single book in the Hebrew Bible that supports the kinds of cultic abuses that are categorized in this oracle.

Exegesis

56.9-12. Three groups are singled out for condemnation: צפים,[2] הזים[3] and רעים. רעים ('shepherds') refers to political leaders, צפים and הזים refer either to prophets[4] or to priests and prophets.[5] These are generic labels for the leaders of the community. Contrary to Hanson's contention that Third Isaiah is anti-hierocrat/Zadokite polemic, this oracle attacks a whole host of people, none of which are specifically identified as priests, much less the Zadokites.[6] The oracle makes use of the idiom of

---

1. *Dawn*, p. 194.
2. *Kethib* צפו, *qere* צפיו, i.e., 'his watchers'. Various textual emendations have been proposed due to the fact that the pronominal suffix has no apparent antecedent. The proposals differ depending on who the speaker is assumed to be. The identity of pronominal antecedents is a common problem encountered in Third Isaiah.
3. Probably emend to חזים with 1QIsa.
4. Blenkinsopp, *A History of Prophecy in Israel*, p. 246.
5. Hanson, *Dawn*, p. 196; R.N. Whybray, *Isaiah 40–66* (NCB; London: Marshall, Morgan & Scott, 1980; Grand Rapids: Eerdmans, 1975), p. 200.
6. There is no denying that the Hebrew Bible reflects a history of antagonism between various priestly groups. Among these the Levite–Zadokite battles were

pre-exilic prophecy to describe conditions in the restoration era.[1] This is significant for our purposes because it shows that the religious practices that the pre-exilic prophets condemned were still on the scene in the post-exilic era. The abuses catalogued in Third Isaiah and laid at the feet of the leaders of the restoration community are evidence that 'Israelite' religion was still in a state of transition in the early restoration period. In other words, what the Hebrew Bible describes as the normative religion only became so at a relatively late date. The polemics of Isa. 56.9–57.13 show us that various kinds of (what I would call) 'traditional' religious practices persisted into the restoration period. And just as the pre-exilic prophets blamed the twin catastrophes of 722 and 587 BCE on these practices, so Third Isaiah asserts that the persistence of these same practices in the restoration period is preventing the arrival of YHWH's promised *Endtheophanie*.

57.1-2. Verses 1c-2 are corrupt, and it is virtually impossible to decide what the correct reading should be.[2] Isa. 57.1a-1b introduces two new groups of people, הצדיק ('the righteous one')[3] and אנשי חסד ('pious men' or 'the pious').[4] These are to be seen in contrast to the צפים, חזים and רעים of 56.9-12, and this dichotomy anticipates the ואתם–עבדי dichotomy of Isaiah 65. This is the first example of a common trait of Third Isaiah, the division of the community into the 'righteous' and the 'wicked'.

57.3-13. This may be the most vitriolic passage in the Hebrew Bible. But against whom or against what was it uttered? The group being

---

especially acerbic. But one of the major characteristics of these battles and of the texts in which these battles are reflected is that the protagonists have no qualms whatsoever about naming their opponents. This characteristic, however, is wholly lacking in Third Isaiah and is evidence that the polemics of Third Isaiah concern something different than intra-priestly squabbles.

1.   Many commentators date this oracle to the pre-exilic period because it 'sounds' pre-exilic.

2.   LXX: ἀπὸ γὰρ προσώπου ἀδικίας ἦρται ὁ δίκαιος· ἔσται ἐν εἰρήνη ἡ ταφὴ αὐτου, ἦρται ἐκ τοῦ μέσου.

3.   The reference to the perishing righteous man is very close to Isa. 53. The mystery of the suffering servant of Second Isaiah cannot be limited to Isa. 40–55. Several passages in Isa. 56–66 share thematic similarities with the suffering servant passages, Isa. 50.4-9 and 52.13–53.12. If there is ever a 'solution' to this ancient mystery, it will probably come from studies focused particularly on Third Isaiah.

4.   On this translation, see Duhm, *Das Buch Jesaia*, p. 425.

attacked is identified with the phrase ואתם ('but as for you').[1] The speaker is YHWH.[2] The group known as 'you' is further labeled as בני עננה ('sons of a sorceress')[3] and זרע מנאף ותזנה ('offspring of an adulterer and a whore').[4] The explicit sexual imagery that is introduced here runs throughout the passage and is to be seen as traditional prophetic polemic against the worship of gods other than YHWH.[5] As the text now stands, the antecedent of ואתם is צפים, הזים and רעים, that is, the leaders of the community. A whole host of accusations follows in vv. 4-13, the first of which is 57.5: הנחמים באלים תחת כל עץ רענן שחטי הילדים בנחלים תחת סעפי הסלעים ('you who lust among the oaks,[6] under every luxuriant tree; you who sacrifice your children in the valleys, among the rock-clefts').[7]

Worship among trees and in gardens, a practice common to many ancient religions,[8] was attacked by the prophets as a 'foreign' intrusion. But we now possess evidence indicating that many of the cultic practices labeled 'foreign' by the prophets were, in fact, traditional YHWHistic cultic practices.[9] Although she is not explicitly mentioned in this passage,

---

1. The *waw* is clearly *waw* adversative and, thus, 57.3-13 is to be seen in contrast to the previous verses. For this reason I am skeptical of the claim that 57.3-13 was an independent oracle. Cf. 65.13-14.

2. See 57.6c: העל אלה אנחם ('Can I [YHWH] change my mind in light of all of this?').

3. Cf. Isa. 2.6.

4. Reading וזנה for ותזנה. Cf. Isa. 1.4: זרע מרעים בנים משחיתים ('offspring of evildoers, corrupt sons'); 1.21.

5. Duhm, *Das Buch Jesaia*, p. 426; Whybray, *Isaiah 40–66*, p. 202; Westermann, *Isaiah 40–66*, pp. 321-22. The sexually toned polemic of this passage is reminiscent of Ezek. 16 and 23.

6. The phrase occurs only here. On the translation of באלים, contrast LXX: ἐπὶ τὰ εἴδωλα. The orthography is inconclusive. אלים can come from אל (Ps 29.1; 89.7; in these cases the manuscripts often reflect the variant spelling, אילים) or from איל or from אלה.

7. The polemical pair, the worship of foreign gods and child sacrifice, is also found in 2 Kgs 16.3-4 and 17.16-17.

8. Burkert lists the following types of ancient cult places: caves, peak sanctuaries, tree sanctuaries, house sanctuaries, temples, graves. Regarding tree sanctuaries he states that 'an important part of religious life was enacted out of doors, far from the everyday existence of the settlements; processions would make their way to those places where the deity could appear in dance beneath the tree', W. Burkert, *Greek Religion* (trans. J. Raffan; Cambridge, MA: Harvard University Press, 1985), p. 28. Cf. Isa. 17.10.

9. See Josh. 24.26 and its reference to the אלה ('oak tree') which was located במקדש יהוה ('in the temple/holy place of YHWH').

the reference to worship תחת כל עץ רענן is a possible reference to the
goddess אשרה ('Asherah'). Passages where Asherah and the stereotypical
phrase in question are explicitly linked are 1 Kgs 14.23, 2 Kgs 17.10 and
Jer. 17.2.[1] The phrase also occurs in Deut. 12.2, 2 Kgs 16.4, Jer. 2.20, 3.6,
13 and Ezek. 6.13, but no reference to Asherah is made.[2] What all of
these passages have in common, however, is that each is a piece of polemic against the worship of 'foreign' gods, and the phrase תחת כל עץ רענן
is in each instance a polemical reference to a place of worship, that is, a
cultic site.[3]

The discoveries at Ras Shamra and Elephantine have moved a great many scholars
to argue that pre-exilic Israelite religion was a typical Canaanite religion. See
G.W. Ahlström, *Royal Administration and National Religion in Ancient Palestine*
(Studies in the History of the Ancient Near East, 1; Leiden: Brill, 1982), esp. pp. 75-
83; *idem, Who Were the Israelites?*; M.D. Coogan, 'Canaanite Origins and Lineage:
Reflections on the Religion of Ancient Israel', in Miller, Hanson, and McBride (eds.),
Ancient Israelite Religion, pp. 115-24; W.G. Dever, 'Archaeology and the Bible—
Understanding their Special Relationship', *BARev* 16 (1990), pp. 52-58, 62; *idem*,
'Women's Popular Religion, Suppressed in the Bible, now Revealed by Archaeology',
BARev 17 (1991), pp. 64-65; R. Hestrin, 'Understanding Asherah—Exploring Semitic
Iconography', *BARev* 17 (1991), pp. 50-59; P.K. McCarter, Jr, 'Aspects of the
Religion of the Israelite Monarchy: Biblical and Epigraphic Data', in Miller, Hanson
and McBride (eds.), *Ancient Israelite Religion*, pp. 137-55; Smith, *The Early History
of God*; M. Smith, 'The Common Theology of the Ancient Near East', *JBL* 71
(1952), pp. 135-47; *idem, Palestinian Parties and Politics*; S.M. Olyan, *Asherah and
the Cult of Yahweh in Israel* (SBLMS, 34; Atlanta: Scholars Press, 1988).
    1. We must distinguish between 'Asherah', the actual goddess (1 Kgs 18.19),
and 'the asherah', the cultic symbol of the goddess. 'The asherah' was probably a
stylized wooden tree that represented the goddess.
    2. There are many instances where 'trees' are criticized without further explana-
tion. See, for example, Isa. 1.29-30: כי יבשו מאילים אשר חמדתם ותחפרו מהגנות אשר בחרתם
('They will be ashamed of the oaks which) כי תהיו כאלה נבלת עלה וכגנה אשר מים אין לה
they desired and of the gardens which they chose; you will be like an oak whose leaf
withers, like an unwatered garden'); Hos. 4.13: על ראשי ההרים יזבחו ועל הגבעות יקטרו
They offer') תחת אלון ולבנה ואלה כי טוב צלה על כן תזנינה בנותיכם וכלותיכם תנאפנה
sacrifice on the mountaintops, on the hills they burn incense, under the oak, the poplar,
and the terebinth...'). This probably derives from the fact that the tree was the ancient
Canaanite symbol of the goddess. See Smith, *The Early History of God*, pp. 81-85.
    3. Asherah's role in the religion of Israel and Judah is currently a hotly debated
topic, primarily because of the discoveries at Kuntillet Ajrud and Khirbet el-Qom.
Both of these locations have yielded inscriptions that can be interpreted to mean that
YHWH had a female consort, Asherah. From Ras Shamra we know that Asherah was
the consort of the great god, El. We also know that in the Hebrew Bible YHWH and El

130   *The Opponents of Third Isaiah*

Child sacrifice, mentioned in 57.5b, was another practice common in antiquity.[1] The overwhelming consensus is that this practice was also

are identified. It is, therefore, a logical inference to link YHWH and Asherah. Proving this inference is extremely difficult, however. The current state of the question is summarized in Olyan, *Asherah and the Cult of Yahweh in Israel*. See also A. Angerstorfer, 'Asherah als "Consort of Jahwe" oder Ashirtah?', *Biblische Notizen* 17 (1982), pp. 7-16; J.W. Betlyon, 'The Cult of 'Asherah/'Elat at Sidon', *JNES* 44 (1985), pp. 53-56; W.G. Dever, 'Iron Age Epigraphic Material from the Area of Khirbet el-Kom', *HUCA* 40/41 (1970), pp. 139-204; *idem*, 'Recent Archaeological Confirmation of the Cult of Asherah in Ancient Israel', *Hebrew Studies* 23 (1982), pp. 37-44; *idem*, 'Material Remains and the Cult in Ancient Israel: An Essay in Archaeological Systematics', in C.L. Meyers and M. O'Connor (eds.), *The Word of the Lord Shall Go Forth: Essays in Honor of David Noel Freedman in Celebration of his Sixtieth Birthday* (Winona Lake: Eisenbrauns, 1983), pp. 571-87; *idem*, 'Asherah, Consort of Yahweh? New Evidence from Kuntillet 'Ajrud', *BASOR* 255 (1984), pp. 21-37; J.A. Emerton, 'New Light on Israelite Religion: The Implications of the Inscriptions from Kuntillet 'Ajrud', *ZAW* 94 (1982), pp. 2-20; A. Lemaire, 'Who or what was Yahweh's Asherah?', *BARev* 10 (1984), pp. 42-51. Everyone agrees that Asherah was worshiped in pre-exilic Israel and Judah. But, as Olyan has argued, the inscriptional evidence from Ajrud and el-Qom raises the question of whether the worship of Asherah was 'an element only of popular religion, as many scholars believe, or an aspect of the official cult, or both?', *Asherah and the Cult of Yahweh in Israel*, p. xiii. Iron Age Palestine has yielded a substantial number of nude female figurines, the majority of which come from Jerusalem. In order to evade the implications of these finds, it is common to 'blame' such things on the 'popular religion'. But blaming all of the 'negative' aspects of the religion of Israel on 'popular religion' is a fruitless and misleading endeavor. It is a kind of half-hearted attempt to 'save' the Bible. According to Ahlström, 'We know too little about the actual rituals of any cult place including those of the Solomonic temple, and our knowledge of the beliefs and customs of the common man is scant. Thus, comparison of "popular" religion and the national religion is almost impossible', *Royal Administration*, p. 83. At any rate, the prophets had little concern for the religious practices of the common people. Most of their words were directed at the leaders of the community: kings, priests and other prophets. What we do know is that the existence of the numerous nude female figurines, however they are interpreted, is inconsistent with the witness of the Hebrew Bible, and, as Miller has stated, this raises the theological problem of the 'potential disparity between the official cultus and theology as portrayed in the OT and the actual historical reality', P.D. Miller, 'Israelite Religion', in D.A. Knight and G.M. Tucker (eds.), *The Hebrew Bible and its Modern Interpreters* (Philadelphia: Fortress Press; Chico, CA: Scholars Press, 1985), pp. 201-37 (217-18).

1. See L.E. Stager and S.R. Wolff, 'Child Sacrifice at Carthage—Religious Rite or Population Control?', *BARev* 10 (1984), pp. 31-51. The cemetery at Carthage reveals that 'child sacrifice took place there almost continuously for a period of nearly

well-known in pre-exilic Israel and Judah.[1] Isa. 57.5b is an explicit reference to the ritual slaughter of children and is best interpreted as evidence for the persistence of this pre-exilic practice into the restoration period.

Isa. 57.6-10 is an elaborate development of the image of a prostitute.[2]

600 years', that is, from the eighth to second centuries BCE. Contrary to the traditional scholarly opinion that human sacrifice was gradually replaced by animal sacrifice, the authors claim that the archaeological evidence from Carthage shows the opposite to be true, that 'the demand for human infant sacrifice, as opposed to animal sacrifice, seems to increase rather than decrease with the passage of time', p. 40. Traditional scholarship has also claimed that child sacrifice was usually associated with times of great civic or national crisis, but the authors contradict this assertion as well by arguing that the inscriptions at the Carthage cemetery indicate 'that the commonest reason for child sacrifice was the fulfillment of a vow', p. 44. See also A.R.W. Green, *The Role of Human Sacrifice in the Ancient Near East* (American Schools of Oriental Research Dissertation Series, 1; Missoula, MT: Scholars Press, 1975).

1. See Isa. 30.27-33; Jer. 7.31; 19.5; 32.35; Ezek. 16.20; 20.31; 23.37, 39; Mic. 6.6-7; Gen. 22; Exod. 13.1-2; 22.28-29; Lev. 18.21; 20.2-5; Deut. 12.31; 18.10; 1 Kgs 11.7; 2 Kgs 16.3; 17.17; 23.10; 2 Chron. 33.6; Ps. 106.37-38. The classical treatment of the subject is O. Eissfeldt, *Molk als Opferbegriff im Punischen und Hebräischen und das Ende des Gottes Moloch* (Halle: Niemeyer, 1935). The major points of Eissfeldt's work are that the term 'Molech' refers not to a deity but rather to a type of sacrifice, and that child sacrifice was a legitimate cultic practice in pre-exilic Israel and Judah up until the Josianic reform. See also G.C. Heider, *The Cult of Molek: A Reassessment* (JSOTSup, 43; Sheffield: JSOT Press, 1985); Olyan, *Asherah and the Cult of Yahweh in Israel*, p. 12; Smith, *The Early History of God*, pp. 132-33; M. Smith, 'A Note on Burning Babies', *JAOS* 95 (1975), pp. 477-79. For a discussion of the Pentateuchal laws of the first-born, see Fishbane, *Biblical Interpretation in Ancient Israel*, pp. 181-87. He argues that Exod. 22.28-29 'has preserved a regulation which prescribes and sanctions the donation of first-born males to the God of Israel'. For a challenge to the consensus, see M. Weinfeld, 'The Worship of Molech and of the Queen of Heaven and its Background', *UF* 4 (1972), pp. 133-54; *idem*, 'Burning Babies in Ancient Israel: A Rejoinder to Morton Smith's Article in *JAOS* 95 (1975): 477-79', *UF* 10 (1978), pp. 411-13. He argues that in the legal and historical sources of the Hebrew Bible, whenever the Molech ritual is mentioned the traditional verbs for sacrifice (שׂרף, שׁחט, זבח) are never used. He concludes that the Molech ritual 'had to do with initiation and dedication to foreign cult (Hadad) rather with slaying and burning babies'. Weinfeld, 'Burning Babies', p. 411.

2. Beginning at v. 6 the subject switches from 'you' (second masculine plural) to 'you' (second feminine singular). See *GKC* §47k. Beuken proposes that this woman is 'the mother of the "sons" who were spoken to earlier', 'The Isaianic Legacy of Trito-Isaiah', p. 53. On 57.8c, ותכרת, read with 1QIsa: ותכרותי, i.e., second feminine singular.

The style is reminiscent of Jer. 2.20-37 and Ezekiel 16 and 23. Sexual imagery abounds.[1] The link between the charge of idolatry and the sexual imagery used to illustrate the idolatry is a close one.[2] Perhaps temple prostitution is the issue.[3] Verse 9b evidently refers to necromancy.[4] All of these practices are said to take place על הר גבה ונשא ('on a high and lofty mountain').[5] Because the passage refers only to a single mountain, Hanson has argued that the mountain in question is none other than Mt Zion.[6] This is possible, but 57.5 has already made reference to several cultic sites. The mountain referred to here is more likely used in contrast to the mountain referred to in 56.7 and 57.13, namely, the הר קדשי ('my holy mountain'), which very definitely refers to Mt Zion. Confirmation of this interpretation is the evidence of 65.11 which attacks a group of people who שכחים את הר קדשי ('forget my holy mountain'). In other words, it is an attack upon a group who have abandoned Mt Zion. Such is the case here as well.

Isa. 57.11-13b pronounces judgment on those who have participated in the practices articulated in 57.3-10. Verse 13c announces salvation to another group, a group which has not participated in such practices: והחוסה בי ינחל ארץ ויירש הר קדשי ('but he who takes refuge in me will inherit the land and possess my holy mountain').[7]

1. Isa. 57.7-8: משכבך ('your bed'). This recalls 56.10 and 57.2. 57.8: זכרונך ('your [phallic] symbol'); יד חזית ('you have seen the hand [phallus]'). See Murtonen, 'Third Isaiah—Yes or No?', p. 37; K. Koenen, 'Sexuelle Zweideutigkeiten und Euphemismen in Jes. 57.8', *Biblische Notizen* 44 (1988), pp. 46-53.

2. Concern is expressed throughout the Hebrew Bible that sexual acts not be associated with the cult of YHWH. This is the most probable explanation of Exod. 20.26. When the Bible attacks the neighboring peoples, it is just as much for their sexual practices as it is for their 'idolatry'. See especially Lev. 18 and 20! In this regard, von Rad has spoken of a 'desacralization' of sex in the Bible. Von Rad, *Old Testament Theology*, I, pp. 27-28.

3. See Westermann, *Isaiah 40–66*, p. 324.

4. See also Isa. 59.9; 65.4; Ps. 106.34-48. Smith, *The Early History of God*, pp. 129-31, 137; M.H. Pope, 'The Cult of the Dead at Ugarit', in G.W. Young (ed.), *Ugarit in Retrospect: Fifty Years of Ugarit and Ugaritic* (Winona Lake: Eisenbrauns, 1981), pp. 159-79.

5. Ezek. 18 gives a definition of a צדיק, that is, a righteous man. Ezek. 18.6 states that among the acts that characterize a צדיק is the fact that אל ההרים לא אכל ('he does not eat upon the mountains').

6. *Dawn*, p. 199. So also Beuken, 'The Isaianic Legacy of Trito-Isaiah', pp. 53, 55.

7. The concept of נחלה or 'inheritance' is a major one for Third Isaiah. See 54.17 and 58.14.

57.14-21. These verses follow logically on the heels of 57.13c. It is a
salvation oracle highly reminiscent of Second Isaiah.[1] The recipient of
the proclamation is עמי ('my people'). Unlike Second Isaiah, however,
where Jacob/Israel and the Babylonians were the protagonists, here עמי is
set in contrast with הרשעים ('the wicked') (Isa. 57.20-21). In its present
context עמי is the name given to the people who 'take refuge' in YHWH,
and הרשעים is the name given to the people who participate in the
practices described in 57.3-10.

Isaiah 58.1-14

General Observations
Whereas 57.3-13 and 57.14-21 had as their main thrust the distinguishing
between עמי and הרשעים, ch. 58 is addressed in critical fashion to עמי
בית יעקב ('my people, the house of Jacob'). The passage begins as if it
were an oracle of judgment, but upon further reading it becomes clear
that we are dealing with a 'sermon'[2] or a 'speech of admonition',[3] the
purpose of which is to call the community to a change of behavior. The
central subject matter of the passage concerns the relationship between
ritual fasting and the arrival of YHWH's promised salvation. In this
respect the passage introduces us to what is perhaps the fundamental
theological question dealt with in Third Isaiah: the attempt to come to
terms with the failure of YHWH's promises, as uttered by Second Isaiah,
to materialize.

Exegesis
58.1-4. Contrary to the position of Hanson who sees in this passage a
distinction between two groups, one which fasts in the traditional way
(the Zadokite priests) and another which practices social justice in place
of fasting (the visionary disciples of Second Isaiah), I would argue on the
basis of 58.1 that the oracle is addressed to the community as a whole and
no division among the people is envisioned. Verse 1 makes it clear that
the people who are being charged with improper fasting are none other
than YHWH's own people, that is, עמי בית יעקב.[4] In other words, the

1.   Westermann, *Isaiah 40–66*, p. 327.
2.   Whybray, *Isaiah 40–66*, p. 212.
3.   Westermann, *Isaiah 40–66*, p. 333.
4.   The עמי of 58.1 recalls 57.14. These are not to be confused with the בני עננה of
57.3. See Whybray, *Isaiah 40–66*, p. 212.

addressees of this oracle are the same as in Isaiah 40–55. The phrase in
58.2, כגוי אשר צדקה עשה ('as if they were a nation that practices
righteousness') supports the contention that no specific group is singled
out for criticism but rather the people as a whole. While it is certainly
true that the verbs דרש and קרב can serve as cultic technical terms, and
thus in certain instances would point to specifically priestly activities, this
oracle makes no attempt to single out any specific group, and as a result
it appears that these terms have a more generic sense here. I contend
that the kind of situation envisioned in this oracle would be one similar
to that described in 2 Chron. 20.3-4 where it is stated that ויירא ויתן יהושפט
את פניו לדרוש ליהוה ויקרא צום על כל יהודה ויקבצו יהודה לבקש מיהוה גם מכל ערי
יהודה באו לבקש את יהוה ('Jehoshaphat was afraid; he turned to seek YHWH
and proclaimed a fast throughout Judah. Judah assembled to inquire of
YHWH, from all of the cities of Judah they came to inquire of YHWH').

Verse 3a records the anguished question of the restoration community:
למה צמנו ולא ראית ענינו נפשנו ולא תדע ('Why, when we fast, do you take no
notice, why, when we afflict ourselves, do you not regard it?').[1]
Although the prophet responds to this question in 58.3b-4 with the
charge that the people's fasting has been corrupted by various social
abuses,[2] there is absolutely no reason to challenge the sincerity of this
question or of the people who raised it. On the contrary, the prophet
accepts the question as legitimate and seeks to give an answer to it.

---

1.   The very same voice will be heard again in 63.7–64.11.
2.   See also Zech. 7, a passage that is strikingly similar to this one. There is a
common tendency among Protestant scholars to see the temple cult and the concern
for social justice as mutually exclusive. It is this tendency that enables scholars to
operate with a cut-and-dried prophet–priest dichotomy. We see this tendency in the
schema of Hanson. Because of their obvious ties to the restoration temple, Hanson
places the prophets Ezekiel and Zechariah into the hierocratic group. His assumption
is that the hierocratic tradition was, at best, indifferent to social justice concerns. There
is no question that Zechariah the prophet was a major supporter of the restoration
temple. For my purposes, however, it is interesting to note Zechariah's preaching on
social justice in Zech. 7.8-14. The similarity of these two passages was pointed out by
J. Skinner, *The Book of the Prophet Isaiah: Chapters XL–LXVI* (Cambridge:
Cambridge University Press, 1954), p.180. This devotee of the temple (or of 'temple
theology' if you will) was every bit as concerned about social justice as any other
prophet. The same could also be said about Ezekiel when one looks at the witness of
Ezek. 18. And finally, Ps. 15 and Ps. 24 make it quite clear that the practice of social
justice is the criterion for admittance to the temple. See J.D. Levenson, *Sinai and Zion*
(Minneapolis: Winston Press, 1985), pp. 169-76.

Here it is important to note the distinction between this interpretation and that of Hanson. Hanson argues that the cry in 58.3a reveals the fundamental flaw in the theology of the hierocratic tradition: it is an attempt to 'manipulate' the deity through cultic observance and can best be characterized as pagan superstition.[1] He argues further that over against this type of cult, the visionaries are posing an alternative cult, a cult 'of meekness and mercy'. But the problem with this interpretation is its assumption that 'manipulation' of the deity is the point at issue; in other words, that the prophet of Isaiah 58 is proposing a 'non-manipulative' form of religion to replace the 'manipulative' one.[2] As can be seen from the exegesis below, however, this completely misses the point. The point at issue is the validity of the proclamation of Second Isaiah. The people being addressed in this oracle are people who were intimately familiar with Second Isaiah's proclamation and who want to know what has gone wrong!

58.5-12. Verses 5-7 approach the question of fasting in typical prophetic hyperbolic fashion by juxtaposing acts of social justice with the common rituals of fasting.[3] The prophet's intention is not to assert that fasting as such is illegitimate but rather to emphasize the importance of doing social justice. As justification for this interpretation, it should be noted that, in Jewish tradition, Isaiah 58 serves as the Haftarah for, of all things, Yom Kippur! Some would argue that this practice is merely an example of simplistic harmonization. I would argue, however, that the practice of reading Leviticus 16 and Isaiah 58 side by side reveals a deep knowledge of the purpose behind hyperbolic prophetic speech.

Isa. 58.8-12 goes on to provide the answer to the question raised in 58.3a. Both the prophet and the people he is addressing agree that the realization of YHWH's promises is dependent on behavior. If one understands by 'manipulation' the attempt to encourage YHWH to act,

---

1. *Dawn*, p. 110.
2. A strong case could be made that doing social justice is also a means of 'manipulating' the deity!
3. Another example of prophetic hyperbole can be seen in Isa. 1.10-20. 1.14a: חדשיכם ומועדיכם שנאה נפשי ('I hate your new moons and festivals'); also 1.15a: ובפרשכם כפיכם אעלים עיני מכם ('when you spread out your hands I will hide my eyes from you'). The prophet uses various cultic acts (prayer included!) as foils for his proclamation of social justice.

then it is clear that the ritual fasting of the people is no more 'manipulative' than what the prophet himself is proposing. The disagreement is not over the issue of 'manipulation' but rather over the question of what kind of behavior on the part of the people will encourage (or 'manipulate') YHWH into acting on his promises. The prophet simply takes the traditional position that basic acts of social justice are the precondition for the realization of YHWH's promised salvation,[1] and he accomplishes this by stating his position in terms of an if-then proposition.[2] Another way to state the issue is to say that there can be no realization of YHWH's promised salvation apart from the doing of basic acts of social justice.[3]

58.13-14. Since Duhm these two verses have been regarded as a later addition because of the change in subject matter from fasting to Sabbath. It is commonly argued that the idea of Sabbath may have been suggested by the fact that the final word of 58.12, לשבת, can be read as from שׁוב or from שׁבת.[4] Others argue that Sabbath observance is simply incompatible with the teaching of 58.3-12.[5] Duhm's position was early on challenged by Volz who stated, 'The affirmation of the Sabbath as the center of religious communal life is completely compatible with the rejection of ceremonial fasting'.[6] Volz's argument has been picked up by Sekine who finds no evidence that 58.13-14 is redactional:

1.   This position is 'traditional' in the sense that it is commonly held throughout the Hebrew Bible. The teaching is 'at home' in Leviticus just as much as it is in Jeremiah or Amos. Hanson's contention that 'priestly theology' or 'temple theology' is being attacked here is dependent on the false assumption that social justice was solely the concern of the prophets. A position similar to Hanson's and suffering from the same false assumption is expressed by Pauritsch: 'Angesichts der Stellen 58, 2ff. und 66, 1ff. scheint eine kultfeindliche Einstellung vorzuherrschen. Doch erweist sich dieser erste Eindruck als Irrtum. Es wird nicht der Kult kritisiert, sondern der kultische Mensch', *Die neue Gemeinde*, p. 237.
2.   This if-then proposition is reminiscent of the blessings and curses of the covenant in Lev. 26 and Deut. 28.
3.   While it is true that Second Isaiah does not deal with social justice issues, it does not follow that Second Isaiah was, therefore, unconcerned with social justice.
4.   Whybray, *Isaiah 40–66*, p. 218.
5.   Smart, *History and Theology in Second Isaiah*, p. 30.
6.   Volz, *Jesaja II*, pp. 228-29 (translation mine). See also Skinner, *The Book of the Prophet Isaiah*, p. 186; Watts, *Isaiah 34–66*, pp. 276-77.

Whereas the direct answers in vv. 3b-5 described the relationships with people and with God in negative form, the indirect answers in vv. 6ff. portray both of these relationships in positive form. Verses 6-7 and 9b-10a describe the ideal relationship with people, and in my opinion v. 13 describes the ideal relationship with God.[1]

The insights of Volz and Sekine are complemented by Achtemeier. Beginning with the observation that 58.1-14 is framed by twin references to 'Jacob', she argues that the passage is a unity 'held together by a series of contrasts'. The contrasts are as follows:

Those who seek their own pleasures (vv. 3, 13) are not pleasing to Yahweh (v. 5). They must choose what he chooses (v. 6). Then they will be able to delight themselves in the Lord (v. 14). It does no good to afflict themselves in penance (vv. 3, 5) if they are afflicting others (vv. 7, 10). If they satisfy others, Yahweh will satisfy them (vv. 10, 11).[2]

As in 56.1-8 so here Sabbath observance occupies an exalted status. So exalted in fact is Sabbath observance that the realization of YHWH's promised salvation is said to depend on it. The phrase, אם תשיב משבת רגליך עשות חפציך ביום קדשי, probably refers to the carrying on of 'business'.[3] The Sabbath day itself is called ענג ('delight')[4] and is regarded as יום קדש and קדוש יהוה ('YHWH's holy day').[5]

58.1-14. Taken as a whole, 58.1-14 is to be seen as a unified composition addressed to the restoration community that asserts that practicing elementary social justice and observing the Sabbath are the necessary prerequisites for the realization of YHWH's promises of salvation.

---

1.   Sekine, *Die Tritojesajanische Sammlung*, p. 130 (translation mine); see also his complete discussion on pp. 128-31.

2.   E. Achtemeier, *The Community and Message of Isaiah 56–66* (Minneapolis: Augsburg), pp. 59-61.

3.   D.J.A. Clines, *I, He, We, and They: A Literary Approach to Isaiah 53* (JSOTSup, 1; Sheffield: JSOT Press, 1976), pp. 44-45; Westermann, *Isaiah 40–66*, p. 340.

4.   The only other occurrence of this noun is at Isa. 13.22.

5.   Construct phrases with the root קדש are common in Third Isaiah. Apart from those already listed above in the exegesis of 56.1-8, see also 62.12: עם הקדש ('the holy people'); 63.10-11: רוח קדשו ('his holy spirit'); 63.15: זבל קדשך ('your holy abode'); 63.18: עם קדשך ('your holy people'); 64.9: ערי קדשך ('your holy cities').

Isaiah 59.1-21

General Observations

The passage divides neatly into three parts: accusation (1-8), confession (9-15a), theophany (15b-20). Although it has been described as 'a most curious and odd creation',[1] Hanson is to be followed in his description of the passage as a salvation-judgment oracle. From a theological point of view, the passage is closely related to Isaiah 58. Both presuppose the same poor economic conditions.[2] Both deal with the problem of the seeming failure of YHWH to act on the promises that were articulated by Second Isaiah, and both attempt to explain the reason why. Both assert that YHWH's 'inactivity' has been caused by the behavior of the people; in other words, the argument is that the fault does not lie with YHWH (or with Second Isaiah!) but with the people. The overall relationship between chs. 58 and 59 can be described as follows: 'While in ch. 58 it is a question of how one attains salvation, in ch. 59 the issue is why one has not attained it'.[3]

Exegesis

59.1-8. The section subdivides into vv. 1-3 (second person) and vv. 4-8 (third person).[4] The section is a prophetic accusation made against a group of people who have evidently been claiming that YHWH is incapable of carrying out his promises made through Second Isaiah. The second person masculine plural pronouns in vv. 1-3 link up with ch. 58 and allow us to conclude that it is still עמי בית יעקב who are being addressed. The people are charged with numerous abuses: עונת ('transgressions'), חטאות ('sins'), שקר ('lies'), עולה ('injustice'). The statement כי כפיכם נגאלו בדם ('your palms are defiled with blood')[5] is strongly reminiscent of Isa. 1.15, ידיכם דמים מלאו ('your hands are full of blood'). The accusations are so broad that they are obviously intended to cover

---

1. Westermann, *Isaiah 40–66*, p. 344.
2. Blenkinsopp, *A History of Prophecy in Israel*, pp. 247-48.
3. Sekine, *Die Tritojesajanische Sammlung*, pp. 229-30 (translation mine).
4. This change in pronouns has led many to conclude that vv. 4-8 are a later addition. See Elliger, *Die Einheit des Tritojesaja*, pp. 15-20; Volz, *Jesaja II*, pp. 230-31.
5. MT נגאלו is a mixed form. Read with *BHS* as simple *niphal.*

all aspects of the people's life, and there is no warrant for limiting them solely to the cultic sphere.[1]

Verses 4-8 are surely metaphorical, the intention of which is to describe the complete breakdown of justice.[2] To limit these accusations to one specific group within the restoration community, namely the Zadokite priests, is at best to enter into sheer speculation, and at worst to do violence to the text.

Verses 1-8, along with 56.9–57.13 and ch. 58, serve to qualify the proclamation of Isa. 40.1-2. Conditions in the restoration community have made it impossible for the prophet to speak of YHWH's judgment as something confined to the past. Second Isaiah's scheme of judgment followed by exile followed by restoration is now qualified by the announcement of a new act of judgment which must precede the promised restoration. And it is the announcement of this new act of judgment that distinguishes the proclamation of Isaiah 56–66 from that of 40–55.

59.9-15a. The phrase על כן ('therefore') links this section to the preceeding one. Although the form is that of a communal lament, there is, nevertheless, no claim of innocence on the part of the speaker.[3] Instead, the accusations of the preceding section are more or less reiterated in the form of a confession. Verses 9-11 describe in lament form the present state of affairs. Verse 9, על כן רחק משפט ממנו ולא תשיגנו צדקה ('therefore justice is far from us and righteousness does not overtake us'), v. 11b, נקוה למשפט ואין לישועה רחקה ממנו ('we wait for justice, but there is none, for salvation, but it is far from us'), and v. 14, והסג אחור משפט וצדקה מרחרק תעמד ('justice is turned away and righteousness stands afar off'), directly recall (and presuppose) the bold proclamation of 56.1: שמרו משפט ועשו צדקה כי קרובה ישועתי לבוא וצדקתי להגלות ('keep justice and practice righteousness, for my salvation and my righteousness are about to be revealed'). The purpose of these verses is to contrast the present situation with that which was announced in 56.1. But whereas at the beginning of the oracle the assumption on the part of the people was that YHWH's inactivity was due to a lack of power on his part, the

---

1. Regarding the phrase, וחטאותיכם הסתירו פנים ('your sins have hidden the Presence'), see the discussion in Chapter 3 of Hanson's exegesis of ch. 59.

2. MT הזורה in 59.5b is odd. For possible solutions, see GKC §80i and Duhm, *Das Buch Jesaia*, p. 441.

3. Contrast this with Isa. 63.7–64.11.

verses which follow, vv. 12-15a, form a communal confession of sin, which, in agreement with 59.1-8, proclaims that the explanation for YHWH's inactivity lies not with YHWH but with the sins of the people.[1] This, in turn, establishes the ongoing validity of the proclamation of 56.1.[2]

At this point reference must be made to Hanson's interpretation of this passage. As already discussed in Chapter 3, he reads 59.1-8 as an attack on the Zadokite cult. But in addition, he interprets 59.9-15a as a lament spoken not by the Zadokites, but rather by the minority group which was supposedly opposing the Zadokites. This, however, is a very strange interpretation, and it destroys the logic of the passage. The logic of the passage is simple. In 59.1-8 the people (i.e., עמי בית יעקב) are accused of various offenses, and in 59.9-15a it is the very same people who respond with a confession of sin. Contrary to Hanson's reading, the people speaking in 59.9-15a are not referring to someone else's sins but rather their own. This is supported by the fact that all of the pronouns in 59.9-15a are first person plural. I would also argue that the voice that is speaking in 59.9-15a is the very same voice that is in evidence in 58.3: למה צמנו ולא ראית עניגו נפשינו ולא תדע ('Why, when we fast, do you take no notice, why, when we afflict ourselves, do you not regard it?'). In other words, the same people are speaking in 58.3 as are speaking in 59.9-15a. The difference is that in 59.9-15a the people are giving the answer to the question which they themselves had raised in 58.3.[3] The reason that YHWH takes no notice of their fasting is כי רבו פשעינו נגדך וחטאותינו ענתה בנו ('because our transgressions are numerous in your sight and our sins speak against us').

59.15b-20. This section forms the climax of the passage. In response to the confession of the people, a theophany is announced. In 59.17 YHWH is pictured as a warrior going to battle: וילבש צדקה כשרין וכובע ישועה בראשו וילבש בגדי נקם תלבשת ויעט כמעיל קנאה ('YHWH clothes himself with

---

1. It is perhaps worth noting that the words used in 59.12 to describe the sins of the people, פשעינו ('our revolts'), חטאותינו ('our sins') and עונתינו ('our iniquities'), are the very same words used in the initial oracle of the book of Isaiah, 1.2-4.

2. This is an extremely important point. In spite of the fact that Isa. 56–66 reflects the frustration of the restoration community over the delay in realizing YHWH's promised salvation, the validity of the proclamtion that 'YHWH's salvation is near' is upheld throughout.

3. We will hear this same first person plural voice speaking in Isa. 63.7–64.11.

the armor of righteousness, with a helmet of victory on his head; he clothes himself with garments of vengeance, he puts on zeal like a robe'). In 59.18 those marked for defeat are named צריו ('YHWH's adversaries'), איביו ('YHWH's enemies') and איים ('distant lands'),[1] while in 59.20 the beneficiaries of YHWH's act of war are called ציון ('Zion') and שבי פשע ביעקב ('those in Jacob who turn away from transgression'). At first reading, the reference to the איים would seem to implicate the foreign nations in YHWH's judgment and give the passage the character of an oracle against the nations. But when צריו and איביו are read in the light of 59.20, it becomes clear that these terms refer not to foreigners but to those within the restoration community who do not שבי פשע ('turn away from transgression').[2] Isa. 1.24b, 27-28a is closely related to 59.18-20 and offers justification for this interpretation: 1.24b, הוי אנחם מצרי ואנקמה מאויבי ('I will be relieved of my adversaries and take vengeance on my enemies');[3] 1.27-28b, ציון במשפט תפדה ושביה בצדקה ושבר פשעים וחטאים יחדו ועזבי יהוה יכלו ('Zion shall be ransomed in the judgment; those among her who repent, in the retribution. But rebels and sinners shall be crushed, and those who forsake YHWH shall perish').[4]

---

1. איים is lacking in LXX, but the entire v. 18 in LXX is much shorter: ὡς ἀνταποδώσων ἀνταπόδοσιν ὄνειδος τοῖς ὑπεναντίοις. In LXX Isaiah, ὑπεναντίος always translates צר, although elsewhere it also translates איב. Here it evidently translates both. See E. Hatch and H.A. Redpath, *A Concordance to the Septuagint* (2 vols.; Grand Rapids: Baker Book House, 1983), II, p. 1407. The word-pair of צרים and איבים occurs in Isa. 1.24, while in 66.6 איבים occurs alone. Targum, Syriac and Vulgate all support MT.

2. Cf. LXX: καὶ ἥξει ἕνεκεν Σιων ὁ ῥυόμενος καὶ ἀποστρέψει ἀσεβείας ἀπὸ Ιακωβ. The translator evidently read ולשבי as the *hiphil* infinitive, ולשיב. Elision of ה in *hiphil* infinitives with preformative ל can be seen in 1 Sam. 2.33, לאדיב, and Ps. 26.7, לשמע. For other examples, see GKC §53q. This phenomenon is also known from Qumran. See E. Qimron, *The Hebrew of the Dead Sea Scrolls* (HSS, 29; Atlanta: Scholars Press, 1986), p. 48.

3. Commenting on the relationship between 1.24b and 59.18a, Steck points out that '1.24 und 59.18a sind die beiden einzigen Stellen im ganzen Jesajabuch, an denen beide Begriffe (צר und אויב) im Plural und im Sinne von Jahwes Feinden nebeneinanderstehen', 'Jahwes Feinde in Jesaja 59', p. 54 (parentheses mine).

4. On the translation of בצדקה, see the new JPSV. 59.19b is difficult: כי יבוא כנהר צר רוח יהוה נססה בו. The problem centers around the subject of יבוא. Most modern interpreters have relied on LXX and take צר נהר as the subject: 'He (i.e., YHWH) will come like a rushing stream, which the wind of YHWH drives on'. Rofé, however, has pointed out that medieval Jewish exegesis took צר ('enemy') as the subject and translated the passage very differently: 'When the enemy comes as a river, the spirit

59.21. This verse is commonly regarded as secondary and unrelated to its context. Westermann has proposed that it originally belonged at the end of the book,[1] while others see it as an introduction to the following chapters.[2] Whatever the origin of this verse, however, its subject matter is highly provocative. The speaker is YHWH and he is addressing the prophet with an oracle of salvation.[3] What is provocative is the statement on YHWH's part that the prophet has his (i.e., YHWH's) 'spirit' (רוחי אשר עליך). This anticipates the words of the prophet in 61.1, רוח אדני אלהים עלי ('the spirit of the Lord God is upon me') and also recalls 48.16, ועתה אדני יהוה שלחני ורוחו ('now the Lord YHWH has sent me and his spirit'). The point is that the justification for the prophet's message is that he possesses YHWH's spirit, and also that possession of YHWH's spirit passes on from generation to generation: רוחי אשר עליך ודברי אשר שמתי בפיך לא ימושו מפיך ומפי זרעך ומפי זרע זרעך אמר יהוה מעתה ועד עולם ('my spirit which is upon you and my words which I have placed in your mouth shall not depart from your mouth nor from the mouth of your children nor from the mouth of your children's children for ever, says YHWH'). In other words, the messengers may change, but the message stays the same. It is this conviction on the part of the various voices that speak in Isaiah 1–66 that bind the book together as a unified whole.

59.1-20 (21). As stated above, chs. 58 and 59 deal with the problem of the seeming failure of YHWH to act on the promises that were articulated by Second Isaiah, and both assert that YHWH's 'inactivity' has been caused by the behavior of the people. But whereas ch. 58 was

---

of the Lord will put him to flight'. He argues that while such a rendering of רוח יהוה נוססה בו is problematic on both grammatical and contextual grounds, the Jewish exegetes were correct in understanding צר as the subject of יבא but erred in following the Masoretic pointing. צר should not be read as 'enemy' but rather as 'envoy', i.e., צ(י)ר. Such a pointing is supported by 1QIsa (צור), where *waw* and *yod* have probably been confused, and by Isa. 5.28, 57.9 and 63.8-9. Rofé understands this 'envoy' to be a figure similar to the 'messenger' of Mal 3.1. See A. Rofé, 'Isaiah 59.19 and Trito Isaiah's Vision of Redemption', in J. Vermeylen (ed.), *The Book of Isaiah, Le Livre d'Isaïe* (BETL, 81; Leuven: Leuven University Press, 1989), pp. 407-10.

1.   Westermann, *Isaiah 40–66*, p. 352.
2.   Pauritsch, *Die neue Gemeinde*, p. 94.
3.   See W.A.M. Beuken, 'Servant and Herald of Good Tidings', in Vermeylen (ed.), *The Book of Isaiah*, p. 423.

basically an exhortation to the people to 'amend their ways', ch. 59 goes well beyond that and posits a terrifying new act of judgment on YHWH's part. When taken as a whole, ch. 59 makes the theological assertion that confession leads to salvation, but this salvation only comes after a new act of judgment on YHWH's part, an act of judgment that will separate the 'righteous' from the 'wicked'. But if we were to leave it at that, we would miss the cutting edge of the passage. It is Hanson who has identified this oracle as a salvation-judgment oracle, and the point of his description is that the new act of judgment on YHWH's part is not the kind of judgment traditionally proclaimed by the prophets. Instead, what we have here is the announcement of a judgment that will divide 'Israel' from 'Israel'.[1]

Isaiah 60–62

Numerous exegetes have referred to chs. 60–62 as the center or the nucleus of Third Isaiah. It is also well known that from both a stylistic and a theological perspective the chapters closely resemble Isaiah 40–55, and it can even be said that chs. 60–62 are dependent on Isaiah 40–55 for their interpretive context.[2] In addition, it has recently been shown that chs. 60–62 draw heavily on material from First Isaiah, that is, that First Isaiah's words undergo a studied reapplication in Isaiah 60–62, the purpose of which is to state that certain prophecies of Isaiah of Jerusalem are either about to be fulfilled or are about to be reversed.[3]

The subject matter of these three chapters concerns the rebuilding/ restoration/glorification of Zion/Jerusalem. As was discussed in Chapter 3, Hanson has described Isaiah 60–62 as a 'program of restoration' that was written in conscious opposition to the program of restoration of Ezekiel 40–48. According to him, the former program is 'prophetic', 'visionary' and 'inclusive', while the latter is 'priestly', 'pragmatic' and 'exclusive'. Hanson's summarization of these two programs of restoration has been vigorously critiqued by Blenkinsopp who argues that

---

1. Beuken, 'Servant and Herald of Good Tidings', pp. 423-24.
2. See Steck, 'Tritojesaja im Jesajabuch', pp. 373-79; Zimmerli, 'Zur Sprache Tritojesajas'.
3. See Fishbane, *Biblical Interpretation in Ancient Israel*, pp. 495-99. Compare Isa. 62.4 with 1.7; 62.10-12 with 11.10; 60.1-2, 17-18 with 9.1, 3; 60.3, 5, 14, 17 with 2.1-4.

144   *The Opponents of Third Isaiah*

Hanson has misconstrued the nature of Third Isaiah in general and Isaiah 60–62 in particular:

> It is important to note that throughout Third Isaiah prophetic-eschatological faith is focused on Temple and altar (e.g., Isa. 60.7, 13; 61.6; 62.9). There is therefore no opposition in principle between the bearers of this faith and the Temple authorities and no evidence that the former were anticultic.[1]

It would be wrong to use Blenkinsopp's argument to support the assertion that there are no points of tension between Isaiah 60–62 and Ezekiel 40–48. But Blenkinsopp's insights can be used against Hanson's contention that Isaiah 60–62 and Ezekiel 40–48 are representative of two distinct and mutually exclusive 'religious mentalities'.

If one wants to compare Third Isaiah's vision of restoration with Ezekiel's, then it is important to consider more than just Ezekiel 40–48. If one brings Ezekiel 33–37 into the picture, it becomes evident that the 'religious mentality' expressed there is actually quite similar to Isaiah 60–62. Both share the conviction that the time of judgment against Israel is passed.[2] Both understand the restoration to be a period of radical reversal. Both share a common vision of exiled Israelites streaming back to their homeland.[3] Both share a common (almost exclusive) focus upon Jerusalem and the temple.[4] And both share an intensely negative attitude toward foreigners.[5] The only substantial difference in outlook between

1. Blenkinsopp, *A History of Prophecy in Israel*, p. 247.
2. Isa. 60.10 and Ezek. 34.11-16.
3. Isa. 60.4 and Ezek. 34.13; 36.8, 12.
4. Isa. 60.1, 13; 62.1; etc., and Ezek. 37.26-28. The prophet Haggai is well-known for his message: בנו הבית ('Build the temple!'). He is also often criticized for having an *ex opere operato* theology. But is he really any more enthusiastic about the blessings that will result from the building of the temple than the author of Isa. 60–62? On this issue, Pauritsch has stated, 'Schliesslich sei erwähnt, dass die Vorstellung von Haggai, der neue Tempel werde die Stätte der eschatologischen Herrlichkeitserscheinung Jahwes sein (Hag. 2.6ff.), mindestens auch in Jes. 60.1ff. im Hintergrund steht', *Die neue Gemeinde*, p. 237.
5. Isa. 60.10, 12!; 61.5; 62.8 (where בני נכר and איביך are used synonomously); and Ezek. 34.28; 35; 36.1-7. In addition, see Ezek. 38-39. Isa. 61.2 is especially enlightening. The prophet announces that part of his mission is לקרא שנת רצון ליהיה ויום נקם לאלהינו ('to proclaim YHWH's year of favor, the day of vengeance for our God'). Westermann has accurately pointed out that the phrase יום נקם recalls the ancient prophetic concept of יום יהוה ('the day of YHWH'). But then he follows this statement by saying, 'Here there is no idea of God's taking vengeance on Israel's foes', Westermann, *Isaiah 40–66*, p. 367. To argue in this way is to miss the entire

Isaiah 60–62 and Ezekiel 33–37 is that Ezekiel posits the restoration of
the Davidic dynasty and the reunification of the nations of Judah and
Israel.[1]

It remains to critique Hanson's claim that Isaiah 60–62 and Ezekiel
hold mutually exclusive views about the concepts of 'holiness' and
'priesthood'. Regarding the issue of priesthood, Hanson states,

> The promise of the visionary is that *the whole nation* 'will be named the
> priests of Yahweh, the ministers of our God' (Isa. 61.6); the realist
> carefully regulates: '…mark well those who may be admitted to the temple
> and all those who are to be excluded from the sanctuary…; [the Levites]
> shall not come near to me, to serve me as priest…' (Ezek. 44.5, 13);
> '…the sons of Zadok…alone among the sons of Levi may come near to
> the Lord to minister to him' (Ezek. 40.46; cf. 44.15).[2]

According to his interpretation, Isa. 61.6 represents an 'astonishing
democratization of the formerly exclusive sacerdotal office…'[3] Hanson
evidently understands this passage to imply the abolition of the priesthood in Israel. But that can hardly be the case, because in the final oracle
of Third Isaiah the prophet foresees a time when certain foreigners will
become כהנים לוים (Levitical priests)![4] Obviously there has to be another
way to understand 61.6. In my view, it is best to read 61.6 as synonomous with (or proclaiming the fulfillment of) Exod. 19.6: ואתם תהיו לי
ממלכת כהנים וגוי קדוש ('You shall be to me a kingdom of priests, a holy
nation'). Childs's description of Exod. 19.6 holds true for Isa. 61.6 as
well: 'Israel as a people is…dedicated to God's service among the
nations as priests function with a society'.[5] In other words, it is precisely

---

thrust of prophetic theology in general and restoration theology in particular. Isa. 60–
62 proclaims the message of a שנת רצון for Israel and of a יום נקם for her enemies. See
Isa. 34.8; 63.4. Stated in another way, to the prophetic mind good news for someone
implies bad news for someone else. See, for example, how Isa. 47 functions within
the Second Isaiah corpus. In the Hebrew Bible the message of the restoration of
Israel always includes the twin elements of the vindication of YHWH and the
humiliation of his enemies.

1.   Ezek. 34.23-24; 37.15-28. On the possibility that Third Isaiah also envisions
the resurgence of 'Greater Israel', see Blenkinsopp, 'Second Isaiah', p. 93.

2.   *Dawn*, pp. 72-73.

3.   *Dawn*, p. 68.

4.   Isa. 66.21. My argument holds even if Isa. 61.6 and 66.21 are not from the
same hand.

5.   B.S. Childs, *The Book of Exodus: A Critical, Theological Commentary*
(OTL; Philadelphia: Westminster Press, 1974), p. 367.

an elevated estimation of the institution of the priesthood that makes
statements such as these possible in the first place.

Regarding the issue of 'holiness', Hanson states,

> The visionary exults, 'Your people shall all be righteous...' (Isa. 60.21);
> 'They will be called "The Holy People"...' (Isa. 62.12); the realist
> meticulously explains that holiness is reserved for the few and that it must
> be safeguarded by ordinances...(Ezek. 44.19, 23; 46.20).[1]

But is it really the case that Ezekiel holds that 'holiness is reserved for
the few?' Ezek. 37.28 reads: וידעו הגוים כי אני יהוה מקדש את ישראל בהיות
מקדשי בתוכם לעולם ('When my sanctuary is in their [i.e., Israel's] midst
forever, the nations will know that I, YHWH, sanctify Israel'). Here it is
clearly stated, just as in Isa. 62.12, that the attribute of holiness applies to
all members of Israel, and this derives from the existence of YHWH's
temple in Jerusalem.[2]

There is no question that Ezekiel 40–48 occupies a unique place in the
theology of the Hebrew Bible. There is also no question that the so-
called 'Zadokite stratum'[3] within Ezekiel 40–48 contains material that is
unparalleled in the Hebrew Bible. But Hanson's contention that Isaiah
60–62 was written in conscious opposition to Ezekiel's program of
restoration is highly problematic. Virtually all of Hanson's examples
from Ezekiel 40–48 are taken from the Zadokite stratum. The problem
with this approach is that the Zadokite stratum is at odds with numerous
texts throughout the Hebrew Bible, but of all of the passages that would
normally come to mind, Isaiah 60–62 is not one of them. There simply is
no evidence that Isaiah 60–62 is fighting an intra-priestly battle. As was
shown above, the passages from Isaiah 60–62 that Hanson brings find
very close parallels in Ezekiel 33–37, and the 'religious mentality' behind
these sections is quite similar.

What, then, can be said about the relationship between Isaiah 60–62
and Ezekiel 40–48? Levenson has described Ezekiel 40–48 as 'a
depiction in detail of the society announced in the more conventional

---

1.   *Dawn*, p. 73.

2.   Note the play on words between מקדש ('he who makes holy') and מקדשי ('my
holy place').

3.   The phrase was coined by H. Gese, *Der Verfassungsentwurf des Ezechiel
(Kap. 40–48) traditionsgeschichtlich untersucht* (BHT, 25; Tübingen: Mohr, 1957).
According to Gese, the stratum consists of Ezek. 44.6-31; 40.46b; 43.19; 45.4-5;
46.19-21, 24; 48.11.

prophecies of restoration in chs. 33–37'.[1] In other words, Ezekiel 33–37 and 40–48 are related in terms of the general and the specific. Although it could be done, it would be misguided to make a point by point comparison between the two and then try to demonstrate that because the latter is more detailed and specific that it is therefore representative of a different 'religious mentality', one that is obsessed with 'minute details'.[2] I would argue in a similar vein that Isaiah 60–62 is representative of one of those 'more conventional prophecies of restoration', one that speaks of the restoration in general terms and utilizes language common to many traditions. We simply do not know what the author of Isaiah 60–62 would have thought about the specifics of the program of Ezekiel 40–48. Hanson's contention that the author of Isaiah 60–62 abhorred 'the obsession with the minute details of the rebuilt temple' and 'the tedious measurements of the dimensions of walls and gates'[3] tells us much more about Hanson than it does about the author of Isaiah 60–62!

Isaiah 63.1-6

General Observations
There is virtual unanimity among scholars that 63.1-6 forms a single unit, but there is major disagreement as to how and to what extent this passage relates to what precedes and what follows it.[4] As regards the form of the passage, I follow Hanson in his identification of it as a 'Divine Warrior Hymn'.[5] The passage is mythico-apocalyptic in character and reflects a world in which YHWH acts alone against the forces that oppose him. These forces are symbolized by the name 'Edom'.

Exegesis
63.1. It was long ago suggested that מאדום and מבצרה should be emended to מְאָדָּם[6] and מִבָּצֵר.[7] Accordingly, instead of reading, 'Who is this who

---

1. Levenson, *Theology of the Program of Restoration*, p. 161.
2. *Dawn*, p. 73.
3. *Dawn*, p. 73.
4. Steck has argued that 63.1-6 may at one time have served as the end of the book of Isaiah, 'Beobachtungen zu Jesaja 56–59', pp. 228-46.
5. *Dawn*, p. 203. It is conspicuous that any explicit mention of God is lacking in this passage. See the discussion in Volz, *Jesaja II*, p. 262.
6. Cf. Nah. 2.4; Exod. 25.5; 26.14; 35.7, 23; 36.19; 39.34.
7. Cf. LXX: βοσορ.

comes from Edom, clothed in red garments from Bozrah?', the reading would be, 'Who is this who comes all stained with red, redder than a grape-gatherer?' The history of the discussion of this *crux* has been summarized by Sekine, along with the modern consensus that MT is to be maintained.[1] This verse is an example of the exilic and post-exilic tendency to regard Edom as the arch-enemy of Israel.[2]

63.2. אדם ('red') plays on אדום, and כדרך בגת ('like him who treads the wine press') is a traditional image of God's judgment.[3] Here, the linking up of the wine-press imagery with Edom/Bozrah may be related to the similarity between בצרה ('Bozrah') and בציר ('vintage').[4]

63.3-6. Verse 3 presents numerous problems for the interpreter.[5] 1QIsa has a substantially different text: פורא דרכתי לבדי ומעמי אין איש אתי וכול מלבושי גאלתי ('I trod the wine-press alone and none of my people was with me, and I polluted all of my garments'). There are two major differences to note. First, 1QIsa has עמי ('my people') instead of MT עמים ('peoples'), and secondly, 1QIsa lacks ואדרכם באפי וארמסם בחמתי ויז נצחם על בגדי ('I trod "them" in my anger and trampled "them" in my wrath, "their" blood spurted upon my garments'). While the meaning of MT is ambiguous, 1QIsa is not. The point of 1QIsa is that the Lord goes forth to judgment without the aid of his people. Against whom? Against the עמים named in 63.6. Thus, 1QIsa distinguishes between the עמי of 63.3

1. Sekine, *Die Tritojesajanische Sammlung*, pp. 140, 146.
2. See Isa. 34.6, in which the same word-pair, בצרה/אדום, occurs, and in a virtually identical sense. See also Obadiah, Mal. 1.2-5. This raises the interesting question of the relationship of this view of Edom to that which comes to expression in Genesis. Genesis clearly attempts to cultivate a certain degree of sympathy toward Esau/Edom in his dealings with his twin brother Jacob/Israel. In fact, a major point of this cycle of traditions appears to be to posit a reconciliation between Jacob/Israel and Esau/Edom. One wonders if such a thing as this would have found any reception at all after the events of 587 BCE.
3. Cf. Lam. 1.15; Joel 4.13.
4. *Dawn*, p. 206.
5. MT ואדרכם, וארמסם and ויז are all pointed as simple imperfects, though one would expect the imperfect consecutive. It is best to understand these as examples of a 'dogmatic emendation...in order to represent historical statements as promises', GKC §107b. Cf. Isa. 42.6; 43.28; 51.2. אגאלתי can be understood as a mixed form or an Aramaism, but a better explanation is that this form is also a dogmatic emendation whereby the א serves to indicate 'the change of the perfect into the imperfect', so as to bring this verb into harmony with the pointing of the three previous verbs. GKC §53p.

and the עמים of 63.6. But in MT it is precisely the עמים of 63.3aα against whom the judgment described in 63.3aβ-b is carried out.[1] According to this reading, the עמים of 63.3a and the עמים of 63.6 would refer to the same group.

There is, however, another way to understand MT, depending on how one construes the ו in the phrase ומעמים אין איש אתי. Is it a simple copula, in which case the phrase would be a restatement of דרכתי לבדי? Or is it causative, in which case the phrase would be giving the reason that judgment was carried out on the peoples? In the latter case the translation would be something like 'Because the peoples were not with me (i.e., because they did not follow my ways), therefore I trod them in my anger...'

It is difficult to come to a decision. The reading of 1QIsa is usually rejected because it has no support in the textual tradition.[2] But as is well known, this reasoning is far from airtight. 1QIsa may represent a very early variant reading. On the other hand, if one rejects 1QIsa, there remains the problem of the ambiguity of MT. For our purposes it is important to note that no matter which interpretive decision is made, who it is exactly who is being judged remains unclear. In spite of the fact that 63.6 explicitly states that the object of God's judgment is עמים, the question still remains: Who are they?[3]

Perhaps more than any other, this oracle illustrates the problem we have in interpreting Third Isaiah. The problem arises from the fact that for the most part in Third Isaiah the traditional distinction between Israel and the nations is blurred, and everything turns on the issue of who exactly is included under the rubric of עמי ('my people').[4] Therefore, although this oracle appears to take the traditional form of an oracle against the nations, the fact that it occurs in the context of Isaiah 56–66 argues against reading it in a traditional way. The answer to the question of who it is who is being judged is dependent on how one interprets Isaiah 56–66 as a whole. One thing, however, is clear. The passage posits

---

1. From a purely grammatical point of view, עמים of 63.3aα must be the antecedent of the pronouns in 63.3aβ and 63.3b. If this were not the case, one would expect the pronominal suffixes to agree with פורה.

2. Interestingly, *BHS* does not even list 1QIsa as a variant reading. *BHK*, however, did.

3. Even if we accept 1QIsa, the problem still remains that the identities of עמי and עמים are not self-evident. See Isa. 65.10.

4. The identification of this problem in Third Isaiah is the great contribution of Hanson.

a new act of judgment which must precede the realization of the
promises made in Isaiah 40–55 and 60–62, and it is the positing of this
new act of judgment that is a major defining characteristic of Third
Isaiah.

Isaiah 63.7–64.11

General Observations

The passage is a rhetorically moving communal lament containing several
key elements: (1) 63.7-9, recollection of YHWH's merciful acts toward
his people in the ancient past; (2) 63.10, acknowledgment of the people's
rebellion against YHWH and his becoming the enemy of his own people;
(3) 63.11-14, recollection of God's merciful acts toward his people in the
Exodus; (4) 63.15–64.11, plea for YHWH to intervene on behalf of his
people against their (and his) enemies in the present time of desolation,
coupled with a confession of sin.[1] The passage is highly reminiscent of
Lamentations and like Lamentations most probably originated in exilic
Judah. This explains why there are 'no substantial links between Isa.
63.7–64.12 and Deutero-Isaiah'.[2]

Exegesis

63.7-14. Verses 7-9 comprise a brief recitation of the *magnalia dei*.
Verse 9 is difficult. LXX construes בכל צרתם ('in all their troubles') with
63.8b: καὶ ἐγένετο αὐτοῖς εἰς σωτηρίαν ἐκ πάσης θλίψεως, and then
renders לא צר ומלאך פניו הושיעם as οὐ πρέσβυς οὐδὲ ἄγγελος, ἀλλ'
αὐτὸς κύριος ἔσωσεν αὐτούς ('neither a messenger nor an angel but
rather the Lord himself saved them'). While מלאך פניו ('the angel of his
presence') is certainly possible, it requires that לא be read as לו. LXX

---

1.   Regarding the compositional history of the passage, see the detailed discussions in Pauritsch, *Die neue Gemeinde*, pp. 146-64; Sekine, *Die Tritojesajanische
Sammlung*, pp. 148-64; Westermann, *Isaiah 40–66*, pp. 385-98.

2.   Williamson, 'The Concept of Israel in Transition', p. 151. This is an
important point. The passage is occupied with the questions: Is there any hope for a
sinful people? Have the people's sins cut them off from God forever? In other words,
the passage raises the very questions that Second Isaiah was designed to answer. But
in its present location, coming as it does after the proclamation of Second Isaiah, the
passage reveals something of the state of mind of the restoration community for
whom the message of Second Isaiah had become highly problematic. Thus, it can be
said that 'eine Phase der Enttäuschung liegt zwischen der Verheissung Deuterojesajas
und dem stürmischen Gebet in Jes 63.19f.', Kraus, 'Die ausgebliebene
Endtheophanie', p. 326.

requires no changes at all and is therefore to be preferred. Furthermore, the idea that it is YHWH's פנים ('presence') that is the active agent is consistent with Deut. 4.37 and Exod. 33.14.[1]

In 63.10 the speaker records Israel's response to YHWH's acts of faithfulness: והמה מרו עצבו את רוח קדשו ויהפך להם לאויב הוא נלחם בם ('But they rebelled,[2] they grieved his holy spirit;[3] so he became their enemy, he himself fought against them'). This echoes the message of the Deuteronomistic History and all of the pre-exilic prophets.[4] Although 63.7–64.11 is often compared with lament psalms like Psalm 44, the comparison is not all that helpful. The lament in Psalm 44 arises out of a protestation of innocence and in essence is a challenge to God's justice. But here the speaker acknowledges that God's actions were justified.

In 63.11-14 the speaker returns to a recitation of the *magnalia dei*, specifically the events of the exodus. Verse 11 is beset with textual difficulties. ויזכר ('he recalled') is problematic. Grammatically speaking, YHWH would be the subject, but this makes no sense.[5] The context and 63.7 suggest that ואזכר ('yet I shall recall') should be read.[6] משה עמו is probably to be read משה ועמו ('Moses and his people').[7] The textual tradition strongly favors emending המעלם ('he who brought them up') to המעלה ('he who brought up').[8] MT רעי is plural, the antecedent of which is evidently עמו. If we read the singular, רעה, with LXX, then the antecedent would be משה.[9] This is too close to call. My translation of

1.   Deut. 4.37: ויצאך בפניו בכחו הגדול ממצרים ('by his presence he brought you out of Egypt, by his great strength'). Exod. 33.14: ויאמר פני ילכו והנחתי לך ('He said, my presence will go [before you] and I will give you rest').

2.   Cf. Ezekiel's constantly recurring description of the people as a בית המרי ('rebellious house').

3.   An extremely rare expression, occurring only here and in Ps. 51.13: ורוח קדשך אל תקח ממני ('Do not take your holy spirit from me!').

4.   For those who lived in the exilic or post-exilic eras, these words could only refer to the catastrophe of 587 BCE.

5.   Interpreters have long recognized this and the translations reveal a dizzying array of attempts to make sense out of this form.

6.   See the discussions in Elliger, *Die Einheit des Tritojesaja*, and Volz, *Jesaja II*.

7.   Syriac has מושא עבדה ('Moses, his servant') and this is the choice of many interpreters. The new JPSV takes משה as a participle, 'he who draws out from the water', thus requiring no textual emendation. If this is the case, then משה would be a play on words with the actual name of Moses which occurs in the next verse.

8.   This, in fact, is the reading of 1QIsa.

9.   That is, the reference would be to Moses, 'the shepherd of the sheep'. If this reading is adopted, then another difficulty arises. 'Where is he who brought the

63.11 is as follows: 'Yet I shall recall the days of old, the days of Moses and his people. Where is he who brought the shepherds of his sheep up from the sea? Where is he who put his holy spirit in their midst?'

63.15–64.11. These verses form the lament proper, but they share two striking characteristics with 63.7-14. The first is that the speaker, an anonymous 'I', operates with the traditional distinction between Israel and the nations. On the one hand there are בית ישראל (63.7), עמי/עמך (63.8, 14; 64.8) and עבדיך (63.17), while on the other there are צריך and גוים (64.1). The second characteristic is that God's judgment on his people is not challenged but rather is accepted as justified due to the sins of the people.[1] The question at issue in the lament is whether God's judgment on his people is forever, whether God will remain the enemy of his people forever, and the purpose of the lament is to beg God to turn once again in mercy toward his people. Verses 9-11 are especially effective. In 64.9-10 the speaker calls to God's attention the desolation of the temple and the holy city. The purpose of this recitation appears to be to challenge God's honor. The lament then concludes in 64.11 with the anguished question: העל אלה התאפק יהוה תחשה ותעננו עד מאד ('YHWH, will you restrain yourself in the light of all of this? Will you continue to remain silent? Will you continue to afflict us terribly?').[2] I contend that the voice that is speaking here is the very same voice that raised the question in 58.3a.

Three verses, 63.16-18, require closer inspection. As stated in Chapter 3, Hanson has argued at length that these verses reflect a situation in which the speaker of the lament is protesting the exclusion of him and his group from the cult by the Zakokite priests. He states,

---

shepherd of the sheep up from the sea?', could be a reference to the Exodus, but it could also be a reference to the rescue of the child Moses from the Nile river. This was first suggested by Duhm. See Isa. 18.2 and 19.5 where ים ('sea') is used for the Nile.

1. See 63.10; 64.4b-6. The confession in 64.4b-6 recalls that of 59.9-15a.
2. The conclusion of the lament is almost identical with the conclusion to the book of Lamentations. Lam. 5.20-22: למה לנצח תשכחנו תעזבנו לארך ימים השיבנו יהוה אליך ונשוב חדש ימינו כקדם כי אם מאס מאסתנו קצפת עלינו עד מאד ('Why have you forgotten us completely? Why have you forsaken us for so long? Return us to you, YHWH, and we will return; renew our days as of old. Or have you utterly rejected us? Are you too angry with us?').

> The referent of the designations Abraham and Israel can be taken most
> naturally as the central Israelite community of this period, that is, the group
> returning from exile under the leadership of the Zadokite priests.[1]

He thus interprets 63.16 in terms of the rejection of one group within
the restoration community by another group within the restoration
community. This, however, destroys the logic of the lament. To be sure,
the lament does deal with the subject of 'rejection', but the one who is
doing the rejecting is YHWH! Accordingly, the issue in the lament is not
exclusion from the cult but rather the destruction of the cult. Contrary
to Hanson, there is absolutely no evidence that 'Abraham' and 'Israel'
are to be taken as pejorative designations.[2] As stated above, the speaker
of the lament operates throughout with the traditional distinction
between Israel and the nations.[3] His theological problem is the fact that
in taking the side of the nations, YHWH has become the enemy of his
own people, and he wants to know if that situation is going to continue
forever. Thus he cries out, 'We are still your people, O God. Acknowledge
us!' Stated simply, the 'battle' in this lament is between the speaker and
his God. Hanson's interpretation misses this completely.

In 63.17 Hanson interprets the reference to עבדיך ('your servants') as
evidence of a rift in the restoration community. But once again he
misses the point that the speaker is speaking on behalf of the community
as a whole. This is proven by the statement in 64.8: עמך כלנו ('we are all
your people'). עבדיך ('your servants'), שבטי נחלתך ('the tribes of your
inheritance'), עמך ('your people'), בית ישראל ('the house of Israel') are all
used synonomously.[4]

Verse 18 is of major importance to Hanson.[5] Scholars have long
noticed that the adverb, למצער ('for a little while'), is somewhat awkward
if the second half of the verse is speaking about the destruction of the
temple at the hands of the Babylonians. To say that the Israelites held
possession of the temple for only 'a little while' would be a gross

---

1.   *Dawn*, pp. 92-93.

2.   See Williamson, 'The Concept of Israel in Transition', p. 151.

3.   See Blenkinsopp, *A History of Prophecy in Israel*, p. 277; Williamson, 'The
Concept of Israel in Transition', pp. 151-52.

4.   See my exegesis below of Isa. 65 for a further critique of Hanson's
interpretation of 63.16.

5.   In spite of protestations to the contrary, Hanson is probably correct in arguing
that MT should not be emended. See his detailed discussion on the textual problems
of this verse in *Dawn*, pp. 84-85.

understatement. As a result, various textual emendations have been proposed to alleviate this difficulty. Hanson argues, however, that this should lead us to look for a different way of understanding the verse rather than seeking to emend it. He proposes that למצער is a reference to the exilic period when the Levites, most of whom were not exiled to Babylonia, were in control of the cult on the site of the destroyed temple in Jerusalem. The second half of the verse, צרינו בוססו מקדשך ('our adversaries have desecrated your sanctuary'), would then be seen as an antagonistic reference to the Zadokites who took control of the sanctuary after they returned from exile.

Two criticisms of this argument are in order. The first is that such an interpretation places an incredible amount of weight on the little word למצער, and the second is that if the speaker wanted to describe a 'takeover' of the cult by a rival priestly group, צרינו בוססו מקדשך would be a strange way of saying it. Indeed, one would have to ask Hanson if the phrase in 64.10, בית קדשינו ותפארתנו אשר הללוך אבתינו היה לשרפת אש ('our holy and glorious house, the house in which our fathers praised you, has been burned with fire'), also refers to a Zadokite takeover! The most natural way of reading 63.18 is to read it as it has always been read, though without emendation, as a reference to the Babylonian destruction of the temple and the temple city. The painful aftermath of this event and the haunting theological problem that it raised are what is at issue in this lament. The problem of YHWH's enmity toward his own people was so acute for the speaker that he was led to describe the entire history of the Solomonic temple as but 'a little while'.

Isaiah 65.1-25

General Observations

The question of the literary unity of this passage is unanswered. Virtually every commentary on Third Isaiah proposes a different compositional history and structure. In my view, however, the passage can be read smoothly and logically from beginning to end, and I follow Hanson in his contention that it is an original prophetic unit.[1] Form-critically the passage is a salvation-judgment oracle.

I contend that 65.1-25 was composed from the very beginning as an

---

1. See *Dawn*, p. 135. For different views, see Sehmsdorf, 'Studien zur Redaktionsgeschichte von Jesaja 56–66', pp. 517-30; Sekine, *Die Tritojesajanische Sammlung*, pp. 165-78.

answer to the lament in 63.7–64.11, and therefore I differ with most
others who argue that 65.1-25 was originally an independent composition
and that its juxtaposition to 63.7–64.11 was secondary. Hanson has
stated that although 65.1-25 does in fact appear to be an answer to 63.7–
64.11, in the final analysis the relationship between the two passages is
superficial. This is so, he argues, because the attack on cultic abuses in
65.1-25 does not really answer the questions raised by the lament. I
would argue, however, that the passage does answer the lament and that
the positions taken in 65.1-25 cannot be understood apart from 63.7–
64.11. The primary function of 65.1-25 is to attack the fundamental
presupposition of the speaker of the lament, the assertion that עמך כלנו
('we are all your people'). To this assertion 65.1-25 responds by saying,
'No, you are not!'

What happens essentially in 65.1-25 is that all of the traditional terms,
such as 'YHWH's people', 'YHWH's servants' and 'YHWH's chosen',
are redefined. To be sure, Hanson has recognized and elucidated this
process of 'redefinition' in ch. 65, but he has missed the point that 65.1-
25 functions as a criticism of the claims made in 63.7–64.11. In other
words, it is precisely those who raised the lament in 63.7–64.11 who
meet with words of judgment in ch. 65. Hanson's scheme, whereby it is
the visionary disciples of Second Isaiah who are behind both 63.7–64.11
and ch. 65, results in a logical absurdity.

The function of ch. 65 over against 63.7–64.11 is summarized by
Steck:

> Isaiah 65–66 breaks open the entire empirical Israel's solidarity in the
> confession of sin, as it is expressed in chaps. 63–64, discards the
> deuteronomistic goal of all Israel's return and participation in salvation,
> and reduces the idea of the servants of Yahweh (63.17) to the pious (64.4;
> 65.8ff.; 66.2, 5ff.), and that of the people of Yahweh to the people who
> seek him.[1]

In other words, the relationship between 63.7–64.11 and ch. 65 is not
that of the theological progression of a single tradition, as Hanson would

---

1. Steck, 'Tritojesaja im Jesajabuch', p. 401 (translation mine). Notice that he
includes ch. 66 in the discussion. His claim is that Isa. 65–66 is a literary unity and is,
as a whole, both a response to the lament in 63.7–64.11 and a conscious ending to the
book of Isaiah. See Steck, 'Beobachtungen zur Anlage von Jes 65–66', pp. 103-16.
See also L. Liebreich, 'Compilation of the Book of Isaiah', *JQR* 46 (1955–56),
pp. 259-77; Sweeney, *Isaiah 1–4*, pp. 21-25.

have us believe, but rather the former serves as the foil for the proclamation of the latter.

Exegesis
65.1-7. When viewed as YHWH's answer to the confession and lament in 63.7–64.11, the rhetorical effect of these verses is striking. The people who so passionately referred to themselves as 'God's people' are now (in 65.1) called by God גוי לא קרא בשמי ('a nation that does not call upon my name') and (in 65.2) עם סורר ('a stubborn people'). There then follows in rapid fashion a series of accusations regarding cultic abuses within the restoration community, and these accusations are strikingly reminiscent of those in 57.3-13.

Verse 3b: זבחים בגנות ומקטרים על הלבנים ('those who offer sacrifice in gardens, who burn incense on the bricks').[1] Sacrifice in gardens most probably refers to a fertility rite and may be related to the cult of Adonis, the Syrian vegetation deity.[2] Though the evidence is circumstantial, burning incense on bricks is a possible reference to a rite honoring Tyrian Asherah.[3] 1QIsa preserves a tantalizing alternative reading for this verse: המה זובחים בגנות וינקו ידים על האבנים ('they offer sacrifice in the gardens and suck hands on the stones'). 'Hands' and 'stones' are well known euphemisms, and whether this reading is original or not, it points to a very early interpretation of the rites involved as sexual in nature.[4] Verse 7 is similar to v. 3b. It states that the present עון ('transgression') of the people is identical with that of their ancestors: they worship (קטר) other deities on the mountains and hills.

Verse 4a: הישבים בקברים ובנצורים ילינו ('those who sit in tombs and spend the night inside the mountains').[5] The practice is evidently that of consulting or caring for the dead.[6] Verse 4b: האכלים בשר החזיר ופרק פגלים כליהם

---

1. See Isa. 1.29.
2. See Isa. 17.10-11; Smith, *The Early History of God*, p. 158; Burkert, *Greek Religion*, pp. 176-77. The cult of Adonis was closely related to that of Babylonian Tammuz, and we know that Tammuz had his devotees in Judah. See Ezek. 8.14.
3. See M. Dahood, 'Textual Problems in Isaiah', *CBQ* 22 (1960), pp. 406-408; Whybray, *Isaiah 40–66*, p. 269.
4. See Brownlee, *The Meaning of the Qumran Scrolls*, pp. 234-35; A. Rubinstein, 'Notes on the Use of the Tenses in the Variant Readings of the Isaiah Scroll', *VT* 3 (1953), pp. 94-95.
5. The translation is that of Dahood, 'Textual Problems in Isaiah', pp. 408-409. He divides בנצורים into בין צורים. Cf. LXX: ἐν τοῖς σπηλαίοις.
6. Cf. Isa. 8.19-20. See Volz, *Jesaja II*, p. 282. He draws attention to the

('those who eat swine, whose bowls contain pieces of unclean things'). The offenses are evident to anyone familiar with the dietary laws of Leviticus and Deuteronomy. In fact, all of the accusations leveled in 65.1-7 are well known from the pre-exilic prophets and from the Pentateuch.

Hanson has argued that all of these accusations are to be taken metaphorically, that is to say, they are not to be read as describing the actual cultic practices of the restoration community, and that what is really at issue here is an attack against the priestly theology undergirding P and Ezekiel 40–48, a theology characterized by 'self-righteousness' and 'exclusivism'. Hanson's identification of the group being attacked here is based primarily on his interpretation of Isa. 65.5 and the fact that this verse places three priestly *termini technici* (קרב‎, נגש‎, קדש‎) into the mouths of the accused. But this interpretation of the passage involves a rather ingenious exegetical sleight-of-hand. In effect, what he argues is that all of the cultic accusations in 65.3-4 are to be read metaphorically with the exception of the accusation in 65.5. It alone is to be taken literally! But the text itself provides no warrant for such an interpretive move. Beginning in 65.2 and running through 65.5 the group being attacked is identified with a series of participles: זבחים‎, המכעיסים‎, ההלכים‎, האמרים‎, האכלים‎, הישבים‎, מקטרים‎. The accusation in 65.5a, האמרים קרב אליך אל תגש בי כי קדשתיך‎, ('those who say, "keep to yourself, do not touch me, because I am holier than you"') is simply the final element in a long list of cultic accusations. Hanson is forced to read all of the accusations (except one!) as metaphorical because he realizes that saddling the post-exilic Zadokite priesthood with actually having practiced such things would be sheer 'Blödsinn'. But in my view that is a rather tortured way of going about things. A simpler and more consistent way of dealing with this passage is to assume that the accusations actually mean what they say and that the passage provides evidence that certain well-known pre-exilic cultic practices persisted into the restoration period. When seen in this light, the passage is to be understood as a late stage in the ongoing struggle to establish the 'orthodox' cult of YHWH, a struggle which only came to an end with the promulgation of the Pentateuch. The passage has nothing to do with the topics of such relative insignificance as 'exclusivism' and 'self-righteousness'.

similarity of the practices described here with those of the mystery religions, especially Attis, Osiris and Mithras. See also Kaufmann, *The Religion of Israel*, pp. 311-16.

158   *The Opponents of Third Isaiah*

65.8-16a. Verse 8 is the key verse in the chapter: כה אמר יהוה כאשר ימצא
התירוש באשכול ואמר אל תשחיתהו כי ברכה בו כן אעשה למען עבדי לבלתי השחית הכל
('Thus says YHWH, just as new wine can be found in the grape cluster,
and it is said, "do not destroy it because there is some good in it", so I
will act for the sake of my servants and not destroy everything'). This
passage asserts that not everyone in the community is to be implicated
in the accusations leveled in 65.1-7. Whereas the speaker in 63.17 used
the phrase 'YHWH's servants' as a description of the community as a
whole, here YHWH himself responds with the claim that only those who
do not participate in the kinds of cultic acts described in 65.1-7 can be
called by that name. In 65.9 those who are destined to participate in the
realization of the promises of Second Isaiah and take possession of
YHWH's holy mountain[1] are called עבדי ('my servants'), בחירי ('my
chosen'), עמי אשר דרשוני ('my people who seek me'). These terms are all
expressly polemical in nature and the people so designated are to be
distinguished from those who, in 65.11, are called עזבי יהוה השכחים את
הר קדשי ('you who forsake YHWH, who forget my holy mountain').[2]
This 'forsaking' and 'forgetting' is defined in 65.11b: הערכים לגד שלחן
והממלאים למני ממסך ('you who spread a table for Gad and mix a drink for
Meni'). This is an explicit statement that Gad and Meni, the gods of
fortune and fate, were worshiped in the restoration community.[3] This
accusation is to be added to those that have already been enumerated in
65.1-7.

What we are witnessing here is a major transition in the theology of
the Hebrew Bible. Salvation is no longer conceived purely in national
terms. The content of such designations as 'YHWH's people', 'YHWH's
chosen', 'YHWH's servants' and בני ישראל, has been radically altered,
and one's membership in בני ישראל is no longer simply a matter of
birthright. Only those who properly adhere to the cult of YHWH, as this
cult is understood by the author, are to be considered 'YHWH's
servants', while those who engage in cultic acts like those described in

1. Reading הרי as singular, in agreement with וירשוה ('they shall take possession
of it').
2. Cf. Isa. 1.28: ועזבי יהוה יכלו. The concept of 'forsaking YHWH' is a major one
for the Chronicler. See 1 Chron. 28.9; 2 Chron. 7.19, 22; 12.5; 13.10, 11; 15.2;
24.18, 20, 24, 25; 29.6; 34.25.
3. For statistics on the occurrences of the names, Gad and Meni, in Israelite
inscriptions, see J.H. Tigay, *You Shall Have No Other Gods: Israelite Religion in the
Light of Hebrew Inscriptions* (HSS, 31; Atlanta: Scholars Press, 1986), pp. 13, 66-67,
69.

65.1-7, 11b, and 57.3-13 and so on are to be excluded. In other words, the content of the terms 'YHWH's chosen', 'YHWH's servants' and 'YHWH's people' has become almost exclusively theological.[1] This theological transition is clearly expressed in 65.13-16 where the twin proclamation of salvation and judgment cuts right through the heart of the restoration community.[2] It is exactly as Hanson has stated: 'The glorious promises of Second Isaiah which applied to the servant Israel have been narrowed to a small segment within Israel, and the classical forms of the judgment and salvation oracles have been fused to account for the new division within the people'.[3]

65.16b-25. Drawing on elements of the proclamation of both First and Second Isaiah, these verses are a proclamation of salvation for YHWH's servants.[4] Scholars have long puzzled over the meaning of 65.17a: כי הנני בורא שמים חדשים וארץ חדשה ('Behold, I create new heavens and a new earth!'). It is either viewed as a gross exaggeration on the part of the author or as an isolated apocalyptic fragment. What is clear, however, is that there is an intimate connection between 65.17a and 65.18b: כי הנני בורא את ירושלם גילה ועמה משוש ('Behold, I create Jerusalem rejoicing and her people exulting'). Levenson has argued that in the P source of the Pentateuch, the temple was regarded 'as a microcosm, a miniature

1. This may be a partial explanation for why Third Isaiah has no need of a Davidide. Something like this is also going on in Ezek. 40–48 where the king, or rather the נשיא ('prince'), is conceived as ruling over 'a kingdom without politics'. Levenson, *Theology of the Program of Restoration*, p. 111. The Chronicler, also, emphasizes the liturgical function of the Davidic monarchy at the expense of its political function. See P.R. Ackroyd, *Exile and Restoration* (Philadelphia: Westminster Press, 1968), p. 252.

2. Isa. 65.15-16 presents two difficulties. The first is how to construe the phrase והמיתך אדני יהוה ('the Lord YHWH will kill you'). The best proposal I have found is that of the new JPSV which takes this phrase as the content of the curse referred to earlier in the verse. The second difficulty concerns the twice recurring phrase באלהי אמן. Drawing on 2 Cor. 1.17-20 and Rev. 3.14, Blenkinsopp proposes that 'those who bless themselves in the land will bless themselves by the God Amen' refers to the new name which is to be given to God's people, that is, those who say 'yes' to God. Blenkinsopp, *A History of Prophecy in Israel*, pp. 277-78.

3. *Dawn*, p. 153.

4. Westermann contends that the passage proclaims salvation to the whole nation. Westermann, *Isaiah 40–66*, p. 411. But this is true only if these verses are read in isolation. In their present context they very clearly are meant to be a proclamation of salvation for that group which has been described in the previous verses as 'YHWH's servants'.

160   *The Opponents of Third Isaiah*

world'.[1] He has also suggested that in several places in the Hebrew Bible, the phrase שמים וארץ ('heaven and earth') may 'be an appellation of Jerusalem or its Temple'.[2] Given the similarity in wording between 65.17a and 18b, this raises the intriguing possibility that creating a new heaven and a new earth is actually a reference to the rebuilding of the temple-city, Jerusalem.[3] In other words, 65.17a and 18b are not mutually exclusive but rather complementary and perhaps even synonomous. Commenting on these two verses, Levenson states,

> Were Jerusalem, the city of YHWH's enthronement, other than a microcosm, these verses would manifest the anomaly that some have sensed in them: is God creating a new world—heaven and earth—or only a new Jerusalem? Is this renewal universal, as v. 17 would indicate, or only Jewish, as v. 18 would have it? In truth, in the minds of Jews for whom the bond of archetype and antitype had not been severed, the dichotomy would have seemed simplistic. The recreation of the temple-city could only have been conceived as a reenthronement of YHWH after a long period in which his palace lay in ruins, and his faithful subjects seemed abandoned and helpless. The reconstruction of the temple-city was not only a recovery of national honor, but also a renewal of the cosmos, of which the Temple was a miniature. It is for this reason that YHWH is here said not to *build* Jerusalem, but to *create* it, just as he creates the new heaven and the new earth.[4]

The remaining verses of the chapter describe the utopian bliss that 'YHWH's people' (65.19, 22) and 'YHWH's chosen' (65.22) will enjoy in the 'new' Jerusalem: the people and YHWH will be in a right relationship (65.23b-24), the people shall enjoy long (65.20, 22b) and prosperous lives (65.21-22a, 23a), Jerusalem shall be at peace (65.19), and the natural world will be at peace (65.25a).[5] All of these things are the blessings that will emanate from 'YHWH's holy mountain' (65.25b).

1. Levenson, *Creation and the Persistence of Evil*, p. 86. See also G.W. Ahlström, 'Heaven on Earth—At Hazor and Arad', in B.A. Pearson (ed.), *Religious Syncretism in Antiquity* (Missoula, MT: Scholars Press, 1975), pp. 67-83.
2. Levenson, *Creation and the Persistence of Evil*, p. 90.
3. In antiquity, temple and city were understood to be homologous. See M. Eliade, *Patterns in Comparative Religion* (New York: Sheed & Ward, 1958), pp. 373-85. See also Isa. 66.6.
4. Levenson, *Creation and the Persistence of Evil*, pp. 89-90.
5. The meaning of ונחש עפר לחמו ('the serpent will have the dust for food') is difficult. Most commentators regard it as a gloss. If it is original, Volz suggests the following meaning: 'Selbst die Schlange wird ein harmloses Tier sein, bloss Tier, nicht mehr Dämon', *Jesaja II*, p. 287.

Isa. 65.1-25 states that the failure of YHWH to act on his promises to restore Jerusalem is to be attributed to the cultic abuses of an anonymous 'you'.[1] The realization of these promises can only take place after YHWH has purged the community of everyone except his true servants.

Isaiah 66.1-24

General Observations

Most scholars agree in seeing 66.17-24 as a separate oracle, but there are major disagreements over 66.1-16. The tendency is to divide this section into several small units. Hanson has shown, however, that alternating words of salvation and judgment cannot be used as criteria for dividing post-exilic prophetic oracles, as has usually been done. Once this is recognized, 66.1-17 can be seen as a single salvation-judgment oracle.[2]

But what of the relationship between 66.1-17 and 66.18-24? It appears to be the case that there has been a conscious attempt to shape ch. 66 as a whole according to the pattern of the first chapter of the book of Isaiah. At the very least, there are an amazing number of lexical similarities between the two chapters. These have been pointed out by Liebreich:

66.1: השמים והארץ	compare 1.2: שמים ארץ
66.3: השור	compare 1.3: שור
66.3: זובח	compare 1.11: זבחיהם
66.3, 20: מנחה	compare 1.13: מנחה
66.3: און	compare 1.13: און
66.3: בחרו	compare 1.29: בחרתם
66.4: אבחר בחרו	compare 1.29: בחרתם
66.4: שמעו	compare 1.19: ושמעתם
66.4: הרע	compare 1.16: רע הרע
66.4: לא חפצתי	compare 1.11: לא חפצתי
66.5: שמעו דבר יהוה	compare 1.10: שמעו דבר יהוה
66.6: לאיביו	compare 1.24: מאויבי
66.8: גוי	compare 1.4: גוי

---

1. See R.P. Carroll, *When Prophecy Failed: Cognitive Dissonance in the Prophetic Traditions of the Old Testament* (New York: Seabury Press, 1979), pp. 150-56.

2. Hanson does not include v. 17, but in my view this verse goes more easily with what precedes than with what follows. Contrast Westermann who takes 66.17 as a totally independent unit, unrelated to its context. Westermann, *Isaiah 40-66*, p. 422.

66.8: ציון	compare 1.27: ציון
66.10, 20: ירושלם	compare 1.1: וירושלם
66.16: ובחרבו	compare 1.20: חרב
66.17: הגנות	compare 1.29: מהגנות
66.22: זרעכם	compare 1.4: זרע
66.23: חדש בחדשו שבת בשבתו	compare 1.13-14: חדש ושבת חדשיכם
66.24: הפשעים	compare 1.28: פשעים
66.24: לא תכבה	compare 1.31: ואין מכבה[1]

Since these similarities run throughout ch. 66 and are not confined to any single section of the chapter, the division of ch. 66 into at least two separate oracles may be an artificial one. To be sure, several different subjects are broached in Isaiah 66, and this gives the chapter a certain degree of complexity. But the solution to the dilemna may be that Isaiah 66 serves a dual purpose: it is both a summary of the message of Isaiah 56–66 and a conclusion to the book of Isaiah as a whole.

Exegesis

66.1-4. These verses present a maze of exegetical difficulties, with the problem beginning in the very first verse: השמים כסאי והארץ הדם רגלי אי זה בית אשר תבנו לי ואי זה מקום מנוחתי ('Heaven is my throne and earth is my footstool,[2] where/what is the house that you can build/are building/will build for me and where/what is my resting place?'[3]). Hanson has proposed that this represents 'a direct repudiation of the temple building campaign of Haggai' in 520 BCE and the theology that undergirds it.[4] Central to this argument is Hanson's claim that Haggai's theology is characterized by the attempt to manipulate YHWH by means of 'cultic orthopraxy', that it is an *ex opere operato* theology, one which operates

1. Liebreich, 'Compilation of the Book of Isaiah', pp. 276-77.
2. This is the only place where the earth is so described. Elsewhere it is always the 'ark' that serves as God's footstool.
3. MT points מקום as an absolute rather than a construct, and thus in apposition to מנוחתי. There is no need to emend.
4. *Dawn*, pp. 173-74. Prior to Hanson, interpretation of this passage fell into four general categories: (1) the passage is from the time of Ezra and constitutes an attack against the Samaritans who are attempting to build their own temple as a rival to the Jerusalem temple, c. 450 BCE (Duhm); (2) the passage dates to c. 520 BCE and is an attack by the prophet against the עם הארץ who desire to participate in the rebuilding of the Jerusalem temple (Elliger); (3) the passage is an attack against an attempt to rebuild the temple during the exile (Smart); (4) the passage is a repudiation of temple building as such and cannot be related to any concrete historical situation (Volz, Westermann; cf. also Acts 7.48-50).

with the simple equation: build the temple and YHWH will bless you. Haggai is representative of a 'religious stance' that is 'centered around the formal worship of the temple'. Over against this 'religious stance', 66.1-2 supposedly posits an alternative 'religious stance', one 'based on an attitude of humility and fear before Yahweh'.[1]

I contend that Hanson's summary of both Haggai's theology and the theology that comes to expression in Isa. 66.1-2 is overly simplistic and highly misleading. Haggai expressly states that the purpose of his prophecy is to attack an attitude that was evidently prevalent in the early restoration community, an attitude that said, 'the time has not yet come to rebuild the temple'.[2] Haggai is incensed that the people have spent their time working on their own houses while YHWH's house lies in ruins, and he argues that this is the explanation for the sorry state of conditions in the restoration community.[3] As Petersen has stated, Haggai's message is one in which 'he is spurring reflection on one essential topic: house/houses'.[4] The underlying assumption at work here cannot be reduced to an obsession with 'cultic orthopraxy', but rather it is the conviction that the rebuilding of YHWH's temple is the cornerstone upon which all hopes for realizing the promises of restoration depend.[5] It is the conviction that YHWH's 'house' is more important than the 'houses' of the people.

Third Isaiah also shares the conviction that the temple is central. This is evidenced by the fact that the theme of the restoration of temple and city is well-nigh omnipresent in Third Isaiah. If we leave Isa. 66.1-2 out

---

1. *Dawn*, p. 170. Hanson sees these two religious stances as having been in tension with one another throughout the history of the monarchy, and he quotes all of the well-known passages: Amos 5.21-24; Mic. 3.12; Isa. 1.10-11; Jer. 7; 11.14-15; 13.13; 26. In justification for claiming that the visionary disciples of Second Isaiah were representative of the anti-cultic religious stance, he states, 'In Second Isaiah, the temple plays virtually no part in the restoration hope', p. 179. But this underestimates the importance of Isa. 44.28-45.1.

2. See Hag. 1.2.

3. See Hag. 1.4-6. This is a significant difference from Ezra, who argues that the reason for the delay in the building of the temple was opposition from the people of the land. According to Haggai, it was not opposition but rather apathy that brought about the delay.

4. Petersen, *Haggai and Zechariah 1–8*, p. 50.

5. See R. Mason, 'The Prophets of the Restoration', in R. Coggins, A. Phillips and M. Knibb (eds.), *Israel's Prophetic Tradition: Essays in Honour of Peter R. Ackroyd* (Cambridge: Cambridge University Press, 1982), pp. 137-54.

of the discussion momentarily, it can be said that there is absolutely nothing in Third Isaiah that stands in contradiction with Haggai's conception of the temple. In fact, Third Isaiah and Haggai speak of the temple in almost identical terms. Hag. 2.6-7 states, כי כה אמר יהוה צבאות עוד אחת מעט היא ואני מרעיש את השמים ואת הארץ ואת הים ואת החרבה והרעשתי את כל הגוים ובאו חמדת כל הגוים ומלאתי את הבית הזה כבוד אמר יהוה צבאות ('Thus says YHWH of hosts, yet a little while longer and I will shake the heavens and the earth and the sea and the dry land, I will shake all the nations, and their choicest things shall come, and I will fill this house with glory, says YHWH of hosts'). This is echoed in Isa. 60.13: כבוד הלבנון אליך יבוא ברוש תדהר ותאשור יחדו לפאר מקום מקדשי ומקום רגלי אכבד ('The glory of Lebanon shall come to you, the cypress, the pine and the box, to beautify the place of my Sanctuary, and I will glorify the place of my feet').

If one interprets Isa. 66.1-2 either as a rejection of temple building as such (which is the most common interpretation) or merely as a rejection of Haggai's temple, then one must also claim that Isa. 66.1-2 stands in contradiction with the rest of Third Isaiah! This is, of course, not impossible, but there is a much more satisfying solution. The first stage of the solution is the translation of Isa. 66.1b, and in particular the phrase אי זה. The most common meaning of this phrase is 'where, then?', though in some cases it is best rendered as 'which?'[1] The demonstrative pronoun זה is added to the interrogative for emphasis. The best translation, therefore, of 66.1b is, 'Where is the house that you can/ would build for me? Where is the resting place (that you can/would build for me)?' There is no warrant for the translation, 'What is *this* house...what is *this* resting place?' When translated in its simplest and most normal way, it becomes clear that the verse is hypothetical[2] and means something like, 'Given the fact that I, YHWH, fill heaven and earth, what sort of house could you possibly build that could contain me?' That this verse is far from any kind of 'anti-temple' polemic is demonstrated by its affinities with 1 Kgs 8.27, a passage attributed to Solomon at the dedication of the first temple: כי האמנם ישב אלהים על הארץ הנה השמים ושמי השמים לא יכלכלוך אף כי הבית הזה אשר בניתי ('Can God really dwell on earth? Behold, heaven and highest heaven cannot contain you, how much less this

---

1. 1 Sam. 9.18; 1 Kgs 13.12; 22.24; 2 Kgs 3.8; Isa. 50.1; Jer. 6.16; Job 28.12, 20; 38.19, 24; Eccl. 2.3; 11.6; Est. 7.5; 2 Chron. 18.23.

2. This is supported by LXX: ποῖον οἶκον οἰκοδομήσετε μοι; ἢ ποῖος τόπος τῆς καταπαύσεώς μου.

house that I have built').[1] 1 Kgs 8.27 is undoubtedly exilic or post-exilic and reflects a debate on the question of where God actually lives. Solomon's speech in 1 Kgs 8.23-53 repeatedly emphasizes that the temple is a place of prayer and that God's true dwelling is in heaven.[2] We have already met with the idea of the temple as a house of prayer in Isa. 56.7. I would argue that Isa. 66.1, Isa. 56.7 and 1 Kgs 8.23-53 all reflect a certain reinterpretation of the temple, but to regard any or all of them as 'anti-temple' would be a gross misnomer.[3]

The passage then continues in 66.2: ואת כל אלה ידי עשׂתה ויהיו כל אלה נאם יהוה ואל זה אביט אל עני ונכה רוח וחרד על דברי ('My hand made all of these things, thus did all these things come into being, oracle of YHWH. Nevertheless, it is to this one that I look, to the humble, to the contrite, to the one who trembles at my word'). Once 66.2 is factored into the equation we see that the purpose of the oracle is simply to set up a contrast in order to elicit a response of great amazement. YHWH made heaven and earth, he is so great that obviously no earthly house could contain him, but in spite of all of that he still regards those of low degree.[4] The intended contrast is between God's greatness and the fact that he stoops to serve the lowly, not between those who are involved in temple building and those who are proponents of a temple-less religion.[5]

---

1. The idea is: O God, a mere house cannot contain you, nevertheless I have built you one anyway!

2. Contrast Ezek. 43.7. There the temple is the place אשר אשכן שם בתוך בני ישׂראל לעולם ('where I [YHWH] will tabernacle in the midst of the Israelites forever'). LXX preserves a different reading, one that is in harmony with 1 Kgs 8.23-53: ἐν οἷς κατασκηνώσει τὸ ὄνομά μου ἐν μέσῳ οἴκου Ισραηλ τόν αἰῶνα.

3. See Levenson, 'From Temple to Synagogue', p. 164. His main point is that, with the reinterpretation of the temple as a place of prayer, 'a new institution has begun to move into the quarters Isaiah knew and the psalmists celebrated. Its name is the "synagogue"'. Elsewhere Levenson has stated that the really remarkable thing about Isa. 66.1-2 is that whereas there are many places in the Hebrew Bible where the temple is described as a world or a microcosm, Isa. 66.1-2 is a passage where the world is described as a temple! See also Levenson, *Creation and the Persistence of Evil*, p. 88.

4. See Isa. 40.22; 57.15; 60.13; 63.15; Ps. 113; 138.6; 146; 147. This idea is of major importance in the Synoptic Gospels. See especially Mary's Magnificat in Luke 1.46-55.

5. Mention should be made of the interpretation of N.H. Snaith, 'Isaiah 40–66: A Study of the Teaching of the Second Isaiah and its Consequences', in H.M. Orlinsky and N.H. Snaith, *Studies on the Second Part of the Book of Isaiah* (VTSup, 14; Leiden: Brill, 1967), pp. 135-264. He contends that the phrase 'where is

As Blenkinsopp has stated, 'The balance between transcendence and intimacy is characteristic of Second Temple discourse about God'.[1]

Whereas the concept of the temple was the dominant topic in 66.1-2, 66.3-4 takes up the subject of what goes on in temples, namely, sacrifice.[2] Isa. 66.3 is every bit as difficult exegetically as 66.1-2:

שׁוֹחֵט הַשּׁוֹר מַכֵּה אִישׁ
זוֹבֵחַ הַשֶּׂה עֹרֵף כֶּלֶב
מַעֲלֵה מִנְחָה דַּם חֲזִיר
מַזְכִּיר לְבֹנָה מְבָרֵךְ אָוֶן

The verse is made up of four pairs of participial clauses. The second member of each pair is simply juxtaposed to the first without any connecting particle. The first member of each pair (a) describes a legitimate form of sacrifice: slaughtering an ox, sacrificing a lamb, making a grain offering, offering incense. The second member of each pair (b) refers to various forms of sacrifice considered aberrant by the Hebrew Bible: killing a man, breaking a dog's neck, offering swine's blood, blessing idols.[3] The exegetical problem is to decide how this juxtaposition of pairs of legitimate and illegitimate sacrifice is to be construed. There are several possibilities. All of the versions equate (b) with (a) by inserting a particle of comparison: כ (1QIsa), ὡς (LXX), *quasi* (Vulgate), אִיךְ (Syriac). Thus, 'he who slaughters an ox is just like him who kills a man...' This translation takes the verse as a condemnation of sacrifice as such. If this is correct, the verse would go beyond anything in the Hebrew Bible.[4] Another possibility is to insert the conjunction 'and'.

---

the house...' means the opposite of what it is usually interpreted to mean. Thus, in 66.1-2, instead of an attack on the temple, what we have is 'an urgent enquiry for the temple, as to why it has not been built. God may have His throne in the heavens, but he needs a resting place on earth', p. 241. Snaith's reading makes 66.1-2 virtually synonomous with the message of Haggai. This is provocative, but it fails to reckon with the relationship between 66.1 and 66.2 and the contrast that is implied there. In other words, it misplaces the emphasis of the passage.

1. Blenkinsopp, *Ezra–Nehemiah*, p. 307.

2. See 2 Chron. 7.12 where the Jerusalem temple is specifically called בֵּית זֶבַח ('a house of sacrifice').

3. Westermann translates מְבָרֵךְ אָוֶן as 'he who blesses the evil power', Westermann, *Isaiah 40–66*, p. 414.

4. Cf. 1 Sam. 15.22; Isa. 1.11; Hos. 6.6; Amos 5.25; Mic. 6.6-8; Ps. 40.7; 50; 51.17-19. With the rise of philosophy, bloody sacrifice came to be seen as highly problematic. The anti-sacrificial attitude of philosophy is quite evident in Paul. See Rom. 12.1.

Thus, 'he who slaughters an ox and kills a man...' This translation understands the verse to be a condemnation of syncretism, but it requires us to add a word not contained in the Hebrew in order to make the case. A third possibility has been suggested by Sasson who argues that (a) is to be understood as past tense and (b) as present tense. Thus, 'he who slaughter*ed* an ox *would now* kill a man...' Sasson's solution implies a condemnation of those who have rejected 'inherited traditions in favor of pagan rituals'.[1] This is an intriguing suggestion, but it is difficult to justify grammatically. There is yet a fourth possibility which has been suggested by Rofé.[2] He argues that (a) is to be understood as the subject and (b) as the predicate. In other words, (a) describes the who and (b) the what. The great advantage of this interpretation is that it can be defended grammatically based on the text as it stands. According to this reading, the subject (a) is none other than 'the priests who serve in the temple',[3] and they are charged with practicing various abominations (b). Biblical Hebrew offers numerous examples of 'the creation of

1. J.M. Sasson, 'Isaiah LXVI 3-4a', *VT* 26 (1976), pp. 199-207. He also makes the helpful suggestion that in the third pair, the participle מעלה does double-duty so as to allow the writer to preserve the four-word sequence for each clause. No emendation is necessary. He also cites the Mari letter, ARM II.37, as evidence that dog sacrifice derives from Hurrian practice. Dog sacrifice is known as well from Greek and Roman sources. Male adults, especially prisoners, were often sacrificed by the Greeks and Romans to ward off military defeat. Swine's blood was used by the Greeks for ritual purification, especially when innocent blood had been shed. He then relates all of this information to a Hittite text which speaks of sacrificing 'a man, a kid, a puppy-dog, and a suckling pig'. It is only in the Hittite archives where sacrifice of humans, dogs and pigs is prescribed for the same ritual. This is an almost exact parallel to Isa. 66.3.

2. A. Rofé, 'Isaiah 66.1-4: Judean Sects in the Persian Period as Viewed by Trito-Isaiah', in A. Kort and S. Morschauser (eds.), *Biblical and Related Studies Presented to Samuel Iwry* (Winona Lake: Eisenbrauns, 1985), pp. 205-17.

3. Rofé, 'Isaiah 66.1-4', p. 208. Two of the sacrificial acts, מעלה מנחה and מזכיר לבנה, were reserved exclusively for the priests. See Num 15.2-16; Lev. 2.2, 9, 16; 5.12; 6.8; 24.7. The other two, שוחט השור and זובח השה, were 'appropriated by the priesthood over time'. Rofé traces a progressive tendency to limit the permission to slaughter sacrifices. In P all Israelites could do so (Lev. 1.2-9, 10-13; 3.1-5, 6-11). Ezekiel, Ezra and Chronicles tend to limit it to the Levites (Ezek. 44.10-11; Ezra 6.20; 2 Chron. 30.16-17). Later the priests claimed the right to slaughter for themselves only. This can be seen already in 2 Chron. 29.23-34. The debate, however, was never settled, as can be seen by the various positions reflected in the Talmud. See *b. Ket.* 106a; *b. Pes.* 64b; *b. Ber.* 31b. See Smart, *History and Theology in Second Isaiah*, pp. 288-89. He also claims that it is the religious leaders of the community who are being attacked here.

synonyms for the names of professions by use of the participle, especially a participle in construct'.[1] In addition, the use of the synonym enables the writer to condemn only certain priests, that is, those currently serving in the temple, and not all priests. Rofé states, 'The rebuke of Trito-Isaiah is thus directed against the priests of his time, and lacking any indication to the contrary, it should be understood that the priests of Jerusalem are referred to'.[2]

At first glance Rofé's proposal sounds like Hanson. Rofé, however, is quick to distance himself from such ideas. He argues, as I have repeatedly done, that 'the establishment of a renewed cult is for Trito-Isaiah an essential factor in the restoration of Israel',[3] and that Third Isaiah's prophecies deal with issues quite different from those which Hanson supposes.[4] Isa. 66.3-4 is attacking a certain group of priests, not 'priestly theology'. Rofé also argues that the polemics of Third Isaiah have much in common with those of Ezra–Nehemiah in that both are united by their opposition to the Jerusalem establishment of priests[5] and notables, by their prohibition against carrying on business on the Sabbath, and by their animosity toward the wealthy who take advantage of the impoverished. Rofé's brilliant summary argument is as follows:

> The agreement between Trito-Isaiah and the views of Ezra and Nehemiah against the Jerusalem establishment explains the origin of his prophecy. In the more than one hundred years since the exile of Jehoiachin, Judaism took shape in the Babylonian exile. This denomination clearly delineates itself from its environment by prohibiting mixed marriages on the one hand, and by the formation of an institutionalized body of נלוים—'Gentiles who join themselves to the Lord'—on the other. It maintains a firm communal solidarity expressed, for example, in the obligation to redeem brethren slaves (cf. Neh 5.8). It strictly enforces cessation of commerce on Sabbath as an extension of the ancient prohibitions against land cultivation. It also nurtures impassionate dreams of rebuilding the city of

1. See Isa. 19.8; 54.16; Jer. 22.30; 33.18; 48.35; Ezek. 27.29; Amos 1.5, 8; Mal. 3.3; *b. Ber.* 28a; *y. Ber.* 5.1.

2. Rofé, 'Isaiah 66.1-4', p. 212.

3. Rofé, 'Isaiah 66.1-4', p. 213.

4. Rofé states that Third Isaiah 'does not censure the cult as being a web of rituals, sacrifices, stringency in matters of purity and impurity, or the confinement of the sacred and its custody in the hands of the Zadokite priests. Trito-Isaiah does not represent a religious movement fundamentally at odds with the priestly faith'. Rofé, 'Isaiah 66.1-4', pp. 212-13.

5. Note also that Malachi savages the priests who have 'turned aside from the way': ואתם סרתם מן הדרך (Mal. 2.8).

Jerusalem which conflict with the more realistic policies of the Jerusalemite notables. Trito-Isaiah represents these ideals. In a Jerusalem controlled by Joiakim (Neh. 12.10), Eliashib and their cohorts, Trito-Isaiah represents a vocal opposition, an opposition of mourners and afflicted (61.2). Some time (a generation?) afterward Nehemiah's time was ripe. However, Nehemiah did not act as an oppositionist but as a ruler. Thanks to his standing in the Persian court he was appointed governor of Judea by Artaxerxes I (465–424 BCE). The dreams of rebuilding Zion became with him a realistic plan for building the walls of Jerusalem. This plan was the basis of a consensus between Nehemiah, the official who came from Susa, and the Jerusalem elite. Afterward, in the wake of this first success, Nehemiah was able to impose other planks of his platform: the shaping of Judaism in the land of Israel in the image of the Eastern Jewish diaspora.[1]

66.5-6. Confirmation of Rofé's thesis that Third Isaiah and Ezra–Nehemiah stand in the same line of tradition has been provided by Blenkinsopp. He has called attention to the occurrence of the rare word החרדים ('those who tremble or quake') in Isa. 66.5.[2] The group singled out as the objects of YHWH's favor are called החרדים אל דברו ('those who tremble at his word'). In Ezra 9.4 virtually the same phrase is used to describe Ezra's support group: כל חרד בדברי אלהי ישראל ('all who tremble at the words of the God of Israel'). And in Ezra 10.3 a similar phrase occurs: החרדים במצות אלהינו ('those who tremble at the commandment of our God'). When this evidence is coupled with the fact that both Third Isaiah and Ezra–Nehemiah are intensely critical of the community leaders because of their involvement with syncretistic cultic practices, it becomes reasonable to conclude that the חרדים of Third Isaiah and the חרדים of Ezra suggest a common group.[3] It is also important to point out that it is the חרדים in Ezra who are behind the move to establish the תורת יהוה ('Torah of YHWH') as the official religion of Judah (Ezra 7.10). Although we can be sure that this 'Torah' was not identical with the Pentateuch,[4] it was undoubtedly very close to it.[5] In addition, one of

1. Rofé, 'Isaiah 66.1-4', pp. 216-17.

2. Blenkinsopp, 'The "Servants of the Lord" in Third Isaiah'.

3. A vastly different evaluation of this evidence has been offered by Sekine. See *Die Tritojesajanische Sammlung*, pp. 59-64.

4. Ezra knows nothing of Yom Kippur, for example.

5. See the careful discussion of this problem in Blenkinsopp, *Ezra–Nehemiah*, pp. 152-57. His conclusion is that Ezra's law 'appears to have been Deut. 12-26, in what precise form we cannot say, supplemented with cultic legislation conventionally attributed to P and H'. See also J. Blenkinsopp, 'The Mission of Udjahorresnet and those of Ezra and Nehemiah', *JBL* 106 (1987), pp. 409-21.

Ezra's primary theological concepts, that of זרע הקדש ('the holy seed'),
occurs elsewhere only in the Isaianic tradition, in Isa. 6.13. When all of
this is coupled with the fact that Ezra was perhaps regarded as the
Zadokite *par excellence* in the restoration period,[1] Hanson's thesis
begins to crumble.

In 66.5 a contrast is drawn between 'those who tremble at YHWH's
word' and their 'brothers', and the animosity between the two groups is
attributed to the tremblers' allegiance to YHWH's name: אמרו אחיכם שנאיכם
מנדיכם למען שמי ('your brothers who hate you and cast you out on
account of my name'). It is surely significant that the 'tremblers' refer
to their opponents as 'brothers'. It points to the fact that the two groups
in question 'are still members of the same community'.[2] Can these
'brothers' be any other than the priests who were savaged in 66.3-4 for
their aberrant cultic practices? Westermann says that this 'may' be the
case, but we ought not presume it.[3] Why not? The logic of the passage
demands that we read it in this way. Just as 'YHWH's servants' in
ch. 65 were contrasted with 'those who forget YHWH's holy mountain',
and just as the former had salvation proclaimed to them while the latter
were condemned, so here 'those who tremble at YHWH's word' are
contrasted with 'your brothers who hate you' (66.5), 'those who have
chosen their own way' (66.4). The conclusion to 66.5, והם יבשו ('but it is
they who will be put to shame'), sounds exactly like 65.13-14. Then in
66.6 the 'brothers who hate you' are given the disparaging title, the one
traditionally reserved for the foreign nations, of איביו ('his, i.e., YHWH's,
enemies'). The logic of the passage is completely lost on Westermann
who asserts that 'the subject here is a divine judgment on foreign
enemies of Israel'.[4]

66.7-17. Verses 7-14a return to the theme of the glorification of Zion
and state that Jerusalem is to be inherited by כל אהביה ('all those who
love her') and כל המתאבלים עליה ('all those who mourn for her'). These
designations are synonomous with החרדים אל דברו. Verse 14b is the key
transitional verse, because in it the transition from the proclamation of

---

1. See Appendix 3.
2. Westermann, *Isaiah 40–66*, p. 416.
3. Westermann, *Isaiah 40–66*, p. 416.
4. Westermann, *Isaiah 40–66*, p. 419. This is a perfect example of what Hanson
calls the tendency to atomize post-exilic prophetic oracles based upon pre-exilic
models.

salvation to the proclamation of judgment occurs. In v. 14bα all of the designations for the group singled out for salvation are subsumed under the title of עבדיו ('his, i.e., YHWH's, servants'). It is they who will inherit Zion, while in 14.bβ it is stated that YHWH's enemies will be destroyed: וזעם את איביו. This theme of judgment against YHWH's enemies is then elaborated in vv. 15-17. Isa. 66.15-16, like 66.6, utilizes the traditional language of judgment against the nations. Contrary to Westermann who argues that 66.17 is an independent unit, having 'no natural connection with what comes before and after it',[1] 66.17 is to be seen as an intimate part of the proclamation of judgment in 66.14bβ-17. It is 66.17 that informs the reader that YHWH's impending judgment is not intended primarily for the foreign nations but rather for those within the restoration community who practice aberrant cultic acts: המתקדשים והמטהרים אל הגנות אחר אחד בתוך אכלי בשר החזיר והשקץ והעכבר יחדו יספו נאם יהוה ('Those who sanctify themselves and purify themselves for the gardens, after one in the midst,[2] who eat swine's flesh and detestable things[3] and mice, shall perish together, oracle of YHWH'). These accusations are of a piece with those of 66.3-4, 65.1-7, 11 and 57.3-13. What all of the cultic accusations in Third Isaiah have in common is that they are all summarily condemned in the Pentateuch.

66.18-24. Whereas 66.1-17 focused directly on the restoration community, 66.18-24 turns toward the diaspora. There are manifold similarities with 56.1-8.[4] Verse 18 is corrupt,[5] but the general idea is clear: the nations shall stream to Jerusalem. That this streaming to Jerusalem contains a note of judgment is indicated by the fact that 66.19 speaks of פליטים ('survivors').[6] These survivors shall then be sent to the nations[7] as heralds of YHWH's כבוד ('glory'). In Isa. 40.5 the manifestation

1. Westermann, *Isaiah 40–66*, p. 422.
2. The phrase recalls Ezek. 8.7-11. *Qere*, 1QIsa, and many manuscripts read the feminine, אחת, suggesting a priestess. So Whybray, *Isaiah 40–66*, p. 288.
3. See Lev. 11.
4. See Sekine, *Die Tritojesajanische Sammlung*, p. 57.
5. See the commentaries for various proposals.
6. See 45.20 and Sehmsdorf, 'Studien zur Redaktionsgeschichte von Jesaja 56–66', pp. 563-65.
7. A distinction is evidently implied between two different groups of nations. Perhaps the first group refers to nations located near Jerusalem and the second to those far away. So Whybray, *Isaiah 40–66*, p. 290. For a similar list, see Gen. 10.2-5; 1 Chron. 1.5-7.

of YHWH's glory is expressly linked to the new act of redemption proclaimed by Second Isaiah. There it is stated: ונגלה כבוד יהוה וראו כל בשר יחדו ('YHWH's glory shall be revealed and all flesh shall see it together'). A similar meaning is probably implied here. The idea is that the nations must see what YHWH has done for Israel. Isa. 66.20: והביאו את כל אחיכם מכל הגוים מנחה ליהוה...על הר קדשי ירושלם...כאשר יביאו בני ישראל את המנחה בכלי טהור בית יהוה ('and they shall bring all your brothers out of all the nations to my holy mountain Jerusalem as an offering to YHWH, just as the Israelites bring an offering in a clean vessel to YHWH's temple'). 'They' refers to the פליטים of 66.19. 'Your brothers' undoubtedly refers to dispersed Israelites. The comparison is striking. Just as the native Israelites bring the מנחה to the temple, so these פליטים will bring the dispersed Israelites *as* a מנחה to the temple. This is perhaps a midrash on Isa. 56.7.[1]

Verse 21 is a classical *crux*: וגם מהם אקח לכהנים ללוים אמר יהוה ('And I will even take some of them for[2] levitical priests,[3] says YHWH'). What is the antecedent of מהם? Grammatically, the case could be made for either the פליטים or the אחים, so the answer must be based on the context. Most commentators prefer the former and see this verse as a 'radical reversal of the traditional attitude towards foreigners'.[4] But this interpretation is linked to the conviction that the overall attitude toward foreigners in 66.18-24 is a positive one. I would contend that, although foreigners play a prominent role in 66.18-24, they are viewed throughout as subservient, much in the same way as they are in Isaiah 60–62. It is consistent with this picture to see 66.21 as referring to diaspora Israelites. The point of the verse, therefore, would be to say that 'the monopoly of the Jerusalem priests will thus be broken'.[5] This interpretation, in turn,

---

1.   See also Isa. 60.4-9. Westermann regards 66.20, 22-24 as incompatible with vv. 18-19, 21, because of the former's emphasis on sacral matters. The incompatibility, however, resides only in his own theological presuppositions.

2.   1QIsa adds ליא ('for myself').

3.   Literally, 'for priests, for Levites'. The ל may be repeated to indicate that ללוים stands in apposition with כהנים, so GKC §131h, or it may reflect a scribal attempt to distinguish the Levites from the priests. Some manuscripts and the versions make this explicit by inserting the word 'and'. MT represents the *lectio difficilior* and is intelligible as it stands. It is, however, impossible to decide if the nouns are supposed to be determinate or not.

4.   So Whybray, *Isaiah 40–66*, p. 292.

5.   Rofé, 'Isaiah 66.1-4', p. 212.

explains the transition to 66.22 where it is stated, כן יעמד זרעכם ושמכם
('thus shall your seed and your name be established').[1]

Verses 23-24 combine elements of 'everlasting worship' and
'everlasting judgment'.[2] The latter concept is unique in the Hebrew Bible
and is to be seen as 'the earliest idea of hell as the state of perdition'.[3] In
spite of Smart's claim that vv. 15-24 'form a most unsatisfactory
conclusion to the chapter and the book',[4] the final two verses reinforce
the message with which the book began, that those who 'rebel' (פשע)
against YHWH shall perish.

1. This is also the view of Sehmsdorf, 'Studien zur Redaktionsgeschichte von
Jesaja 56–66', p. 567: 'Doch so sehr sich diese Deutung auf V. 20 berufen könnte,
wo die Völker ja bereits eine priesterliche Rolle wahrnehmen, so wenig ist dann das
זרעכם in V. 22 verständlich. Denn es ist kaum zu begreifen, wie durch eine Berufung
von Nichtisraeliten zum Priesterdienst der biologische Fortbestand Israels, das nach
V. 20 hier angeredet wird (אחיכם), gesichert sein könnte.'
2. Westermann, *Isaiah 40–66*, p. 428. See Zech. 12; 14; Joel 4; Zeph. 3.8;
Isa. 13–14; 24–27. The linking of new moon and Sabbath in 66.23 is paralleled in
Num. 28.9-15 and recalls Isa. 1.13. See also Amos 8.4-6
3. Westermann, *Isaiah 40–66*, p. 428.
4. Smart, *History and Theology in Second Isaiah*, p. 290.

Chapter 5

CONCLUSION: THE OPPONENTS OF THIRD ISAIAH

The fundamental exegetical claim of Hanson's *The Dawn of Apocalyptic* is that the polemical oracles of Third Isaiah represent an attack on the Zadokite restoration program of Ezekiel 40–48 in particular and on priestly, Pentateuchal theology in general. But because the latter is not simply a logical extension of the former, this twin claim of Hanson's is problematic. One could certainly have been anti-Zadokite without at the same time having been opposed to the cult as such. This inconsistency, however, runs throughout Hanson's work and is never resolved.[1]

In spite of all of the pains that Hanson has gone through in order to set up a dichotomy between the Zadokites on the one hand and the visionary disciples of Second Isaiah and disenfranchised Abiatharite Levites on the other, it is clear that the real dichotomy that he works with is between 'prophetic' theology/religion and 'priestly' theology/religion. It would be fair to say that Hanson is not interested in the Zadokites and the Levites as such but rather in the theology, and more precisely the 'religious mentality' that each supposedly represented. For him priestly theology[2] is essentially an *ex opere operato* theology, one that is characterized by the attempt to manipulate the deity through pagan superstition. Prophetic theology, however, relies solely on God's word and God's direct intervention.[3] Establishing a distinction between

1. See Carroll, 'Twilight of Prophecy'.
2. 'Priestly theology' refers to the theology of P, Ezek. 40–48, Haggai and Zech. 1–8.
3. This prophet–priest dichotomy is well-nigh omnipresent in Protestant biblical scholarship, deriving primarily from Wellhausen. The following quote from C.H. Dodd, *The Epistle of Paul to the Romans* (London: Hodder & Stoughton, 1932), p. 165, is typical: 'The righteousness of Leviticus is, in the main, hard and mechanical, and its emphasis is on ceremonial with no moral value. The Deuteronomic code, which was sponsored on its promulgation by the prophetic school, has much more of the prophetic spirit in it; it bases righteousness on the love of God which

these two 'mentalities' is important to Hanson because one of his central scholarly interests is in pointing out areas of theological tension within the Bible. Isaiah 56–66 and Ezekiel 40–48 are for him a supreme example of this theological tension. He regards these two collections of

should be provoked by His grace towards his people'. On the issue of what the prophets actually were and did, see G.W. Ahlström, 'Some Remarks on Prophets and Cult', in J.C. Rylarsdam (ed.), *Transitions in Biblical Scholarship* (Essays in Divinity, 6; Chicago: University of Chicago Press, 1968), pp. 113-29; Barton, *Oracles of God*; D.L. Petersen, 'Ways of Thinking about Israel's Prophets', in D.L. Petersen (ed.), *Prophecy in Israel* (Issues in Religion and Theology, 10; Philadelphia: Fortress Press; London: SPCK, 1987), pp. 1-21.

One would be on firm ground to assert that a prophet–priest dichotomy, though common among modern scholars, is unknown in the Hebrew Bible. When it comes to condemnation, the Bible typically condemns both prophets and priests alike. See, among numerous examples, Isa. 28.7. But perhaps the greatest problem with this dichotomy is that in the case of the three most famous prophets, Isaiah, Jeremiah and Ezekiel, the prophetic role/identity and the priestly role/identity significantly overlap. Also, Second Isaiah has numerous points of contact with the priestly tradition. See R.R. Wilson, 'The Community of Second Isaiah', in C.R. Seitz (ed.), *Reading and Preaching the Book of Isaiah* (Philadelphia: Fortress Press, 1988), pp. 53-70; C. Stuhlmueller, *Creative Redemption in Deutero-Isaiah* (AnBib, 43; Rome: Biblical Institute Press, 1970). The prophet Malachi attacks the priesthood not out of any conviction that prophecy is good and priesthood is bad, but precisely because the priesthood of his day was not living up to his own high expectations of what priesthood ought to be. On the other hand, when prophets or priests are attacked it is not because of their adherence to 'prophetic' theology or 'priestly' theology, but because of their adherence to a cult and/or god which the biblical writer considers aberrant.

It is evident that Hanson belongs to the school of thought that asserts that the end or the 'death' of prophecy was brought about by the ascension of the priesthood in the post-exilic period. This position can also be attributed to the legacy of Wellhausen. The living word of prophecy is seen to have been crushed by the dead letter of the priestly Torah. A new version of this position has been articulated by Carroll, *When Prophecy Failed*, who argues that prophecy ended or died because it 'failed'. He refers specifically to the failure of prophetic promises of salvation to materialize. This position has been effectively critiqued by Mason, 'The Prophets of the Restoration', pp. 141-42. He states, 'It is strange that, if earlier prophecy were regarded as having proved such a "failure", the post-exilic period should have been the time when the present prophetic collections were formed and invested with increasing authority'. He adds, 'In fact, it seems far more likely that prophecy began to die, or change, after the exile, not because of its failure but because of its "success"'. Not only was the Torah written down, but the prophets were as well. Once that had taken place, prophecy was transformed into exegesis. On this whole issue, see Barton, *Oracles of God*.

texts as representing mutually exclusive and irreconcilable theological positions. It has been my goal to contest this provocative claim.

I contend that Hanson's prophet–priest dichotomy is basically useless when it comes to identifying who or what is being attacked in Third Isaiah.[1] With regard to the cultic abuses that are condemned by Third Isaiah, I have argued that there is not a single book in the Hebrew Bible that supports these kinds of cultic acts, and certainly not the P tradition! What does this imply? Hanson would have us believe that Third Isaiah is an attack on Zadokite cultic religion and especially the theology that undergirds it, that is, the Pentateuch and Ezekiel 40–48. He refers to the protagonists as representatives of two distinct religious mentalities, the visionary and the hierocratic, with the visionary being primarily identified with the prophetic tradition.[2] But in my view Hanson's thesis is simply a new version of a very old theological assertion. It is the assertion that the two major sections of the Hebrew Bible, תורה and נביאים, represent two distinct religious mentalities. It is the assertion that it was the *prophets* who were 'the carriers of authentic YHWHism',[3] a YHWHism that was directly opposed to the priestly, legal and temple-

---

1. The same could also be said regarding Hanson's curious tendency to associate the notion of 'inclusivity' with the prophetic tradition and 'exclusivity' with the priestly. Accordingly, the great sin of the Zadokites is that they were 'exclusive'. At times Hanson even speaks of Third Isaiah and the prophetic tradition as if they were synonomous with modern-day egalitarianism. But if there is anything that can be said with absolute and total conviction about the Hebrew Bible, it is that Israel's prophets were anything but modern day egalitarians. As Levenson has stated, 'Those who read either the Hebrew Bible or the New Testament from the vantage-point of social history alone will find little to encourage them if the values by which they assess this literature derive from an egalitarian theory of social justice. They should, however, have the honesty to acknowledge that the ways of the biblical God are not the ways of egalitarian man. For it is essential to recognize that the action of God as conceived in the Hebrew Bible and the New Testament alike is mediate, that is to say, exercised through human agents whose prominence could not have been predicted and whose role in the divine drama sets them off from their equals.' Levenson, *Theology of the Program of Restoration*, p. 148. Levenson's scathing critique should not be misconstrued to imply that the Hebrew Bible can be read without any social history vantage point. That would be to misunderstand him completely. His concern is, rather, to criticize reading the Bible exclusively from the vantage point of social history. The problem with this latter approach is its tendency to be highly reductionistic.

2. Excluding of course Ezekiel, Haggai and Zech. 1–8!

3. J.D. Levenson, 'The Temple and the World', *JR* 64 (1984), pp. 275-98, p. 277.

centered Pentateuch. But both this old argument and Hanson's new version of it commit the same error, and that is that they miss the forest for the trees. To be sure, the Hebrew Bible is a pluriform document and the history of its transmission is singularly complex, but on certain key theological issues, what I would call 'the forest', it is thoroughly uniform. As an alternative to Hanson, I maintain that what is being attacked in Third Isaiah in general and in passages like Isa. 57.3-13, 65.1-7, 11-15, 66.3-4, 17 in particular, is the very same thing that is attacked in manifold places throughout the Hebrew Bible, namely, the traditional, syncretistic cult of YHWH.[1] To put it simply, those who interpret the Hebrew Bible according to a תורה versus נביאים schema, and this is essentially what Hanson has done, only in a more sophisticated way, have failed to see that these two sections (even these two 'mentalities', if you will) have far more in common with one another than they have apart.[2] As Levenson has stated, 'the prophetic groups, with whom the sympathies of the modern biblical theologians lie, were not the bearers of some radically different mode of consciousness from that of the often execrated Temple party'.[3] On the contrary, 'they are to be located at a different point within the self-same culture'.[4] This is never more true than with the issue of the cultic polemics of the Hebrew Bible. תורה and נביאים are together an apology for the city of Jerusalem and its temple cult as outlined in the Pentateuch.[5]

The distinction between my thesis and that of Hanson is great. By painting the Hebrew Bible as resulting from ongoing conflicts between visionary (prophetic) and hierocratic (priestly) elements, and by elucidating the polemics of Third Isaiah according to this same dichotomy, I would argue that Hanson has focused our attention on an issue of relative inconsequence and has missed what is the fundamental issue in the cultic polemics of the Hebrew Bible, namely, the battle with the traditional, syncretistic cult of YHWH, a battle in which the priestly, Pentateuchal tradition and the prophetic tradition fought on the same side!

---

1. This is Morton Smith's phrase. See Smith, *Palestinian Parties and Politics*. See below for an explication of the term 'syncretism'.

2. This is, I think, the proper meaning of the old rabbinic dictum that נביאים serves to comment upon and interpret תורה.

3. But this is precisely what Hanson wants us to believe.

4. Levenson, 'The Temple and the World', p. 291.

5. Another way to put this is that the canonical prophets are orthodox Jewish prophets!

This proposal is consistent with results that are currently coming out of studies on the history of Israelite and Judean religion. In summarizing the present state of the question, P. Kyle McCarter has forcefully argued that the shape of the religion espoused by the final form of the Hebrew Bible was not the official religion of the pre-exilic period but only one 'branch' of that religion. He states,

> Of the competing parties in preexilic Yahwism only one was vindicated by history, and its thought is preserved in the Bible. But the biblical writers themselves indicate that the branch of preexilic religion they are embracing was a dissenting viewpoint during much of the Israelite monarchy. It was championed by the prophetic party but excluded from the official circles of the court and Temple except during the reigns of a few kings whom the writers regard as reformers.[1]

Morton Smith has referred to the 'branch' of pre-exilic YHWHism that the final shape of the Hebrew Bible endorses as the 'Yahweh-alone party'.[2] It was this group that opposed the traditional cult of Israel and Judah, a cult that was characterized by a syncretistic form of worship, that is, the worship of YHWH along with other deities.[3]

Smith has argued that only such an understanding of the historical development and transformation of Israelite religion, that is, that the religion espoused by the Hebrew Bible was not the official religion of

---

1. McCarter, 'Aspects of the Religion of the Israelite Monarchy: Biblical and Epigraphic Data', p. 137. See Appendix 4.

2. He uses the term 'party' to mean 'a body of like-minded individuals; it does not imply formal organization', Smith, *Palestinian Parties and Politics*, p. 10. According to Smith, the 'Yahweh-alone party' was devoted to the exclusive worship of YHWH, and it is this party whose theology is represented as the official theology of the Hebrew Bible as we have it today. Smith's thesis of a 'Yahweh-alone party' has been picked up and developed by Bernhard Lang, *Monotheism and the Prophetic Minority: An Essay in Biblical History and Sociology* (Sheffield: Almond Press, 1983); *idem*, 'Neues über die Geschichte des Monotheismus', *TQ* 163 (1983), pp. 54-58; *idem*, 'Zur Entstehung des biblischen Monotheismus', *TQ* 166 (1986), pp. 135-42.

3. The term 'syncretism' often carries with it a pejorative nuance. It usually implies the 'pollution' or 'contamination' by something foreign of that which was originally 'pure'. The standard definition of syncretism is: 'the union of religious phenomenon [*sic*] from two historically separate systems or cultures', Smith, *The Early History of God*, p. xx. For Morton Smith, however, syncretism carries with it no value judgment. It is simply used as a term to define the opposite of the exclusive worship of YHWH.

the pre-exilic period, makes it possible to account 'for one of the most important, peculiar and neglected characteristics of the Old Testament: the representation of the Israelites as constantly in conflict with the demands of their own religion'.[1] It is this characteristic that sets the Hebrew Bible apart from all other ancient literature. As Smith states, 'that constantly recurrent national apostasy should be made the leitmotif of an entire literature is something unparalleled in antiquity; it requires explanation'. The explanation is that the tradition that comes to expression in the final form of the Hebrew Bible is 'the tradition of a minority party which has lived its life in conflict with the majority of its people and has seen its brief moments of victory again and again reversed by the return of the majority to their traditional ways'.[2] This is precisely what we find in Third Isaiah. Our exegesis has shown that the polemics of Third Isaiah closely resemble those of the pre-exilic prophets. A logical explanation for this state of affairs is not that various oracles of Third Isaiah are to be assigned a pre-exilic date, but rather that Third Isaiah provides evidence that many typical pre-exilic cultic practices persisted into the restoration period. In other words, the battle with the traditional, syncretistic cult of YHWH which is so prominently in evidence in pre-exilic texts was still being waged in the restoration period.

The fact that all of the cultic practices attacked by Third Isaiah are summarily condemned not only by the pre-exilic prophets but also by the Pentateuch is of crucial significance. First of all, it shows that Third Isaiah and the 'priestly' Pentateuch, at least in regard to these basic cultic issues, are in total agreement. And secondly, if the Pentateuch had already been established as the official religious document of Judah and Jerusalem, all that Third Isaiah would have had to do in order to make its case is appeal to it. But it does not. The most logical inference is, therefore, that the Pentateuch had not yet been established as the official religious document of Judah and Jerusalem at the time when the oracles of Third Isaiah were composed.

My proposal suggests that Third Isaiah is representative of the interests and the theology of the Babylonian גולה; in other words, that Third Isaiah was written *by* the very group that Hanson claims it was written *against!* In one respect this is not new. Numerous scholars have interpreted the restoration period under the rubric of a Babylonian–Palestinian

1. Smith, *Palestinian Parties and Politics*, pp. 35-36.
2. Smith, *Palestinian Parties and Politics*, pp. 35-36.

dichotomy and have argued that Third Isaiah is a representative of the theology of Babylonian diaspora Judaism.[1] Where we differ with previous proposals is in regard to the evaluation of the 'Palestinian' aspect of this dichotomy. The most common interpretation has seen Third Isaiah as opposing either the Samaritans or a group of people who were later to become the Samaritans.[2] The other major alternative views Third Isaiah's opponents as either the 'pagan' peoples of Palestine or as representatives of Israelite 'popular' religion.[3]

The anti-Samaritan hypothesis suffers from two major flaws. The first is that, properly speaking, the origins of 'Samaritanism' are to be located in the Hellenistic and Hasmonean periods.[4] The second and more important flaw in the hypothesis is that it misconstrues what was at issue in the strife between Jews and Samaritans. The Samaritans were not proponents of the kinds of cultic practices that are attacked in Third Isaiah. They were just as much opposed to child sacrifice, the worship of Gad and Meni, necromancy and so on, as were the Jews of Jerusalem. On issues such as these the Samaritan Pentateuch and the Jewish Pentateuch are in harmony.[5] Where they differ is in regard to the question of the locus of the legitimate site of the cult of YHWH: is it Jerusalem or is it Gerizim? To be sure, later Jewish tradition associated all kinds of abuses with the Samaritans, and later Samaritan tradition associated all kinds of abuses with the Jews, but most of this polemic can be traced to the attempt on the part of both traditions to demonstrate their respective antiquity. Each tradition attacks the other in the same way. The claim is made that 'our' religion is ancient and pure, 'yours' is new and corrupt. Those who see either the Samaritans or the forerunners of the Samaritans

---

1.   Ezek. 11.14-21 and 33.23-29 provide important evidence of animosity between the Babylonian and Palestinian communities. The animosity centered on two issues: (1) what does exile imply about one's status as people of God? (2) does the land of Israel belong to those who were exiled or to those who were not?

2.   This anti-Samaritan hypothesis is to be attributed to Duhm. The most recent defender of the hypothesis is Snaith, 'Isaiah 40–66'.

3.   This thesis originated with Elliger.

4.   See the discussion of the 'Samaritan Schism' in Chapter 2.

5.   See Purvis, *The Samaritan Pentateuch*, p. 12. He argues that 'Samaritanism' is dependent on or is an offshoot from orthodox Judaism. The point is that if one wants to describe the Samaritans as heretics, one would have to concede that 'they were extremely orthodox—even fundamentalistic—heretics'. See also Blenkinsopp, 'Yahweh and Other Deities', p. 365.

as the people who are being attacked in Third Isaiah have simply taken over at face value the later Jewish polemic regarding the pagan origins of Samaritanism.

The second hypothesis suffers from similar flaws. It operates out of the still common presupposition that the kinds of cultic acts attacked in Third Isaiah never had a legitimate place in the cult of YHWH, or conversely that a YHWH cult that did contain such things was never legitimate. On that basis it is concluded that Third Isaiah must be attacking either paganism or the unofficial 'popular' religion of the people. But modern research into the history of the religion of Israel and Judah has seriously called this presupposition into question, and it ought to be abandoned.

My proposal emphasizes that Third Isaiah was not fighting against some sort of 'pagan' (non-YHWHistic) religion but rather against traditional, syncretistic YHWHists, people whose religious practices had a long history in the (pre-exilic) kingdoms of Israel and Judah. It is this that gives the cutting-edge to the oracles of Third Isaiah, in that it is precisely traditional members of the people Israel who are being excluded from the community. Hanson is correct in asserting that the standard prophetic mode of viewing the world as divided into two parts, Israel on the one hand and the nations on the other, undergoes a fundamental change in Third Isaiah, and he is also correct that this change in prophetic world-view manifests itself in a bitter, intra-community struggle in which 'Israel' is divided off from 'Israel', but he is wrong both in regard to the identity of the protagonists and with respect to the theological issues that are at stake in the struggle.

The underlying theological structure with which Third Isaiah works was formed in the Babylonian diaspora. The oracles are intimately related to those of Second Isaiah, the great prophet of the exile, whose most basic theological assertion is that YHWH alone is God: אני יהוה ואין עוד ('I am YHWH, there is no other').[1] Third Isaiah goes beyond Second Isaiah, though, in that Third Isaiah redefines YHWH's people as those who abstain from various kinds of traditional, syncretistic cultic acts. This redefinition was to become complete with the promulgation of the priestly Pentateuch. The Pentateuch enshrined once and for all time the theological convictions of Second Isaiah and elucidated how the faithful follower of YHWH is to worship him properly. Once this interpretive

---

1.   Isa. 43.11; 44.6, 8; 45.5, 6, 14, 21, 22; 46.9.

move had taken place, it can be said, at least theoretically, that 'Israel' ceased to be 'a national-ethnic entity' and became 'a confessional community'.[1] The oracles of Third Isaiah are to be seen as playing an integral role in this process.

1.   Blenkinsopp, 'Yahweh and Other Deities', p. 363.

Even conservative estimates agree that many biblical books were composed in their entirety during the Persian period: Haggai, Zechariah, Malachi, Chronicles, Ezra, Nehemiah, Jonah, Ecclesiastes, Song of Songs, Job, probably Joel and Ruth, and perhaps Esther. Substantial portions of other books also date to this period: Dan. 1–6, Isa. 56–66, Prov. 1–9 and many Psalms. Of these Persian period works, only Haggai, Zechariah, Ezra, Nehemiah and Esther consciously and explicitly identify themselves as such. The vast majority of Persian period biblical texts are either anonymous or pseudonymous works.

Perhaps the major issue in the study of the Hebrew Bible concerns the dating of the Pentateuch, specifically the sources of the Pentateuch, and more specifically the relative dating of the Priestly source. The primary text for the investigation of this problem remains J. Wellhausen, *Prolegomena to the History of Ancient Israel*.[1] Simply stated, Wellhausen argued that the Prophets precede the Law. He began his massive work with this provocative statement: 'In the following pages it is proposed to discuss the place in history of the "law of Moses;" more precisely, the question to be considered is whether that law is the starting-point for the history of ancient Israel, or not rather for that of Judaism, i.e., of the religious communion which survived the destruction of the nation by the Assyrians and Chaldeans' (p. 1). The most thorough response to Wellhausen has been the one mounted by Y. Kaufmann, *The Religion of Israel*.[2] Kaufmann accepted the source-critical division of the Pentateuch made famous under the names of Graf and Wellhausen but vehemently disagreed on the dating of these sources, arguing for the great antiquity of JE and P. He stated the goal of his work as follows: 'The Torah—it will be shown—is the literary product of the earliest stage of Israelite religion, the stage prior to literary prophecy. Although its compilation and canonization took place later, its sources are demonstrably ancient—not in part, not in their general content, but in their entirety, even to their language and formulation' (pp. 1-2). The subsequent literature is truly immense, and there is nothing approaching a consensus. For example, the major work of M. Weinfeld, *Deuteronomy and the Deuteronomic School*,[3] argues that P precedes D. Meanwhile the work of Van Seters threatens to reformulate all of the issues. He has argued for an exilic

---

1. Repr.; Gloucester, MA: Peter Smith, 1983.
2. (Trans. and abridged M. Greenberg; Chicago: University of Chicago Press, 1960), especially pp. 153-211.
3. (Oxford: Clarendon Press, 1972), pp. 179-89.

dating of those Abrahamic traditions that are usually ascribed to J and dated to the early monarchical period.[1]

In spite of the disagreement on the dating of the Pentateuchal sources, there is general agreement, however, regarding the final redaction of the Pentateuch. Scholars who are inclined toward the position of Wellhausen are willing to concur with the opposition that the Pentateuch contains material that dates from the entire history of the nations of Israel and Judah, while scholars who incline toward Kaufmann concur that the Pentateuch, in its final shape, is a product of the Persian period and that the person of Ezra played a significant role in this process. But the fundamental issue, the relationship between pre-exilic Israelite religion and post-exilic 'Israelite' religion, that divides these two camps still remains: Was the post-exilic religion basically a continuation of that which had gone before (so Kaufmann), or was it a fundamentally new and different religion (so Wellhausen)?

1. See J. Van Seters, *Abraham in History and Tradition* (New Haven: Yale University Press, 1975); *idem*, 'Confessional Reformulation in the Exilic Period', *VT* 22 (1972), pp. 448-59. Van Seters's thesis has received recent support from T.L. Thompson, *The Early History of the Israelite People: The Archaeological and Written Evidence* (Leiden: Brill, 1992).

APPENDIX 2

In spite of the fact that the historical books of the Hebrew Bible relate virtually nothing about conditions in exile, a substantial Judaite presence in Mesopotamia during the Babylonian and Persian periods is well established, based upon the occurrence of Hebrew personal names in Mesopotamian documents. Morton Smith has stated, 'Their (i.e., Hebrew personal names') increasing frequency during the late Babylonian and early Persian periods presumably reflects the arrival of Judean exiles in Babylonia and their gradual rise in social and economic life'.[1] But Smith adds the qualification that certain things must be taken into account when using this evidence: first, non-Judaites could and did adopt Hebrew names for themselves, and secondly, some Judaites had Babylonian names, for example, Zerubbabel and Sheshbazzar.

The main evidence for a substantial Judaite presence in Mesopotamia is the Murashu family archive from Nippur which contains a trove of over 650 cuneiform tablets reflecting the business activities of the Murashu family. The archive dates from 455 to 403 BCE. Out of some 200 settlements in the area of Nippur, Judaites are linked to 28. Judaites are known to have been land owners, business agents, witnesses to contracts, managers, shepherds, slaves. Though the majority belonged to the lower classes of the society, in general the Judaites prospered relatively well in Babylonia.[2]

According to Josephus, conditions in exile were good enough that many Judaites actually refused to return home after the edict of Cyrus because they did not want to give up their property: Ταῦτα Κύριου καταγγείλαντος τοῖς Ἰσραηλίταις, ἐξώρμησαν οἱ τῶν δύο φυλῶν ἄρχοντες τῆς Ἰούδα καὶ Βενιαμίτιδος οἵ τε Λευῖται καὶ οἱ ἱερεῖς εἰς τὰ Ἱεροσόλυμα· πολλοὶ γὰρ κατέμειναν ἐν τῇ Βαβυλῶνι, τὰ κτήματα καταλιπεῖν οὐ θέλοντες (*Ant.* 11.8).

The most remarkable fact about the Judaite contingent in Babylonia was that it, and it alone, among ancient exiled peoples was able to maintain its ethnic and religious identity over a period of many centuries. Babylonia under the Achaemenids was a melting pot of peoples and cultures, and as a result it usually required only a short amount of time for a foreign group to be thoroughly assimilated into the surrounding society, both religiously and culturally. Judaites were only one of many groups that had been exiled to Mesopotamia, but the other groups, through assimilation, disappeared from history rather rapidly. The Judaites, on the other hand, maintained

1.   M. Smith, 'Jewish Religious Life in the Persian Period', in Davies and Finkelstein (eds.), *The Cambridge History of Judaism*, I, p. 220 (parentheses mine).
2.   So E. Bickermann, 'The Babylonian Captivity', in Davies and Finkelstein (eds.), *The Cambridge History of Judaism*, I, pp. 346-48.

themselves as a 'distinct social group' in Mesopotamia from the sixth century BCE until the Middle Ages.[1] This is not at all to deny Babylonian and Persian influence on these people. That there was substantial influence is clear from the fact that the creation story in Gen. 1.1-2.4a shares so much common material with the Babylonian creation epic, Enuma Elish. In addition, post-exilic Hebrew adopted Babylonian names for the months of the year. Studies on Jewish apocalyptic writings have long pointed to Persian Zoroastrianism to account for the phenomenon of apocalyptic in the period of the second temple. Because the dating of the emergence of Zoroastrianism is still an open question, studies that attempt to demonstrate Zoroastrian 'influence' on the Hebrew Bible are always vulnerable to the charge of anachronism. But there are a number of provocative theological parallels between Zoroastrianism and the P-source in the Pentateuch, and these surely indicate some kind of mutual exchange of ideas.[2] Morton Smith has argued that the cosmology and the political propaganda of Isa. 40–48 is heavily influenced by Persian thought.[3] For this reason Josephus's claim that Isa. 44.28–45.1 had actually come to the attention of Cyrus may not be as far-fetched as it first appears.

---

1.   See Smith, 'Jewish Religious Life in the Persian Period', pp. 222-23.
2.   See M. Boyce, 'Persian Religion in the Achemenid Age', in Davies and Finkelstein (eds.), *The Cambridge History of Judaism*, I, pp. 279-307.
3.   See M. Smith, 'II Isaiah and the Persians', *JAOS* 83/4 (1963), pp. 415-21.

APPENDIX 3

The genealogy provided for Ezra in Ezra 7.1-5 is provocative, the express purpose of which appears to be to place Ezra in the high-priestly lineage extending back through Zadok to Aaron. This genealogy is similar, though not identical, to 1 Chron 5.27-41.

1 Chron. 5.27-41	Ezra 7.1-5
Levi	
Kohath	
Amram	
Aaron	Aaron the High Priest (כהן הראש)
Eleazar	Eleazar
Phinehas	Phinehas
Abishua	Abishua
Bukki	Bukki
Uzzi	Uzzi
Zerahiah	Zerahiah
Meraioth	Meraioth
Amariah	
Ahitub	
Zadok	
Ahimaaz	
Azariah	
Johanan	
Azariah	Azariah
Amariah	Amariah
Ahitub	Ahitub
Zadok	Zadok
Shallum	Shallum
Hilkiah	Hilkiah
Azariah	Azariah
Seraiah	Seraiah
Jehozadak	**Ezra**

Various attempts have been made to account for the descrepancies, for example, through dittography, haplography, or both, none of which are satisfying.[1] Both lists are obviously selective and not exhaustive. The Ezra genealogy in its present form, even if corrupt, still makes the vital link with Zadok son of Ahitub and Aaron.[2] Koch

---

1. See F.M. Cross, 'The Priestly Houses of Early Israel', in *Canaanite Myth and Hebrew Epic*, pp. 206-15.
2. See 2 Sam. 8.17; 1 Chron. 6.37-38; 9.11; Neh. 11.10.

thinks it possible that Ezra actually came to Jerusalem as High Priest.[1] This is contested by Blenkinsopp,[2] who claims that Ezra was not High Priest and that the genealogy is fictive, the purpose of which was to establish continuity between Ezra and the pre-exilic priesthood. Whether the genealogy is fictive or not is beside the point. Clearly there is more going on here than merely linking the message and function of Ezra with the pre-exilic priesthood. Both 1 Esdras and Josephus explicitly refer to Ezra as High Priest: 1 Esd. 9.39-40: Εσδρας ὁ ἀρχιερεύς; Josephus, *Ant.* 11.121: Ἔσδρας πρῶτος ἱερεύς. Later Jewish tradition made much of the Ezra genealogy, and this can be seen in the backdating of Ezra to the exilic period, a move no doubt necessitated by a literal reading of the statement that Ezra was the son of Seraiah.[3]

1. See Koch, 'Ezra and the Origins of Judaism', esp. pp. 190-93.
2. *Ezra–Nehemiah*, pp. 135-36, 172.
3. See 4 Ezra 3.1, 29.

Strong hints as to what the official religion of the pre-exilic period looked like can be derived from an analysis of the reforms of Hezekiah and Josiah. Hezekiah is said to have removed the high places, destroyed the pillars, cut down the Asherah, and broken Nehushtan to pieces (see 2 Kgs 18.4). Everything about the 'discovery' of the book of the law during the reign of Josiah points to Josiah as having been a religious innovator. Subsequent to the 'discovery', Josiah purged the temple of all the vessels that were used in the worship of Baal and Asherah. In addition he deposed the priests who served at the high places, priests who made offerings to Baal, the sun, the moon and the stars. He purged the temple of cult prostitutes and destroyed the high places throughout the land. He defiled the Topheth and removed the horses that the kings of Judah had dedicated to the sun (see 2 Kgs 23.4-14).[1] In Jer. 44 it is stated that a contingent of exiles in Egypt blames Jerusalem's demise at the hands of the Babylonians on Josiah's reform. The implication of their argument is that Josiah had abandoned the traditional religion. The description of the pre-exilic temple cult in Ezek. 8 also provides further evidence regarding the nature of the traditional, official religion of Judah and Jerusalem. Furthermore, Ezekiel insists that the worship of the second temple must be different from that of the first.[2]

Mention should be made of the book by Tigay, *You Shall Have No Other Gods*, and of his essay, 'Israelite Religion: The Onomastic and Epigraphic Evidence'.[3] Tigay's thesis is that the anti-polytheism polemic in the Hebrew Bible is really no more than hyperbole and that polytheism itself was quite rare in ancient Israel. He is led to this conclusion because the representation of deities other than YHWH/El in both Israelite onomastica and epigraphy is meager. According to Tigay, so much space is devoted to attacking polytheism in the Hebrew Bible not because it was widespread but because of the theological significance that it had for the biblical writers. He regards the situation in the Hebrew Bible as analogous to modern Jewish polemics against the 'Jews for Jesus' movement, that is, statistically speaking, the movement represents only a miniscule number of people, but an immense amount of time and effort is spent discrediting it in Jewish circles. His major conclusion is, 'If

---

1. For a discussion of Josiah's reform, see G.W. Ahlström, 'An Archaeological Picture of Iron Age Religions in Ancient Palestine', *StudOr* 55 (1984), pp. 117-44; *idem, Royal Administration*, pp. 74-81.

2. See M. Smith, 'The Veracity of Ezekiel, the Sins of Manasseh, and Jeremiah 44.18', *ZAW* 87 (1975), pp. 11-16.

3. In Miller, Hanson and McBride (eds.), *Ancient Israelite Religion*, pp. 157-94.

we had only the inscriptional evidence, I doubt that we would ever imagine that there existed a significant amount of polytheistic practice in Israel during the period in question' (i.e., during the monarchy).[1] In response, it must be said that Tigay's evidence ought not to be pushed too far. All that can be said with assurance in light of his study is that YHWH was the main and/or national god during the monarchic period, but this tells us very little about the specifics of the pre-exilic cult. It is one thing to say that pre-exilic Israel was essentially monolatrous, but it is quite another to extrapolate from that that pre-exilic religion was essentially identical with the religion described in the Pentateuch. A very helpful discussion of these issues is provided by Smith, *The Early History of God*. He argues that pre-exilic religion was shaped by the dual processes of 'convergence' and 'differentiation'. Convergence is understood as a development whereby 'various deities and/or some of their features' coalesced or converged into the figure of YHWH. In the case of YHWH and El, for example, this happened at a very early date. The process of convergence is intriguing, as evidenced by the fact that 'Yahwistic polemic assumed that Yahweh embodied the positive characteristics of the very deities it was condemning'. Differentiation, on the other hand, was a process whereby various 'features of early Israelite cult were later rejected as Canaanite and non-Yahwistic' (pp. xxiii-xxiv). It is this process of differentiation that is strongly in evidence in Third Isaiah.

---

1.   'Israelite Religion', p. 178.

BIBLIOGRAPHY

Primary Texts

Biblia Hebraica (ed. R. Kittel *et al.*; Leipzig: J.C. Hinrichs, 1913).

Biblia Hebraica (ed. R. Kittel *et al.*; Stuttgart: Württembergische Bibelanstalt, 1937).

Biblia Hebraica Stuttgartensia (ed. K. Elliger *et al.*; Stuttgart: Deutsche Bibelgesellschaft, 1983).

Biblia Sacra: Iuxta Vulgatam Versionem (ed. B. Fischer *et al.*; Stuttgart: Deutsche Bibelgesellschaft, 3rd edn, 1983).

Die Bibel oder die ganze Heilige Schrift des Alten und Neuen Testaments: Nach der deutschen Übersetzung Martin Luthers (N.p.: National Publishing Company, 1967).

Josephus (trans. H.St.J. Thackeray, R. Marcus and L.H. Feldman; LCL; Cambridge: Harvard University Press, 1956–65).

Scrolls from Qumran Cave 1: The Great Isaiah Scroll, The Order of the Community, The Pesher to Habakkuk (ed. F.M. Cross, D.N. Freedman and J.A. Sanders; Jerusalem: Albright Institute of Archaeological Research, The Shrine of the Book, 1974).

Septuaginta (ed. A. Rahlfs; Stuttgart: Deutsche Bibelgesellschaft, 1935).

Syriac Bible (N.p.: United Bible Societies, 1979).

Tanakh: The Holy Scriptures. The New JPS Translation according to the Traditional Hebrew Text (Philadelphia: Jewish Publication Society, 1985).

The Bible in Aramaic. II. The Latter Prophets according to Targum Jonathan (ed. A. Sperber. Leiden: Brill, 1962).

Reference Works

Brown, F., S.R. Driver and C.A. Briggs, *A Hebrew and English Lexicon of the Old Testament: With an Appendix Containing the Biblical Aramaic* (Oxford: Clarendon Press, 1906).

Charles, R.H. (ed.), *The Apocrypha and Pseudepigrapha of the Old Testament in English: With Introductions and Critical and Explanatory Notes to the Several Books* (2 vols.; Oxford: Clarendon Press, 1913).

Charlesworth, J.H. (ed.), *The Old Testament Pseudepigrapha* (2 vols.; Garden City, NY: Doubleday & Co., 1983–85).

Conybeare, F.C., and St.G. Stock, *Grammar of Septuagint Greek: With Selected Readings from the Septuagint According to the Text of Swete* (Boston: Ginn & Co., 1905; repr.; Peabody, MA: Hendrickson, 1988).

Even-Shoshan, A., *A New Concordance of the Bible: Thesaurus of the Language of the*

Bible; Hebrew and Aramaic; Roots, Words, Proper Names, Phrases and Synonyms (Jerusalem: Kiryat Sepher, 1985).

Hatch, E., and H.A. Redpath, *A Concordance to the Septuagint* (2 vols.; Grand Rapids: Baker Book House, 1983).

Holladay, W.L., *A Concise Hebrew and Aramaic Lexicon of the Old Testament: Based upon the Lexical Work of Ludwig Koehler and Walter Baumgartner* (Grand Rapids: Eerdmans, 1971).

Jastrow, M., *A Dictionary of the Targumim, the Talmud Babli and Yerushalmi, and the Midrashic Literature* (2 vols.; New York: Pardes Publishing House, 1950).

Kautzsch, E., and A.E. Cowley (eds.), *Gesenius' Hebrew Grammar* (Oxford: Clarendon Press, 2nd edn, 1910).

Koehler, L., and W. Baumgartner, *Lexicon in Veteris Testamenti Libros* (Leiden: Brill, 1953).

Jellicoe, S., *The Septuagint and Modern Study* (Oxford: Oxford University Press, 1968; repr.; Ann Arbor, MI: Eisenbrauns, 1978).

Liddell, H.G., and R. Scott, *A Greek–English Lexicon* (rev. H.S. Jones and R. McKenzie; Oxford: Clarendon Press, 9th edn, 1940).

Pritchard, J.B. (ed.), *Ancient Near Eastern Texts Relating to the Old Testament* (Princeton: Princeton University Press, 3rd edn, 1969).

Qimron, E., *The Hebrew of the Dead Sea Scrolls* (Harvard Semitic Studies, 29; Atlanta: Scholars Press, 1986).

Segal, M.H., *A Grammar of Mishnaic Hebrew* (Oxford: Clarendon Press, 1927).

Smith, J.P., *A Compendious Syriac Dictionary: Founded upon the 'Thesaurus Syriacus' of R. Payne Smith* (Oxford: Clarendon Press, 1903).

Smyth, H.W., *Greek Grammar* (rev. G.M. Messing; Cambridge, MA: Harvard University Press, 1956).

Swete, H.B., *An Introduction to the Old Testament in Greek* (rev. R.R. Ottley; Cambridge: Cambridge University Press, 1914; repr.; Peabody, MA: Hendrickson, 1989).

Secondary Literature Consulted

Abramowski, R., 'Zum literarischen Problem von Jesaja 56–66', *TSK* 96/97 (1925), pp. 90-143.

Achtemeier, E., *The Community and Message of Isaiah 56–66* (Minneapolis: Augsburg, 1982).

Ackroyd, P.R., *Exile and Restoration* (Philadelphia: Westminster Press, 1968).

—'Historical Problems of the Early Achaemenian Period', *Eastern Great Lakes Biblical Society Proceedings* 4 (1984), pp. 54-56.

—'An Interpretation of the Babylonian Exile. A Study of 2 Kings 20, Isaiah 38–39', *SJT* 27 (1974), pp. 329-52.

—'Isaiah I–XII: Presentation of a Prophet', in J.A. Emerton *et al.* (eds.), *Congress Volume, Göttingen 1977* (VTSup, 29; Leiden: Brill, 1978), pp. 16-48.

—*Israel under Babylon and Persia* (London: Oxford University Press, 1970).

—'The Jewish Community in Palestine in the Persian Period', in Davies and Finkelstein (eds.), *History of Judaism*, pp. 130-61.

—Review of P.D. Hanson, *The Dawn of Apocalyptic*, *Int* 30 (1976), pp. 412-15.

Ahlström, G.W., 'An Archaeological Picture of Iron Age Religions in Ancient Palestine', *StudOr* 55 (1984), pp. 117-45.

—'Heaven on Earth—At Hazor and Arad', in B.A. Pearson (ed.), *Religious Syncretism in Antiquity* (Missoula, MT: Scholars Press, 1975), pp. 67-83.

—*Royal Administration and National Religion in Ancient Palestine* (Studies in the History of the Ancient Near East, 1; Leiden: Brill, 1982).

—'Some Aspects of Historical Problems of the Early Persian Period', *Eastern Great Lakes Biblical Society Proceedings* 4 (1984), pp. 54-56.

—'Some Remarks on Prophets and Cult', in J.C. Rylarsdam (ed.), *Transitions in Biblical Scholarship* (Essays in Divinity, 6; Chicago: University of Chicago Press, 1968), pp. 113-29.

—*Who Were the Israelites?* (Winona Lake, IN: Eisenbrauns, 1986).

Alt, A., 'Die Rolle Samarias bei der Entstehung des Judentums', in *Kleine Schriften zur Geschichte des Volkes Israel* (3 vols.; Munich: C.H. Beck'sche Verlagsbuchhandlung, 1953), II, pp. 316-37.

Angerstorfer, A., 'Asherah als "Consort of Jahwe" oder Ashirtah?', *Biblische Notizen* 17 (1982), pp. 7-16.

Avigad, N., *Bullae and Seals from a Post-Exilic Judean Archive* (trans. R. Grafman; Qedem, 4; Jerusalem: 'Ahva' Co-op Press, 1976).

—'The Contribution of Hebrew Seals to an Understanding of Israelite Religion and Society', in Miller, Hanson and McBride (eds.), *Ancient Israelite Religion*, pp. 195-208.

Avi-Jonah, M., *The Holy Land from the Persian to the Arab Conquest* (Grand Rapids: Eerdmans, 1966).

Banwell, B.O., 'A Suggested Analysis of Isaiah XL–LXVI', *ExpTim* 76 (1964–65), p. 166.

Barstad, H., 'Lebte Deuterojesaja in Judäa?', *Norsk Teologisk Tidsskrift* 83 (1982), pp. 77-86.

—'On the So-called Babylonian Literary Influence in Second Isaiah', *SJT* 2 (1987), pp. 90-110.

Barton, J., *Oracles of God* (New York: Oxford University Press, 1986).

Bastiaens, J., W. Beuken and F. Postma, *Trito-Isaiah: An Exhaustive Concordance of Isa. 56–66, Especially with Reference to Deutero-Isaiah: An Example of Computer Assisted Research* (Amsterdam: VU Uitgeverij, Free University Press, 1984).

Begrich, J., 'Das priesterliche Heilsorakel', *ZAW* 52 (1934), pp. 81-92.

Berger, P.L., 'Charisma and Religious Innovation: The Social Location of Israelite Prophecy', *American Sociological Review* 28 (1963), pp. 940-50.

Betlyon, J.W. 'The Cult of 'Asherah/'Elat at Sidon', *JNES* 44 (1985), pp. 53-56.

Beuken, W.A.M., 'Isa. 55, 3-5: The Reinterpretation of David', *Bijdragen* 35 (1974), pp. 49-64.

—'Isa. 56.9–57.13—An Example of the Isaianic Legacy of Trito-Isaiah', in J.W. van Henten, H.J. de Jonge, P.T. van Rooden and J.W. Wesselius (eds.), *Tradition and Re-Interpretation in Jewish and Early Christian Literature: Essays in Honor of Jürgen C.H. Lebram* (Leiden: Brill, 1986), pp. 48-64.

Bickerman, E.J., 'The Babylonian Captivity', in Davies and Finkelstein (eds.), *The Cambridge History of Judaism*, pp. 342-58.

Blenkinsopp, J., *Ezra–Nehemiah: A Commentary* (OTL; Philadelphia: Westminster Press, 1988).

—*A History of Prophecy in Israel* (Philadelphia: Westminster Press, 1983).
—'Interpretation and the Tendency to Sectarianism: An Aspect of Second Temple History', in E.P. Sanders (ed.), *Jewish and Christian Self-Definition* (Philadelphia: Fortress Press, 1981), pp. 1-26.
—'The Mission of Udjahorresnet and those of Ezra and Nehemiah', *JBL* 106 (1987), pp. 409-21.
—'Old Testament Theology and the Jewish-Christian Connection', *JSOT* 28 (1984), pp. 3-15.
—*The Pentateuch: An Introduction to the First Five Books of the Bible* (AB; Garden City, NY: Doubleday, 1992).
—*Prophecy and Canon* (Notre Dame: University of Notre Dame Press, 1977).
—'Second Isaiah—Prophet of Universalism', *JSOT* 41 (1988), pp. 83-103.
—'The "Servants of the Lord" in Third Isaiah', *Proceedings of the Irish Biblical Association* 7 (1983), pp. 1-23.
—'The Structure of P', *CBQ* 38 (1976), pp. 275-92.
—'Yahweh and Other Deities: Conflict and Accommodation in the Religion of Israel', *Int* 40 (1986), pp. 354-66.
Bowman, J., 'Ezekiel and the Zadokite Priesthood', *Transactions of the Glasgow University Oriental Society* 16 (1955–56), pp. 1-14.
Boyce, M., 'Persian Religion in the Achemenid Age', in Davies and Finkelstein (eds.), *History of Judaism*, pp. 279-307.
Brettler, M., '2 Kings 24.13-14 as History', *CBQ* 53 (1991), pp. 541-52.
Bright, J., *A History of Israel* (Philadelphia: Westminster Press, 2nd edn, 1972).
Brown, R.E., Review of P.D. Hanson. *The Dawn of Apocalyptic*, *CBQ* 38 (1976), pp. 389-90.
Brownlee, W.H., 'The Manuscripts of Isaiah from which DSIsa was Copied', *BASOR* 127 (1952), pp. 16-21.
—*The Meaning of the Qumran Scrolls for the Bible: With Special Attention to the Book of Isaiah* (New York: Oxford University Press, 1964).
Brueggemann, W., 'Isaiah 55 and Deuteronomic Theology', *ZAW* 80 (1968), pp. 191-203.
—'Unity and Dynamic in the Isaianic Tradition', *JSOT* 29 (1984), pp. 89-107.
Burkert, W., *Greek Religion* (trans. J. Raffan; Cambridge, MA: Harvard University Press, 1985).
Burn, A.R., *Persia and the Greeks: The Defense of the West, 546–478 BC* (New York: Minerva Press, 1962).
Carroll, R.P., 'Prophecy and Society', in Clements (ed.), *The World of Ancient Israel*, pp. 203-25.
—'Twilight of Prophecy or Dawn of Apocalyptic?', *JSOT* 14 (1979), pp. 3-35.
—*When Prophecy Failed: Cognitive Dissonance in the Prophetic Traditions of the Old Testament* (New York: Seabury, 1979).
Childs, B.S., *The Book of Exodus: A Critical, Theological Commentary* (OTL; Philadelphia: Westminster Press, 1974).
—*Introduction to the Old Testament as Scripture* (Philadelphia: Fortress Press, 1979).
Clements, R.E., 'Beyond Tradition History: Deutero-Isaianic Development of First Isaiah's Themes', *JSOT* 31 (1985), pp. 95-113.
—*Isaiah 1–39* (NCB; repr.; London: Marshall, Morgan and Scott; Grand Rapids: Eerdmans, 1987).

—*Isaiah and the Deliverance of Jerusalem* (JSOTSup, 13; Sheffield: JSOT Press, 1980).

—'The Prophecies of Isaiah and the Fall of Jerusalem in 587 BC', *VT* 30 (1980), pp. 421-36.

—'The Unity of the Book of Isaiah', *Int* 36 (1982), pp. 117-29.

Clements, R.E. (ed.), *The World of Ancient Israel* (Cambridge: Cambridge University Press, 1989).

Clines, D.J.A., *I, He, We, and They: A Literary Approach to Isaiah 53* (JSOTSup, 1; Sheffield: JSOT Press, 1976).

Cody, A., *Ezekiel. With an Excursus on Old Testament Priesthood* (Old Testament Message, 11; Wilmington, DE: Michael Glazier, 1984).

—*A History of Old Testament Priesthood* (AnBib, 35; Rome: Pontifical Biblical Institute, 1969).

Coggins, R.J., 'The Origins of the Jewish Diaspora', in Clements (ed.), *The World of Ancient Israel*, pp. 163-81.

Conrad, E.W., 'The Community as King in Second Isaiah', in J.T. Butler, E.W. Conrad and B.C. Ollenburger (eds.), *Understanding the Word* (JSOTSup, 37; Sheffield: JSOT Press, 1985), pp. 99-111.

—*Reading Isaiah* (Overtures in Biblical Theology; Philadelphia: Fortress Press, 1991).

Coogan, M.D., 'Canaanite Origins and Lineage: Reflections on the Religion of Ancient Israel', in Miller, Hanson and McBride (eds.), *Ancient Israelite Religion*, pp. 115-24.

Cowley, A., *Aramaic Papyri of the Fifth Century BC* (repr.; Osnabrück: Otto Zeller, 1967 [1923]).

Crenshaw, J., 'Popular Questioning of the Justice of God in Ancient Israel', *ZAW* 82 (1970), pp. 380-85.

Cross, F.M., 'Aspects of Samaritan and Jewish History in Late Persian and Hellenistic Times', *HTR* 59 (1966), pp. 201-11.

—*Canaanite Myth and Hebrew Epic: Essays in the History of the Religion of Israel* (Cambridge, MA: Harvard University Press, 1973).

—'The Discovery of the Samaria Papyri', *BA* 26 (1963), pp. 110-21.

—'Papyri of the Fourth Century BC from Daliyeh', in D.N. Freedman and J.C. Greenfield (eds.), *New Directions in Biblical Archaeology* (Garden City, NY: Doubleday, 1969), pp. 41-62.

—'A Reconstruction of the Judean Restoration', *JBL* 94 (1975), pp. 4-18.

Dahood, M., 'Textual Problems in Isaiah', *CBQ* 22 (1960), pp. 400-409.

Dandamayev, M. 'Babylonia in the Persian Age', in Davies and Finkelstein (eds.), *The Cambridge History of Judaism*, I, pp. 326-42.

Davies, P.R., 'The Social World of the Apocalyptic Writings', in Clements (ed.), *The World of Ancient Israel*, pp. 251-71.

Davies, W.D., and L. Finkelstein (eds.), *The Cambridge History of Judaism*. I. *Introduction; The Persian Period* (Cambridge: Cambridge University Press, 1984).

Delcor, M., Review of P.D. Hanson, *The Dawn of Apocalyptic*, *Bib* 57 (1976), pp. 577-79.

Dever, W.G., 'Archaeology and the Bible—Understanding their Special Relationship', *BARev* 16 (1990), pp. 52-58, 62.

—'Asherah, Consort of Yahweh? New Evidence from Kuntillet 'Ajrud', *BASOR* 255 (1984), pp. 21-37.

—'The Contribution of Archaeology to the Study of Canaanite and Early Israelite Religion', in Miller, Hanson and McBride (eds.), *Ancient Israelite Religion*, pp. 209-47.

—'Iron Age Epigraphic Material from the Area of Khirbet el-Kom', *HUCA* 40/41 (1970), pp. 139-204.

—'Material Remains and the Cult in Ancient Israel: An Essay in Archaeological Systematics', in Meyers and O'Connor (eds.), *The Word of the Lord Shall Go Forth*, pp. 571-87.

—'Recent Archaeological Confirmation of the Cult of Asherah in Ancient Israel', *Hebrew Studies* 23 (1982), pp. 37-44.

—'Women's Popular Religion, Suppressed in the Bible, now Revealed by Archaeology', *BARev* 17 (1991), pp. 64-65.

Dodd, C.H., *The Epistle of Paul to the Romans* (London: Hodder & Stoughton, 1932).

Driver, G.R., *Aramaic Documents of the Fifth Century BC* (Oxford: Clarendon Press, 1957).

Duhm, B., *Das Buch Jesaia* (Göttingen: Vandenhoeck & Ruprecht, 5th edn, 1968).

Eaton, J., Review of P.D. Hanson, *The Dawn of Apocalyptic*, *ExpTim* 87 (1975–76), pp. 119-20.

Eissfeldt, O., *Molk als Opferbegriff im Punischen und Hebräischen und das Ende des Gottes Moloch* (Halle: Niemeyer, 1935).

—'The Promises of Grace to David in Isaiah 55.1-5', in B. Anderson and W. Harrelson (eds.), *Israel's Prophetic Heritage: Essays in Honor of James Muilenberg* (New York: Harper & Row, 1962).

Eitz, A., 'Studien zum Verhältnis von Priesterschrift und Deuterojesaja' (Inaugural dissertation, Heidelberg, 1969).

Eliade, M., *Patterns in Comparative Religion* (New York: Sheed & Ward, 1958).

Elliger, K., *Deuterojesaja in seinem Verhältnis zu Tritojesaja* (Stuttgart: Kohlhammer, 1933).

—*Die Einheit des Tritojesaja (Jes 56–66)* (BWANT, 45; Stuttgart: Kohlhammer, 1928).

—'Der Prophet Tritojesaja', *ZAW* 49 (1931), pp. 112-40.

Emerton, J.A., 'New Light on Israelite Religion: The Implications of the Inscriptions from Kuntillet 'Ajrud', *ZAW* 94 (1982), pp. 2-20.

Evans, C.A., 'On the Unity and Parallel Structure of Isaiah', *VT* 38 (1988), pp. 129-47.

Fishbane, M., *Biblical Interpretation in Ancient Israel* (Oxford: Clarendon Press, 1985).

Fohrer, G., *History of Israelite Religion* (trans. D.E. Green; Nashville: Abingdon Press, 1972).

—*Introduction to the Old Testament* (trans. D.E. Green; Nashville: Abingdon Press, 1968).

—'Jesaja 1 als Zusammenfassung der Verkündigung Jesajas', *ZAW* 74 (1962), pp. 251-68.

Freedman, D.N., '"Who is Like thee among the Gods?" The Religion of Early Israel', in Miller, Hanson and McBride (eds.), *Ancient Israelite Religion*, pp. 315-35.

Friedman, R.E., *The Exile and Biblical Narrative: The Formation of the Deuteronomistic and Priestly Works* (Chico, CA: Scholars Press, 1981).

—*Who Wrote the Bible?* (New York: Harper & Row, 1987).

Galling, K., 'The "Gola-List" according to Ezra 2/Nehemiah 7', *JBL* 70 (1951), pp. 149-58.

—*Studien zur Geschichte Israels in persischen Zeitalter* (Tübingen: Mohr, 1964).

Gammie, J.G., Review of P.D. Hanson, *The Dawn of Apocalyptic*, *JBL* 95 (1976), pp. 651-54.

Gelston, A., 'The Foundations of the Second Temple', *VT* 16 (1966), pp. 232-35.

Gese, H., *Der Verfassungsentwurf des Ezechiel (Kap. 40–48) traditionsgeschichtlich untersucht* (BHT, 25; Tübingen: Mohr, 1957).

Gosse, B., *Isaïe 13, 1-14, 23 dans la tradition littéraire du livre d'Isaïe et dans la tradition des oracles contre les nations* (OBO, 78; Freiburg: Universitätsverlag; Göttingen: Vandenhoeck & Ruprecht, 1988).

Gray, J., *I and II Kings* (OTL; Philadelphia: Westminster Press, 1970).

Green, A.R.W., *The Role of Human Sacrifice in the Ancient Near East* (American Schools of Oriental Research Dissertation Series, 1; Missoula, MT: Scholars Press, 1975).

Greenfield, J.C., 'Aspects of Aramean Religion', in Miller, Hanson and McBride (eds.), *Ancient Israelite Religion*, pp. 67-78.

Gunneweg, A.H.J., *Leviten und Priester* (Göttingen: Vandenhoeck & Ruprecht, 1965).

—עם הארץ'—A Semantic Revolution', *ZAW* 95 (1983), pp. 437-40.

Hallo, W.W., 'The Origins of the Sacrificial Cult: New Evidence from Mesopotamia and Israel', in Miller, Hanson and McBride (eds.), *Ancient Israelite Religion*, pp. 3-13.

Hanson, P.D., 'Apocalyptic Literature', in D.A. Knight and G.M. Tucker (eds.), *The Hebrew Bible and its Modern Interpreters* (Philadelphia: Fortress Press; Chico, CA: Scholars Press, 1985), pp. 465-88.

—*The Dawn of Apocalyptic* (Philadelphia: Fortress Press, rev. edn, 1979).

—'Israelite Religion in the Early Postexilic Period', in Miller, Hanson, and McBride (eds.), *Ancient Israelite Religion*, pp. 485-508.

—'Jewish Apocalyptic against its Near Eastern Environment', *RB* 78 (1971), pp. 31-58.

—'Old Testament Apocalyptic Re-examined', *Int* 25 (1971), pp. 454-79.

Heider, G.C., *The Cult of Molek: A Reassessment* (JSOTSup, 43; Sheffield: JSOT Press, 1985).

—'A Further Turn on Ezekiel's Baroque Twist in Ezek. 20.25-26', *JBL* 107 (1988), pp. 721-24.

Herbert, A.S., *The Book of the Prophet Isaiah: Chapters 40–66* (Cambridge: Cambridge University Press, 1975).

Herrmann, S., *A History of Israel in Old Testament Times* (trans. J. Bowden; Philadelphia: Fortress Press, 1975).

Hestrin, R., 'Understanding Asherah—Exploring Semitic Iconography', *BARev* 17 (1991), pp. 50-59.

Holladay, J.S., 'Religion in Israel and Judah under the Monarchy: An Explicitly Archaeological Approach', in Miller, Hanson and McBride (eds.), *Ancient Israelite Religion*, pp. 249-99.

Irwin, W.H., 'The Smooth Stones of the Wadi? Isaiah 57:6', *CBQ* 29 (1967), pp. 31-40.

Janssen, E., *Juda in der Exilzeit* (Göttingen: Vandenhoeck & Ruprecht, 1956).

Japhet, S., 'Sheshbazzar and Zerubbabel: Against the Background of the Historical and Religious Tendencies of Ezra–Nehemiah', *ZAW* 94 (1982), pp. 66-98.

—'The Supposed Common Authorship of Chronicles and Ezra–Nehemiah Investigated Anew', *VT* 18 (1969), pp. 330-71.

Jensen, J., 'Yahweh's Plan in Isaiah and in the Rest of the Old Testament', *CBQ* 48 (1986), pp. 443-55.

Jones, D., *Isaiah 56–66 and Joel* (London: SCM Press, 1964).

—'The Traditio of the Oracles of Isaiah of Jerusalem', *ZAW* 67 (1955), pp. 226-46.

Kanael, B., 'Ancient Jewish Coins and their Historical Importance', *BA* 26 (1963), pp. 38-62.

Kaufmann, Y., *The Religion of Israel* (trans. and abridged M. Greenberg; Chicago: University of Chicago Press, 1960).

Kendall, D., 'The Use of Mishpat in Isaiah 59', *ZAW* 96 (1984), pp. 391-405.

Kessler, W., *Gott geht es um das Ganze* (Die Botschaft des Alten Testaments, 19; Stuttgart: Calwer Verlag, 1960).

—'Studie zur religiösen Situation im ersten nachexilischen Jahrhundert und zur Auslegung von Jesaja 56–66', *Wissenschaftliche Zeitschrift der Martin Luther Universität, Halle-Wittenberg* 1 (1965–67), pp. 41-74.

—'Zur Auslegung von Jesaja 56–66', *TLZ* 81 (1956), pp. 335-38.

Knibb, M., 'Prophecy and the Emergence of the Jewish Apocalypses', in R. Coggins, A. Phillips and M. Knibb (eds.), *Israel's Prophetic Tradition: Essays in Honour of Peter R. Ackroyd* (Cambridge: Cambridge University Press, 1982), pp. 155-80.

Knierim, R., 'Criticism of Literary Features, Form, Tradition, and Redaction', in D.A. Knight and G.M. Tucker (eds.), *The Hebrew Bible and its Modern Interpreters* (Philadelphia: Fortress Press; Chico, CA: Scholars Press, 1985), pp. 123-65.

—'Old Testament Form Criticism Reconsidered', *Int* 27 (1973), pp. 435-68.

—'The Vocation of Isaiah', *VT* 18 (1968), pp. 47-68.

Knight, G.A.F. *The New Israel: A Commentary on the Book of Isaiah 56–66* (Grand Rapids: Eerdmans, 1985).

Koch, K., 'Ezra and the Origins of Judaism', *JSS* 19 (1974), pp. 173-97.

—*The Prophets* (trans. M. Kohl; 2 vols.; Philadelphia: Fortress Press, 1983–84).

Koenen, K., 'Sexuelle Zweideutigkeiten und Euphemismen in Jes 57, 8', *Biblische Notizen* 44 (1988), pp. 46-53.

Kraeling, E.G. *The Brooklyn Museum Aramaic Papyri: New Documents of the Fifth Century BC from the Jewish Colony at Elephantine* (New Haven: Yale University Press, 1953).

Kraus, H.-J., 'Die ausgebliebene Endtheophanie: Eine Studie zu Jesaja 56–66', *ZAW* 78 (1966), pp. 317-32.

Kugel, J.L., *The Idea of Biblical Poetry: Parallelism and its History* (New Haven: Yale University Press, 1981).

—'Some Thoughts on Future Research into Biblical Style: Addenda to *The Idea of Biblical Poetry*', *JSOT* 28 (1984), pp. 107-17.

Kuhrt, A., 'The Cyrus Cylinder and Achaemenid Imperial Policy', *JSOT* 25 (1983), pp. 83-97.

Kutscher, E.Y., *The Language and Linguistic Background of the Isaiah Scroll (1QIsa)* (Leiden: Brill, 1974).

Lang, B., *Monotheism and the Prophetic Minority: An Essay in Biblical History and Sociology* (Sheffield: Almond Press, 1983).

—'Neues über die Geschichte des Monotheismus', *TQ* 163 (1983), pp. 54-58.

—'Zur Entstehung des biblischen Monotheismus', *TQ* 166 (1986), pp. 135-42.

Lemaire, A., 'Who or what was Yahweh's Asherah?', *BARev* 10 (1984), pp. 42-51.

Levenson, J.D., *Creation and the Persistence of Evil* (San Francisco: Harper & Row, 1988).

—'From Temple to Synagogue: 1 Kings 8', in B. Halpern and J.D. Levenson (eds.), *Traditions in Transformation* (Winona Lake: Eisenbrauns, 1981), pp. 143-66.

—'The Jerusalem Temple in Devotional and Visionary Experience', in A. Green (ed.), *Jewish Spirituality from the Bible through the Middle Ages* (New York: Crossroad, 1986), pp. 32-61.

—*Sinai and Zion* (Minneapolis: Winston Press, 1985).

—'The Temple and the World', *JR* 64 (1984), pp. 275-98.

—*Theology of the Program of Restoration of Ezekiel 40–48* (HSM, 10; Atlanta: Scholars Press, 1976).

Lewis, T.J., 'Death Cult Imagery in Isaiah 57', *HAR* 11 (1987), pp. 267-84.

Liebreich, L., 'Compilation of the Book of Isaiah', *JQR* 46 (1955–56), pp. 259-77.

Lohfink, N., 'The Cult Reform of Josiah of Judah: 2 Kings 22–23 as a Source for the History of Israelite Religion', in Miller, Hanson and McBride (eds.), *Ancient Israelite Religion*, pp. 459-75.

Long, B.O., 'Prophetic Authority as Social Reality', in G.W. Coats and B.O. Long (eds.), *Canon and Authority* (Philadelphia: Fortress Press, 1977), pp. 3-20.

Maass, F., 'Tritojesaja?', in F. Maass (ed.), *Das ferne und das nahe Wort: Festschrift für L. Rost* (BZAW, 105; Berlin: de Gruyter, 1967), pp. 153-63.

Mannheim, K., *Ideology and Utopia* (trans. L. Wirth and E. Shils; New York: Harcourt, Brace & Co., 1936).

Mason, R., 'The Prophets of the Restoration', in R. Coggins, A. Phillips and M. Knibb (eds.), *Israel's Prophetic Tradition: Essays in Honour of Peter R. Ackroyd* (Cambridge: Cambridge University Press, 1982), pp. 137-54.

McCarter, P.K., Jr, 'Aspects of the Religion of the Israelite Monarchy: Biblical and Epigraphic Data', in Miller, Hanson and McBride (eds.), *Ancient Israelite Religion*, pp. 137-55.

McCullough, W.S., 'A Re-Examination of Isaiah 56–66', *JBL* 67 (1948), pp. 27-36.

McEvenue, S.E., 'The Political Structure in Judah from Cyrus to Nehemiah', *CBQ* 43 (1981), pp. 353-64.

Melugin, R.F., *The Formation of Isaiah 40–55* (BZAW, 141; Berlin: de Gruyter, 1976).

Meyers, C.L., and E.M. Meyers, *Haggai and Zechariah 1–8* (AB, 25b; Garden City, NY: Doubleday, 1987).

Meyers, C.L., and M. O'Connor (eds.), *The Word of the Lord Shall Go Forth: Essays in Honor of David Noel Freedman in Celebration of his Sixtieth Birthday* (Winona Lake: Eisenbrauns, 1983).

Meyers, E.M., 'The Persian Period and the Judean Restoration: From Zerubbabel to Nehemiah', in Miller, Hanson, and McBride (eds.), *Ancient Israelite Religion*, pp. 509-21.

—'The Use of Tora in Haggai 2.11 and the Role of the Prophet in the Restoration Community', in Meyers and O'Connor (eds.), *The Word of the Lord Shall Go Forth*, pp. 69-76.

Milgrom, J., 'Religious Conversion and the Revolt Model for the Formation of Israel', *JBL* 101 (1982), pp. 169-76.

Miller, P.D., Jr, 'Aspects of the Religion of Ugarit', in Miller, Hanson and McBride (eds.), *Ancient Israelite Religion*, pp. 53-66.

—*The Divine Warrior in Early Israel* (Cambridge, MA: Harvard University Press, 1973).

Miller, P.D., Jr, P.D. Hanson and S.D. McBride (eds.), *Ancient Israelite Religion: Essays in Honor of Frank Moore Cross* (Philadelphia: Fortress Press, 1987).

Momigliano, A., 'Biblical Studies and Classical Studies: Simple Reflections about Historical Method', *BA* 45 (1982), pp. 224-28.

Morgenstern, J., 'Isaiah 49–55', *HUCA* 36 (1965), pp. 1-35.

Mosca, P.G., 'Child Sacrifice in Canaanite and Israelite Religion: A Study in Mulk and Molech' (PhD dissertation, Harvard University, 1975).

Mulder, M.J. (ed.), *Mikra* (CRINT, 2.1; Assen/Maastricht: Van Gorcum; Philadelphia: Fortress Press, 1988).

Murtonen, A., 'Third Isaiah—Yes or No?', *Abr-Nahrain* 19 (1980–81), pp. 20-42.

Myers, J.M., *The World of the Restoration* (Englewood Cliffs, NJ: Prentice–Hall, 1968).

Nock, A.D., *Conversion* (London: Oxford University Press, 1933).

—'Eunuchs in Ancient Religion', *ARW* 23 (1925), pp. 25-33.

North, C.R., *The Second Isaiah* (Oxford: Clarendon Press, 1964).

Noth, M., *The History of Israel* (trans. P.R. Ackroyd; New York: Harper & Row, 2nd edn, 1960).

Oded, B., 'Judah and the Exile', in J.H. Hayes and J.M. Miller (eds.), *Israelite and Judean History* (Philadelphia: Westminster Press, 1977), pp. 435-88.

Olmstead, A.T., *History of the Persian Empire* (Chicago: University of Chicago Press, 1948).

Olyan, S.M., *Asherah and the Cult of Yahweh in Israel* (SBLMS, 34; Atlanta: Scholars Press, 1988).

Oppenheimer, A., *The 'am ha-aretz: A Study in the Social History of the Jewish People in the Hellenistic-Roman Period* (Leiden: Brill, 1977).

Pauritsch, K., *Die neue Gemeinde: Gott sammelt Ausgestossene und Arme (Jesaia 56–66)* (AnBib, 47; Rome: Biblical Institute Press, 1971).

Payne, D.F., 'Characteristic Word-play in "Second Isaiah": A Reappraisal', *JSS* (1967), pp. 207-29.

Peckham, B., 'Phoenicia and the Religion of Israel: The Epigraphic Evidence', in Miller, Hanson and McBride (eds.), *Ancient Israelite Religion*, pp. 79-99.

Petersen, D.L., *Haggai and Zechariah 1–8* (OTL; Philadelphia: Westminster Press, 1984).

—'Israel and Monotheism: The Unfinished Agenda', in G.M. Tucker, D.L. Petersen and R.R. Wilson (eds.), *Canon, Theology, and Old Testament Interpretation: Essays in Honor of Brevard S. Childs* (Philadelphia: Fortress Press, 1988), pp. 92-107.

—'Ways of Thinking about Israel's Prophets', in D.L. Petersen (ed.), *Prophecy in Israel* (Issues in Religion and Theology, 10; London: SPCK; Philadelphia: Fortress Press, 1987), pp. 1-21.

Plöger, O., *Theocracy and Eschatology* (trans. S. Rudman; Richmond, VA: John Knox Press, 1968).

Pope, M.H., 'The Cult of the Dead at Ugarit', in G.W. Young (ed.), *Ugarit in Retrospect: Fifty Years of Ugarit and Ugaritic* (Winona Lake: Eisenbrauns, 1981), pp. 159-79.

Porten, B., *Archives from Elephantine* (Berkeley: University of California Press, 1968).

Purvis, J.D., *The Samaritan Pentateuch and the Origin of the Samaritan Sect* (HSM, 2; Cambridge, MA: Harvard University Press, 1968).

Rad, G. von, *Old Testament Theology* (trans. D.M.G. Stalker; 2 vols.; New York: Harper & Row, 1962–65).

Rendtorff, R., 'Between Historical Criticism and Holistic Interpretation: New Trends in Old Testament Exegesis', in J.A. Emerton (ed.), *Congress Volume, Jerusalem 1986* (VTSup, 40; Leiden: Brill, 1988), pp. 298-303.

—'The Composition of the Book of Isaiah', in *Canon and Theology: Overtures to an Old Testament Theology* (trans. M. Kohl; Overtures to Biblical Theology; Minneapolis: Fortress Press, 1993), pp. 146-69.

—*The Old Testament: An Introduction* (Philadelphia: Fortress Press, 1986).

—'Pentateuchal Studies on the Move', *JSOT* 3 (1977), pp. 2-10, 43-45.

Richter, W., 'Zu den "Richtern Israels"', *ZAW* 77 (1965), pp. 40-41.

Ringgren, H., *Israelite Religion* (trans. D.E. Green; Philadelphia: Fortress Press, 1966).

Roberts, J.J.M., 'The Davidic Origins of the Zion Tradition', *JBL* 92 (1973), pp. 329-44.

Rofé, A., 'How is the Word Fulfilled? Isaiah 55.6-11 within the Theological Debate of its Time', in G.M. Tucker, D.L. Petersen, and R.R. Wilson (eds.), *Canon, Theology, and Old Testament Interpretation: Essays in Honor of Brevard S. Childs* (Philadelphia: Fortress Press, 1988), pp. 246-61.

—'Isaiah 66.1-4: Judean Sects in the Persian Period as Viewed by Trito-Isaiah', in A. Kort and S. Morschauser (eds.), *Biblical and Related Studies Presented to Samuel Iwry* (Winona Lake: Eisenbrauns, 1985), pp. 205-17.

Roth, W., *Isaiah* (ed. J.H. Hayes; Knox Preaching Guides; Atlanta: John Knox Press, 1988).

Rubinstein, A., 'Notes on the Use of the Tenses in the Variant Readings of the Isaiah Scroll', *VT* 3 (1953), pp. 94-95.

Russell, D.S., *The Method and Message of Jewish Apocalyptic* (Philadelphia: Westminster Press, 1964).

Sanders, J.A., 'Hermeneutics in True and False Prophecy', in G.W. Coats and B.O. Long (eds.), *Canon and Authority* (Philadelphia: Fortress Press, 1977), pp. 21-41.

Sasson, J.M., 'Isaiah LXVI 3-4a', *VT* 26 (1976), pp. 199-207.

Schunck, K.D., 'Die Richter Israels und ihr Amt', in J.A. Emerton et al. (eds.), *Volume du Congrès, Genève 1965* (VTSup, 15; Leiden: Brill, 1966), pp. 252-62.

Scott, G.R., *Phallic Worship* (London: Luxor Press, 1966).

Scullion, J.J., 'Some Difficult Texts in Isaiah 56–66 in the Light of Modern Scholarship', *UF* 4 (1972), pp. 105-28.

Seeligmann, I.L., *The Septuagint Version of Isaiah* (Leiden: Brill, 1948).

Sehmsdorf, E., 'Studien zur Redaktionsgeschichte von Jesaja 56–66', *ZAW* 84 (1972), pp. 517-76.

Seitz, C.R., 'The Divine Council: Temporal Transition and New Prophecy in the Book of Isaiah', *JBL* 109 (1990), pp. 229-47.

—'Isaiah 1–66: Making Sense of the Whole', in C.R. Seitz (ed.), *Reading and Preaching the Book of Isaiah* (Philadelphia: Fortress Press, 1988), pp. 105-26.

—*Theology in Conflict* (BZAW, 176; Berlin: de Gruyter, 1989).

Sekine, S., *Die Tritojesajanische Sammlung (Jes 56–66) redaktionsgeschichtlich untersucht* (BZAW, 175; Berlin: de Gruyter, 1989).

Skinner, J., *The Book of the Prophet Isaiah, Chapters XL–LXVI* (Cambridge: Cambridge University Press, 1954).

Smart, J.D., *History and Theology in Second Isaiah* (Philadelphia: Westminster Press, 1965).

Smith, J.Z., 'Wisdom and Apocalyptic', in *Map is not Territory* (Leiden: Brill, 1978), pp. 67-87.

Smith, M.S., *The Early History of God: Yahweh and the Other Deities in Ancient Israel* (San Francisco: Harper & Row, 1990).

—'A Note on Burning Babies', *JAOS* 95 (1975), pp. 477-79.

Smith, M., 'The Common Theology of the Ancient Near East', *JBL* 71 (1952), pp. 135-47.

—'Jewish Religious Life in the Persian Period', in Davies and Finkelstein (ed.), *The Cambridge History of Judaism*, I, pp. 219-78.

—*Palestinian Parties and Politics that Shaped the Old Testament* (London: SCM Press, 2nd edn, 1987).

—'II Isaiah and the Persians', *JAOS* 83/4 (1963), pp. 415-21.

—'The Veracity of Ezekiel, the Sins of Manasseh, and Jeremiah 44.18', *ZAW* 87 (1975), pp. 11-16.

Snaith, N.H., 'The Date of Ezra's Arrival in Jerusalem', *ZAW* 63 (1951), pp. 53-66.

—'Isaiah 40–66: A Study of the Teaching of the Second Isaiah and its Consequences', in H.M. Orlinsky and N.H. Snaith, *Studies on the Second Part of the Book of Isaiah* (VTSup, 14; Leiden: Brill, 1967), pp. 135-264.

Snook, L.E., 'Interpreting the Book of Isaiah: Yahweh's Changeless Purpose in the Changing History of Zion', *Word and World* 3 (1983), pp. 448-61.

Soggin, J.A., *Introduction to the Old Testament* (trans. J. Bowden; OTL; Philadelphia: Fortress Press, 1976).

Stager, L.E., and S.R. Wolff, 'Child Sacrifice at Carthage—Religious Rite or Population Control?', *BARev* 10 (1984), pp. 31-51.

Steck, O.H., 'Beobachtungen zu Jesaja 56–59', *BZ* 31 (1987), pp. 228-46.

—'Beobachtungen zur Anlage von Jes 65–66', *Biblische Notizen* 38/39 (1987), pp. 103-16.

—*Bereitete Heimkehr: Jesaja 35 als redaktionelle Brücke zwischen dem ersten und dem zweiten Jesaja* (SBS, 121; Stuttgart: KBW, 1985).

—'Der Grundtext in Jesaja 60 und sein Aufbau', *ZTK* 83 (1986), pp. 261-96.

—'Der Rachetag in Jesaja LXI 2: Ein Kapitel redaktionsgeschichtlicher Kleinarbeit', *VT* 36 (1986), pp. 323-38.

—'Heimkehr auf der Schulter oder/und auf der Hüfte: Jes 49,22b/60,4b', *ZAW* 98 (1986), pp. 275-77.

—'Jahwes Feinde in Jesaja 59', *Biblische Notizen* 36 (1987), pp. 51-56.

—'Jesaja 60,13—Bauholz oder Tempelgarten?', *Biblische Notizen* 30 (1985), pp. 29-34.

—'Tritojesaja im Jesajabuch', in *The Book of Isaiah, Le Livre d'Isaïe* (ed. J. Vermeylen; BETL, 81; Leuven: Leuven University Press, 1989), pp. 361-406.

Stern, E., 'The Archaeology of Persian Palestine', in Davies and Finkelstein (eds.), *The Cambridge History of Judaism*, I, pp. 88-114.

—*The Material Culture of the Land of the Bible in the Persian Period, 538–332 BCE* (Jerusalem: Bialik Institute/Israel Exploration Society, 1982).

—'The Persian Empire and the Political and Social History of Palestine in the Persian Period', in Davies and Finkelstein (eds.), *The Cambridge History of Judaism*, I, pp. 70-87.

Stone, M., 'Ideal Figures and Social Context: Priest and Sage in the Early Second Temple Age', in Miller, Hanson and McBride (eds.), *Ancient Israelite Religion*, pp. 575-86.

Stuhlmueller, C., *Creative Redemption in Deutero-Isaiah* (AnBib, 43; Rome: Biblical Institute Press, 1970).

Sweeney, M., *Isaiah 1–4 and the Post-exilic Understanding of the Isaianic Tradition* (BZAW, 171; Berlin: de Gruyter, 1988).

Talmon, S., 'DSIa as a Witness to Ancient Exegesis of the Book of Isaiah', in F.M. Cross and S. Talmon (eds.), *Qumran and the History of the Biblical Text* (Cambridge, MA: Harvard University Press, 1975), pp. 116-26.

—'The Emergence of Jewish Sectarianism in the Early Second Temple Period', in Miller, Hanson and McBride (eds.), *Ancient Israelite Religion*, pp. 587-616.

Thompson, T.L., *The Early History of the Israelite People: The Archaeological and Written Evidence* (Leiden: Brill, 1992).

Tigay, J.H., *You Shall Have No Other Gods: Israelite Religion in the Light of Hebrew Inscriptions* (Harvard Semitic Studies, 31; Atlanta: Scholars Press, 1986).

—'Israelite Religion: The Onomastic and Epigraphic Evidence', in Miller, Hanson and McBride (eds.), *Ancient Israelite Religion*, pp. 157-94.

Torrey, C.C., *The Chronicler's History of Israel* (New Haven: Yale University Press, 1954).

—*The Second Isaiah* (New York: Charles Scribner's Sons, 1928).

Tournay, R., Review of P.D. Hanson, *The Dawn of Apocalyptic*, *RB* 83 (1976), pp. 150-53.

Troeltsch, E., *The Social Teaching of the Christian Churches* (trans. O. Wyon; New York: Harper & Row, 1960).

Van der Woude, A.S., 'Malachi's Struggle for a Pure Community. Reflections on Malachi 2.10-16', in J.W. Van Henten, H.J. De Jonge, P.T. Van Rooden and J.W. Wesselius (eds.), *Tradition and Re-Interpretation in Jewish and Early Christian Literature* (Leiden: Brill, 1986), pp. 65-71.

Van Seters, J., *Abraham in History and Tradition* (New Haven: Yale University Press, 1975).

—'Confessional Reformulation in the Exilic Period', *VT* 22 (1972), pp. 448-59.

Volz, D.P., *Jesaja II* (KAT, 9; Leipzig: A. Deichertsche Verlagsbuchbuchhandlung D. Werner Scholl, 1932).

Wallis, G., 'Gott und seine Gemeinde: Eine Betrachtung zum Tritojesaja-Buch', *TZ* 27 (1971), pp. 182-200.

Wanke, G., 'Prophecy and Psalms in the Persian Period', in Davies and Finkelstein (eds.), *The Cambridge History of Judaism*, I, pp. 162-88.

Watts, J.D.W., *Isaiah 34–66* (Waco, TX: Word Books, 1987).

Weber, M., *The Sociology of Religion* (trans. E. Fischoff; Boston: Beacon Press, 1963).

Weinberg, J.P., 'Demographische Notizen zur Geschichte der nachexilischen Gemeinde in Juda', *Klio* 54 (1972), pp. 45-58.

Weinfeld, M., 'Burning Babies in Ancient Israel: A Rejoinder to Morton Smith's Article in *JAOS* 95 (1975): 477-79', *UF* 10 (1978), pp. 411-13.

—*Deuteronomy and the Deuteronomic School* (Oxford: Clarendon Press, 1972).

—'The Worship of Molech and of the Queen of Heaven and its Background', *UF* 4 (1972), pp. 133-54.

Wellhausen, J., *Prolegomena to the History of Ancient Israel* (repr.; Gloucester, MA: Peter Smith, 1983).

Westermann, C., *Isaiah 40–66* (trans. D.M.G. Stalker; OTL; Philadelphia: Westminster Press, 1969).

Whybray, R.N., *Isaiah 40–66* (NCB; repr.; London: Marshall, Morgan & Scott; Grand Rapids: Eerdmans, 1987).

—*Thanksgiving for a Liberated Prophet: An Interpretation of Isaiah Chapter 53* (JSOTSup, 4; Sheffield: JSOT Press, 1978).

—*The Heavenly Counsellor in Isaiah xl 13-14* (Cambridge: Cambridge University Press, 1971).

Widengren, G., 'The Persian Period', in J.H. Hayes and J.M. Miller (eds.), *Israelite and Judean History* (Philadelphia: Westminster Press, 1977), pp. 489-538.

Wilcox, P., and D. Paton-Williams, 'The Servant Songs in Deutero-Isaiah', *JSOT* 42 (1988), pp. 79-102.

Williamson, H.G.M., 'The Concept of Israel in Transition', in Clements (ed.), *The World of Ancient Israel*, pp. 141-61.

—'The Composition of Ezra i–vi', *JTS* 34 (1983), pp. 1-30.

—' "The Sure Mercies of David": Subjective or Objective Genitive?', *JSS* 23 (1978), pp. 31-49.

Willi-Plein, I., Review of P.D. Hanson, *The Dawn of Apocalyptic*, *VT* 29 (1979), pp. 122-27.

Wilson, R.R., *Prophecy and Society in Ancient Israel* (Philadelphia: Fortress Press, 1980).

—*Sociological Approaches to the Old Testament* (Philadelphia: Fortress Press, 1984).

—'The Community of the Second Isaiah', in C.R. Seitz (ed.), *Reading and Preaching the Book of Isaiah* (Philadelphia: Fortress Press, 1988), pp. 53-70.

Wonneberger, R., *Understanding BHS: A Manual for the Users of 'Biblia Hebraica Stuttgartensia'* (trans. D.R. Daniels; Subsidia biblica, 8; Rome: Editrice Pontificio Istituto Biblica, 2nd rev. edn, 1990).

Würthwein, E., *The Text of the Old Testament: An Introduction to the 'Biblia Hebraica'* (trans. E.R. Rhodes; Grand Rapids: Eerdmans, 1979).

Zimmerli, W., 'The History of Israelite Religion', in G.W. Anderson (ed.), *Tradition and Interpretation: Essays by Members of the Society for Old Testament Study* (Oxford: Clarendon Press, 1979), pp. 351-84.

—'Sinaibund und Abrahambund: Ein Beitrag zum Verständnis der Priesterschrift', in *Gottes Offenbarung: Gesammelte Aufsätze zum Alten Testament* (Munich: Chr. Kaiser Verlag, 1963), pp. 205-16.

—'Zur Sprache Tritojesajas', in *Gottes Offenbarung*, pp. 217-33.

INDEXES

INDEX OF REFERENCES

OLD TESTAMENT

OTHER ANCIENT REFERENCES

INDEX OF AUTHORS

JOURNAL FOR THE STUDY OF THE OLD TESTAMENT

Supplement Series